D1706845

This study of religious change and cultural fragmentation in contemporary Sri Lanka focuses on a series of new Catholic shrines that attract hundreds of pilgrims. Their fame is based, among other things, on their efficacy as centres for demonic exorcism, for alleviating suffering, and helping people to find jobs. The book examines the rise of these shrines in relation to the historical experience of the Catholic community in Sri Lanka, rather than in terms of narrowly defined religious criteria. Central to this broader non-religious context is the role of power, and especially the impact of post-colonialism on the small Roman Catholic population.

*Cambridge Studies in Social and Cultural Anthropology*

*Editors: Ernest Gellner, Jack Goody, Stephen Gudeman, Michael Herzfeld, Jonathan Parry*

87

Power and religiosity in a post-colonial setting

# POWER AND RELIGIOSITY IN A POST-COLONIAL SETTING

*Sinhala Catholics in contemporary Sri Lanka*

R. L. STIRRAT
*School of African and Asian Studies*
*University of Sussex*

CAMBRIDGE
UNIVERSITY PRESS

Published by the Press Syndicate of the University of Cambridge
The Pitt Buildings, Trumpington Street, Cambridge CB2 1RP
40 West 20th Street, New York, NY 10011–4211, USA
10 Stamford Road, Oakleigh, Victoria 3166, Australia

First published 1992

Printed in Great Britain by Bell and Bain Ltd., Glasgow

*A catalogue record for this book is available from the British Library*

*Library of Congress cataloguing in publication data*

Stirrat, R. L.
  Power and religiosity in a post-colonial setting: Sinhala Catholics in contemporary Sri
Lanka / R. L. Stirrat.
    p.    cm. – (Cambridge studies in social and cultural anthropology: 87)
  Includes bibliographical references and index.
  ISBN 0 521 41555 1
  1. Catholic Church – Sri Lanka – History – 1965–   2. Sri Lanka – Religion – 20th
century.   3. Christian shrines – Sri Lanka.   4. Christian pilgrims and pilgrimages – Sri
Lanka.   I. Title.   II. Series.
BX1646.S75 1992
282'.5493 – dc20   91–39138   CIP

ISBN 0 521 41555 1

CE

*For Rachel*

# Contents

# Maps and figures

**Maps**

**Figures**

# Tables

# Acknowledgements

In writing this book, I have amassed more debts than I care to remember. In Sri Lanka, my gratitude is due first and foremost to the many people who endured my questions and presence with patience and forbearance. Besides the people of Ambakandawila, Pallansena and Vahacotte as well as the devotees at the various shrines, I must mention in particular Father Jayamanne, Bishop Lalith Aponsu, Brother Lambert and others who allowed me to attend their shrines and interview both themselves and their devotees. Father Alex Fernando and Father David Wijetunge first introduced me to the world of Sinhala Catholicism and have always shown an interest in my work. Also, I am grateful to Ben Sooriyabandara for help in recording and translating some of the interview data used in chapter 7. Finally my thanks must be recorded to the University of Peradeniya to which I was affiliated during part of this research, and the staff of the Sri Lanka National Archives for allowing me access to their resources.

The research on which this book is based was funded from a number of sources. Besides the generous support I received from the Economic and Social Research Council, and the Leverhulme Trust, I would also like to thank the Carnegie Trust and the British Academy for smaller grants.

Various friends and colleagues have commented on parts or the whole of the manuscript. These include James Aitken, James Brow, Michael Carrithers, Chris Fuller, Chuck Jedrej, Colin Kirk, Eric Meyer, Jonathan Parry and Jonathan Spencer, and to all I owe my gratitude. I should also like to take this opportunity to thank Ranjani and Gananath Obeyesekere for their interest and friendship over the last twenty years. As ever I cannot thank Elizabeth Nissan enough for her critical comments, suggestions, help and support. Without her help and, in a different way, that of J. Perkins, this work would never have been completed.

In the text that follows, there has been little possibility of using synonyms for places and people. Shrines such as Kudagama and individuals such as Father Jayamanne are too well known in Sri Lanka to be disguised with false names. However, I have changed many personal names of individuals and in some cases deliberately 'scrambled' stories to hide identities. I only hope that I have not offended too many people and that they can at least sympathise with the attempts of a non-Catholic, non-Sri Lankan to understand sympathetically their religious convictions.

# Abbreviations

ACBC    All Ceylon Buddhist Congress
AGA     Assistant Government Agent
AR      Administration Reports
*CM*    *The Catholic Messenger* (also known as *The Messenger*)
GA      Government Agent
OMI     Oblates of Mary Immaculate
OSB     Order of the Sylestrine Benedictines
SEDEC   Social and Economic Development Centre
SLFP    Sri Lanka Freedom Party
SLNA    Sri Lanka National Archives
UNP     United National Party

Note on transliteration

In the text I have used an extremely simple form of transliteration without diacritics. More correct forms are given in the glossary.

# Glossary

| | |
|---|---|
| *āgama* | religion |
| *āngaṭa ätulen* | 'inside the body' |
| *āngaṭa eliyen* | 'outside the body' |
| *anjamankārayā* | lightreader (a technique of fortune telling) |
| *annāvi* | lay leader of congregation |
| *ārakshā karanavā* | to protect |
| *ārakshā pot* | 'books of protection' |
| *ārakshākārayā* | protector |
| *ārūdē* | possessed, 'mounted' (by a spirit) |
| *āsīrvādaya* | blessings, grace |
| *äs vaha* | evil eye |
| *ātmaya* | soul |
| *āvēsa* | possessed, 'entered' (by a spirit) |
| *ayitikārayā* | possessor, owner |
| *balla* | dog |
| *bälma* | glance (usually of a demon) |
| *bandinavā (bändilā)* | to tie (tied) |
| *bāra* | vow |
| *bhakti* | devotion |
| *bhikkhu* | Buddhist monk |
| *boralikkama* | medallion |
| *boru* | lies |
| *dānē* | alms |
| *darshana* | vision |
| *dāvädda* | dowry |
| *dāyaka maṇḍalaya* | parish council |
| *dēvālē* | temple of the gods |

| | |
|---|---|
| *dhātuva* | relic |
| *disṭiya* | look, essence, also the state of being inhabited by a demon |
| *dukkha* | sorrow, suffering |
| *duk vindinavā* | to experience suffering |
| *dum allanavā* | to catch the smoke |
| *ekavagē* | similar |
| *ekayī* | identical |
| *gälavīma* | salvation |
| *garbavasa māniyō* | Our Lady of Good Expectation |
| *gātā* | prayers |
| *gnānasaktiya* | mental power |
| *gōlayō* | disciples, followers |
| *hēvisi* | a type of drum, also used to denote a particular sort of musical band |
| *hrudasāksiya* | conscience |
| *hūniyam* | sorcery, also the name of a god |
| *japamālaya* | rosary (literally, 'muttering beads') |
| *kapumahattayā* | priest of the gods |
| *kapurāla* | priest of the gods |
| *karma* | action, deed, law of rebirth |
| *kaṭa vaha* | evil mouth |
| *kaṭṭadiya* | Sinhala Buddhist exorcist, also, sorcerer |
| *kaṭuva* | thorn, pin |
| *kāvaḍi* | dance in honour of Kataragama |
| *kavi* | verses |
| *kavum* | oil cake |
| *kembura davas* | days of week suitable for worshipping gods |
| *killa* | pollution |
| *konṭaya* | rosary, spear, javelin |
| *lajjāva* | shame |
| *lakuna* | sign, symbol |
| *laukika* | worldly, mundane |
| *leḍā* | patient |
| *lēkama* | secretary |
| *lokkā* | boss |
| *lokottara* | supra-mundane |
| *mala perētayō* | malevolent spirits of the dead |
| *māyam* | possessed, unconscious |
| *misēma* | mission |

| | |
|---|---|
| *misēma sēvaka* | parish priest (literally, 'servant of the mission') |
| *mudalāli* | trader |
| *munivarayā* | saint |
| *muppu* | lay leader of the congregation |
| *nidahas kämätta* | free will |
| *nikan innavā* | a state of inactivity (literally, 'nothing being') |
| *nirvāna* | state of non-being |
| *pāda namaskāraya* | Way of the Cross |
| *panḍuru* | coins tied in cloth which accompany a vow |
| *pasan pot* | passion books |
| *pavula pota* | family book |
| *perahära* | procession |
| *perētayō* | malevolent spirits of the dead (singular form: *perētaya*) |
| *pilli, pilliya* | a type of sorcery |
| *pin* | merit |
| *pirisa* | following |
| *pirit pot* | books containing Pali texts |
| *poya* | the four quarter-days of the lunar calendar |
| *prārthanākārayā* | litany reader |
| *pūjā* | literally, 'sacrifice' but used by Catholics for the mass |
| *rēnda* | the tithe or its substitute paid by the faithful to the Church |
| *sadhara* | fortune |
| *sahōdarayō* | siblings |
| *samayam velāva* | times when demons are active |
| *saṅgha* | order of Buddhist monks |
| *sannyasin* | Hindu world renouncer |
| *siddhastanaya* | holy or sacred place |
| *sirita* | custom, tradition |
| *suddha* | pure, unsullied |
| *suruvama* | religious statue |
| *swāmi, swāminvahansē* | priest |
| *tanikama* | 'aloneness' |
| *tāpasa* | ascetic, penance |
| *telkǟma* | 'oil food' |
| *vandanā gamanā* | pilgrimage (literally, 'worship journey') |
| *varam* | delegated authority, warrant |

| | |
|---|---|
| *vidyāva* | science |
| *vihāra* | Buddhist temple |
| *viksopa mãniyō* | Our Lady of Sorrows |
| *viruddha* | against, opposed |
| *viswāsa* | knowledge, faith, understanding |
| *yakā* | demons |
| *yakshā dōsaya* | 'demon poison' |

Map 1:   Sri Lanka

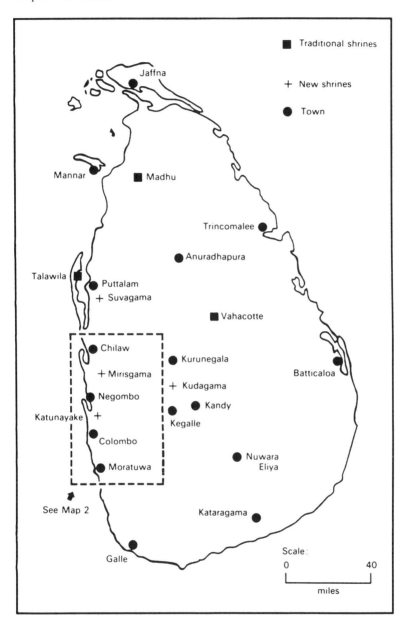

Traditional shrines

+ New shrines

● Town

Jaffna

Mannar

■ Madhu

Trincomalee

● Anuradhapura

Talawila
● Puttalam
+ Suvagama

■ Vahacotte

● Chilaw
+ Mirisgama
● Kurunegala

Batticaloa

+ Kudagama
● Negombo
● Kandy
Katunayake +
Kegalle
● Colombo

● Moratuwa

Nuwara
Eliya

See Map 2

● Kataragama

Scale:
0                40
miles

● Galle

Map 2:   The west coast of Sri Lanka

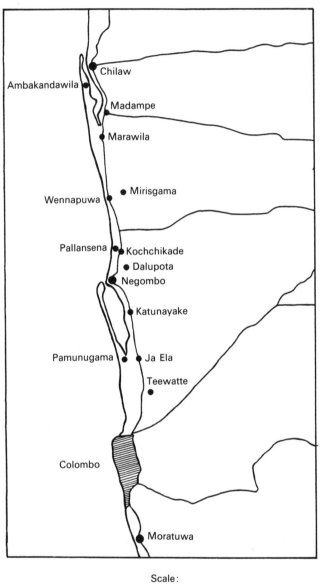

Scale:

0          5          10                    20

miles

# 1

## Introduction

On the first Friday of each month, Rita leaves her home in Pallansena, a suburb about fifteen miles north of Colombo, and travels for more than three hours in a crowded bus to the shrine of Our Lady of Lourdes in a village called Kudagama. Rita has been making this journey almost every month for the last ten years: at one time she was going every week. She goes because she considers this shrine to be the most sacred spot in the whole of Sri Lanka, a place chosen by the Virgin Mary to make her powers known to humanity.

Rita can vividly remember her first visit to Kudagama. She had come with her sister, who was having problems with her daughter. The girl was refusing to go to school and sat around the house doing nothing. Rita's sister had heard of Kudagama and Father Jayamanne, the parish priest. He was said to have remarkable powers and to be able to cure the sick and the distressed. So she asked Rita to come along and keep them company, even though Rita didn't have much faith in such places. 'I was ignorant in those days', says Rita. 'I had no idea of the power of Our Lady or of Father Jayamanne.'

The first time they went to Kudagama, Rita travelled by the regular state-run bus service to Kurunegala and then changed to a smaller bus which ran to Kudagama. She says she first realised how popular the shrine was when they had to fight to get on the Kudagama bus. It was already getting dark, and as the bus climbed the narrow twisting road into the foothills of the central highlands, Rita began to wonder where on earth she was going.

They arrived at Kudagama just after dusk and she could see little of the place. Already a large crowd of men, women and children had gathered close to the bus stop at what she soon realised was the first station of a

Way of the Cross which led up a huge rock past the church of Our Lady of Lourdes to a group of statues representing the Crucifixion. The people were all kneeling, praying with lit candles in their hands. Rita, her sister and niece, bought candles from some small boys and joined the group. Then Father Jayamanne appeared, coming down the hill to join the throng. As the priest began to recite the prayers, Rita began to feel a power going through her body. 'It was like electricity. I had never felt anything like it before. Then I felt a wave of joy. I started crying with love for the Virgin and pity for our dear Lord who died for us.' Then, as if that wasn't enough, something even more dramatic happened. Rita's niece suddenly collapsed and started screaming and wailing. Rita and her sister didn't know what to do, but some other women and a man restrained the girl and told them that she must be possessed by a demon. 'I had never seen anything like it before', said Rita. 'I didn't believe in such things. After all, our priest at home said that such things were all lies.'

Over the weekend Rita saw many more possessed people. She watched them being blessed by Father Jayamanne and the demons being expelled. She saw pins being produced out of people's bodies, pins which had been sent by sorcerers. She met people who had recovered from cancer, who had obtained jobs and had passed exams through the intervention of Father Jayamanne and the Virgin Mary. She heard stories of how Father Jayamanne fought demons and sorcerers; of how the Virgin Mary appeared to him in dreams, and of how she was going to appear at Kudagama as she had appeared at Fatima and Garabandal. She met people who assured her that it was from Kudagama that the Virgin would lead true Catholics in the last battle against the forces of Satan. She also met 'a wise old Italian priest' called Father Paolicci who told her that the reason so many people were possessed by demons, and Catholics suffered so many problems, was because the Church was corrupt and priests were breaking their vows. He told Rita that Father Jayamanne was the only good priest in the whole of Sri Lanka and had been chosen by the Virgin herself to lead the people back to the true religion.

Rita returned to Pallansena full of enthusiasm for the shrine. 'I felt a new person. I now realised that my life had been a sin. I had been ignoring Our Lady. I had forgotten about Christ and his sacrifice.' She began to organise a bus to go to Kudagama each week from Pallansena. The local priest objected. 'He didn't understand. He was afraid of the power of Father Jayamanne', but Rita continued to spread the news of the shrine. She still went to her own parish church but would only take communion from Father Jayamanne. She also stopped going on pilgrimages to the great national shrines of Sri Lankan Catholics, Madhu and Talawila, dismissing them as 'carnivals'.

Over the years Rita has received all sorts of help from Our Lady: she discovered that one of her own children was possessed by a demon which was exorcised at Kudagama; another of her children managed to get a job in Dubai, again with the Virgin's help; when her husband nearly lost his job the Virgin intervened; and when she was ill some holy water from the shrine restored her health. Today she is one of the staunchest supporters of the shrine and claims it changed her life. 'Before I came here', she says, 'I didn't realise what true religion was. I didn't realise why I was unhappy. But now I have peace. Now I know what true religion is.' She points to the miracles which take place each week at the shrine. They are the proof of its sacred power.

The first time I heard about Kudagama was in the summer of 1974 when I was doing fieldwork in a fishing village called Ambakandawila, about twenty miles north of Pallansena. At the time my main preoccupations were with kinship and the economy of small-scale fishing. Although Ambakandawila was a Catholic village I was uninterested in religion. It appeared to me that there was little of significance to say about the religiosity of the fishing families in this village: they simply went to church each Sunday, celebrated the feasts of the Catholic calendar and the sacralised life-cycle rituals, attended the feasts of parishes where they had relations or friends, and went to some of the larger and more famous national shrines. It seemed to me that religion played a minor role in their lives except as an identity marking them off from the Sinhala Buddhists who form the bulk of the population of Sri Lanka.

I was first told about Kudagama by a young priest who had previously been in charge of Ambakandawila but by 1974 had been transferred to the nearby town of Chilaw. For him and for many other priests, the sort of religiosity found at Kudagama was a threat to the changes they were trying to introduce into the post-Vatican II Church in Sri Lanka. They viewed what was happening at Kudagama as a manifestation of idle superstition, the result of priests' failure to educate the laity in the meaning of 'true' Catholicism. But what he had to say about Kudagama, partly based on a visit he had made to the shrine and partly based on what his parishioners had told him about it, made me want to go there. After all, compared with what I had previously seen of Sinhala Catholics, Kudagama promised exotic behaviour and bizarre events. So like Rita, the next Friday I took the crowded bus up from the coast to

Kurunegala, and then an even more crowded bus for the last few miles to Kudagama.

What I saw at Kudagama quickly began to fascinate me. At first what struck me most were the demonically possessed. In over two years in Ambakandawila I had only come across one such case, and that was tame stuff compared with the twenty or thirty cases a day which I saw at Kudagama. I began to be interested in why there were so many demonically possessed people at the shrine, what such possession signified, and how to go about understanding it. Soon, however, my interests widened. In the mid-seventies, Kudagama was attracting thousands of pilgrims each weekend, by no means all in search of relief from demonic possession. Many were coming to the shrine in search of much more mundane goals: jobs, financial success, recovery from sickness and so on, whilst others came simply because they considered Kudagama to be imbued with the divine. Demonic possession was only one aspect of the shrine and, I began to realise, could only be understood in terms of the wider forces which had led to the rise in its popularity. Finally, I became fascinated by the emotional intensity of those who came to Kudagama, a far cry from the restrained forms of religious behaviour I was familiar with from Ambakandawila. The more time I spent there, what had at first seemed exotic became the ordinary, everyday life of Kudagama.

At various points over the next ten years I carried out further pieces of fieldwork in Sri Lanka, all in one way or another concerned with the rise of Kudagama. It rapidly became clear that understanding the shrine and what went on there could not be based on fieldwork at Kudagama alone. Simply in practical terms, the sheer numbers of people at the shrine made fieldwork difficult, but more importantly, by working only at the shrine it proved impossible to situate what was happening at Kudagama within the wider context, not just of Catholic Sri Lanka but also of Sri Lanka as a whole. And so the fieldwork expanded.

I soon discovered that Kudagama was not the only shrine to develop in the 1970s. Rather there was a whole series of such shrines, some flourishing for only a few months before falling from favour, whilst others attracted a regular group of devotees for many years. Although such shrines varied from one to another, the same themes continually recurred: a stress on exorcism of the demonically possessed, a stress on direct contact with the divine through the central figures at these shrines, and a stress on what the devotees saw as a return to traditional Catholicism. Kudagama, although by far the most famous of these shrines, was not a 'one off': rather it was one element of a more general phenomenon.

Whilst continuing to work in the shrines, I also visited the homes of the pilgrims, in part because it was often easier to talk to them away from the hurly-burly of the shrines, and in part to try to understand the backgrounds from which they came. At first this was simply a matter of pursuing individual pilgrims or family groups back to their homes, as disparate as the mansions of middle-class Colombo, the slums of north Colombo and impoverished rural huts. Yet even this was too shrine orientated: such dips into a variety of social milieux told me little of the forces which encouraged some, but not others, towards the sort of religiosity found at Kudagama or the other shrines. And so I decided to focus on three villages, all very different from each other, in an attempt to understand these wider processes.

The first of these, not surprisingly, was Ambakandawila. Here what interested me was why so few people from the village had ever been to Kudagama or any of the other shrines, and why they treated the claims of these shrines with a marked degree of scepticism. Throughout the seventies no more than a handful of people from Ambakandawila went to any of these shrines, and of them only two or three had much credence in the miracles that devotees claimed to take place there. More generally, people in Ambakandawila rejected the forms of religiosity manifest at these shrines, preferring instead much less emotional forms of religious expression.

The second village I concentrated on was Pallansena, Rita's home village. Although only twenty miles from Ambakandawila, Pallansena is a very different sort of community. Situated at the northern end of the periurban area which stretches north along the coast from Colombo, Pallansena is more of a suburb than a village. In the 1970s it consisted of a couple of thousand households, mostly Catholic. Unlike Ambakandawila, where most households depended directly on fishing for their livelihoods, people in Pallansena made a living from a vast range of occupations mainly in the towns and factories between there and Colombo. Although by no means typical of all the villages and towns from which shrines such as Kudagama drew their pilgrims, it did stand in marked contrast to Ambakandawila, for here around half of all households had been to one or other of the shrines, and there was little of the scepticism over the miracles which took place at these shrines that characterised religiosity in Ambakandawila.

Ambakandawila and Pallansena are both on the coast, firmly within the main area of Catholic concentration in Sri Lanka. The third village I worked in, Vahacotte, is situated almost in the centre of Sri Lanka, a

Catholic enclave surrounded by a predominantly Sinhala Buddhist population. Vahacotte was founded in the eighteenth century by Catholic refugees fleeing Dutch persecution and today is a fairly important Catholic pilgrimage centre. Unlike both Ambakandawila and Pallansena, the economic basis of the village is paddy and tobacco growing. Compared with Pallansena, relatively few people from Vahacotte visited Kudagama or any of the other new shrines, yet at the same time there was not the same degree of rejection of them as in Ambakandawila.

Most of what follows is based on my fieldwork in these various shrines and villages, although I should add that it does not consist of three contrasting village studies and I do not attempt to discuss fully religious practice in any of these three villages. Furthermore, just as understanding the rise of Kudagama involved moving out of the shrine into the homes of the devotees, so understanding the present involved at least some attempt to understand the past and the ways in which contemporary Sinhala Catholicism has developed over the last two centuries. Over and over again, people at Kudagama would invoke the past. As far as they were concerned what was going on at the shrine was an attempt to regain the past, to return to what they saw as traditional Catholicism. Just as Kudagama cannot be understood in itself, so the contemporary Catholic community cannot be understood in a timeless present. What was happening in the 1970s was only a series of episodes in the history of the Catholic population in Sri Lanka, and to comprehend these episodes I had also to investigate what had happened in the past and how views of the past had become critical elements in the construction of the present. Thus as well as the fieldwork, I also had to investigate what records of the past were available to me.

There are around one million Roman Catholics in Sri Lanka today. Of these, probably 300,000 are Tamils, either 'Sri Lankan Tamils' or 'Indian Tamils', and I will have very little to say about these groups in this book.[1] Of the rest, except for a small number of Burghers who claim descent from Portuguese and Dutch colonists, all claim to be Sinhala. Excluding some minor inland concentrations such as Vahacotte and groups of Catholics in towns such as Kandy and Nuwara Eliya, most Sinhala Catholics are concentrated in a narrow coastal belt stretching from Panadura south of Colombo to Puttalam in the north. The present distribution of Catholics in Sri Lanka is at least in part a result of the history of the Church in Sri Lanka. The Church first came to Sri Lanka with the Portuguese in the sixteenth century and the coastal areas were those they most firmly controlled. During the Dutch period Catholics were frequently subject to persecution, the Dutch fearing that the Catholics could form a threat to their control over the coasts of the island. However, after the establishment of British rule in the last years of the eighteenth century, Catholics began to enjoy religious toleration, and in the coastal belt the Church regained control over local Catholics.

The minority status of the Catholic community in Sri Lanka is one of the fundamental themes running through this book – and one of the major analytical problems which has to be addressed from the beginning. Writings on religion in Sri Lanka, both anthropological and historical, are both voluminous and excellent. Most have been concerned with Sinhala Buddhists and concentrate on a number of interrelated themes: the nature of 'orthodoxy' in contemporary Sinhala Buddhism, the relationship between Buddhism and the spirit cults, the relationship between Buddhism and Sinhala national identity and the transformation of 'traditional' Sinhala Buddhism over the last century.[2] Yet running through all the work on Sinhala Buddhism has been the close identity between what might be called 'Sinhala Buddhism' and 'Sinhala culture'. Buddhism in itself has been seen as a formative factor on the development of Sinhala culture, and thus recourse is frequently made to implicit ideas of a common Buddhist culture of which Sinhala culture is only one variant, a 'little tradition' within the broader and more inclusive 'great tradition' of the Theravada Buddhist cultures of Southeast Asia.[3]

In many ways, such an approach is not illegitimate. After all, the distinction between 'religion' and 'culture' is at base one which developed in the particular historical circumstances of Christian Western Europe after the Reformation, and in pre-colonial Sri Lanka it did not exist. The Sinhala term *agama* which is now used to denote 'religion' only took on such a specific meaning in the nineteenth century, and even today the boundaries of what constitutes *agama* are still open to doubt, not simply amongst academics but also amongst non-academic Sinhala Buddhists. Yet in the case of Sinhala *Catholics*, the problem becomes particularly acute for whilst they are Sinhala people, speaking the same language as their Buddhist counterparts, a language imbued with Buddhist significance, and sharing much of the same culture with other Sinhala people, they lack one crucial element of what can be seen as central to Sinhala culture: they are not Buddhist.

Put in different terms, Sinhala Catholics exist at the intersection of two analytically separable historical streams. On the one hand they are heirs to a Eurocentric Catholic stream of history, the result of the two great missionary movements of modern times, the first associated with Iberian imperial expansion in the sixteenth century, the second with nineteenth-century colonialism. Sinhala Catholics today are well aware of their Catholic heritage and see themselves as part of the universal Church. From this point of view, the shrines which I shall be discussing in this book and the types of religiosity which they manifest have to be seen in this wider context, the local equivalents to European shrines of the twentieth century such as Fatima in Portugal, Garabandal in Spain or, most recently, Medjugorje in Yugoslavia (Bax 1990). In this sense, the discussion in this book has a relevance far outside the narrow confines of Sri Lanka: at its most general level, it is concerned with the vicissitudes of the Catholic Church in the post-colonial, post-imperial and post-Vatican II world. It is concerned with the ways in which religious activities have retained and even regained a significance which modernisation and secularisation theorists would have appeared to ignore.

Yet at the same time, to view the rise of these shrines as no more than the local manifestation of processes emanating from Rome or Catholic Europe would be to tell only half the story, and the other half is very much Sri Lankan. As I shall show in later chapters, despite all the attempts by the missionaries to create a self-enclosed, hermetically sealed group of Catholics in Sri Lanka, there were always close connections between Sinhala Catholics and members of the majority community. In part this manifested itself in the continuing arguments as to where the proper boundaries of religion lay: what was Catholicism, what was dangerous 'superstition' or 'paganism', and what was simply 'culture' and thus outside the domain of the Church. Yet of equal or perhaps greater importance was that Sinhala Catholics were always members of the Sri Lankan polity, and even if they did have some autonomy under colonial rule, with Independence they were pulled more and more into the main-streams of political and economic developments in Sri Lanka. Thus whilst the shrines discussed in this book can be seen in terms of the wider history of the universal Catholic Church, at the same time they have to be seen in terms of local factors, in terms of what Sinhala Catholics share with their Buddhist neighbours rather than in terms of what sets them apart, as well as in terms of the tension between them.

This tension, this dialectic interplay between Sri Lankan particulars and global generalities, runs through all the chapters which follow, although for purposes of presentation one chapter may stress one theme rather than another. Yet at a more abstract level there is a unifying theme: the importance of power in the analysis of religious thought and behaviour.

As I mentioned earlier, the creation of a separate domain of the 'religious' is a relatively recent phenomenon which developed in a particular historical context. One only needs to reflect on the recent history of the Islamic Middle East to recognise that the sort of division between 'religion' and 'politics' beloved of Western sociologists and politicians is scarcely tenable, whilst even in Britain the continuing arguments between churchmen and politicians make this distinction extremely questionable. In a sense, the fragility of such a distinction is not surprising: after all, both religion and politics are centrally concerned with the nature and practice of power and authority despite all attempts to limit the religious to matters of spirituality, theology, soteriology or whatever. Ultimately, the distinction between 'religion' and 'politics', whether made by churchmen, politicians or academics, is itself ideological.

As far as this book is concerned, the central argument is that understanding the nature of contemporary Catholicism in Sri Lanka, and indeed throughout the world, requires relations of domination to be placed at the centre of the analysis. At the most obvious level, the Catholic Church arrived in Sri Lanka as part of the ideological baggage of the Portuguese invaders. From the beginning, the Church in Sri Lanka was associated with a particular form of colonial intervention. More recently, the rise of Sinhala nationalism has been closely linked to the resurgence of Buddhism and various attempts at the construction of particular Buddhist conceptions of the state, authority and legitimacy. Sinhala Catholics have had little choice but to react to the changing situation. As will become clear in later chapters, the attempts by various Catholics to affirm the distinction between religion and politics have been a failure. Within the Sri Lankan polity which emerged in the years after Independence there was simply no space for such a distinction to emerge.

Yet there is more to the relationship than simply colonial domination and nationalist reaction. Conceptions of power and authority are crucial elements within both the Catholic and Buddhist traditions. In the history of the Buddhist states of Southeast Asia, kingship and the state have been conceptualised in a particular Buddhist form. These images continue to play an important part in the ways in which such states are constituted today and the forms which the grammar of political struggle take.[4] Similarly, ever since the Emperor Constantine's victory at the battle of Milvan Bridge, the Catholic Church has been centrally concerned with attempting to define the nature of political authority and legitimate domination. Indeed, if the distinction between 'religion' and 'politics' is to be used in any analytical sense, the historical picture in both traditions is of religion encompassing politics rather than existing as a separate domain which only rarely interacts with the political.

Such preoccupations with authority and domination are not restricted to the level of the state but also encompass other aspects of social life. Both the Buddhist and Catholic traditions are concerned, to a greater or lesser extent, with regulating moral and ethical conduct. In the Catholic tradition, relations between clergy and laity, the nature of economic relations and relations within the family have all been of critical concern. These areas are also crucially concerned with domination: the relative spheres of authority of clergy and laity; what count as legitimate and illegitimate economic activities; relations of authority within the family. In becoming involved in such matters, the Church has attempted to clothe what is ultimately arbitrary with transcendental reality and significance. The result has been that almost all aspects of life can become imbued with supra-mundane significance. As we shall see in later chapters, a young girl failing her exams, a middle aged woman suffering from arthritis or a young man successfully obtaining a job in Dubai, all become signifiers of this wider, transcendental reality. The preoccupation with legitimate domination and authority breaks down the divide between the macrocosm and the microcosm, between the universe and the individual.

By approaching religion in terms of domination and authority, the frequently used distinctions between 'tradition' and 'modernity' or 'tradition' versus 'change' also become extremely problematic. Earlier I mentioned that one of the main themes in writings on Sinhala Buddhists has been the ways in which Sinhala Buddhism has been transformed over the last century or so. Much of this body of work presents an idealised, often perfectly integrated and highly functionalist view of the role of Buddhism in the past.[5] The result is an extremely static, ahistorical picture of the past which is surely questionable, and even if such an unlikely picture of the unchanging past is true for Buddhist Sri Lanka, it quite clearly is not when one looks at the history of the Catholic Church. What emerges after even the most cursory look at the latter is a picture of continual change, of continual struggle over what is and is not 'true Catholicism' and of major shifts in the dominant interpretations of the Gospels. It is not that there is no continuity, but rather that the continuity of institutions (such as the Church) or of elements (such as the Virgin Mary, the saints) should not be allowed to disguise the discontinuities which are at least as important. The claim that the Church makes to being the bearer of an unchanging tradition is itself part of an attempt to legitimate its own authority. Tradition is thus an aspect of domination and in itself an area of dispute.

Devotees at the shrines discussed in this book claim that they, rather than the contemporary Church, are the true heirs to the Catholic tradition. So when 'tradition' is used in the chapters that follow, it is not used in any strong sense to denote either a continuous unchanging Catholic tradition or an unchanging static past, but rather in a much weaker sense to indicate that there is a thread of historical continuity with the past within which change is what has to be stressed.

Within such a framework, any opposition of the 'ideal' versus the 'actual' is untenable. Attempts to create some essential 'Catholicism' or 'Buddhism' are doomed to failure as analytical constructs. Admittedly, texts can be written which claim to present the true nature of either Buddhism or Catholicism, but such attempts must be seen as selective and particular endeavours, each presenting a partisan position in a continuing dialogue. Rather, the approach taken in this book is that understanding what is called 'religion' involves understanding religious practice. By this I mean that religion is something which people do: for my purposes it does not exist except in so far as people act, speak and reflect as beings in the world, and as such understanding their religious behaviour also involves taking into account other aspects of their lives which are often viewed as being outside religion. This is not to say that all aspects of people's lives will fit neatly together into one totality, a sort of micro-cosmic version of functionalist views of society. There are discontinuities, fractures, inconsistencies and paradoxes in people's lives, for after all, post-colonial Sri Lanka is itself a mass of contradictions and discontinui-ties. But it is through visiting such shrines as Kudagama, through witness-ing and reflecting on the events which take place there, that individuals attempt to reintegrate their fragmented experiences.

Furthermore, by focusing on religious practice, activities at shrines such as Kudagama can be seen as areas of dispute and contention rather than consensus and harmony. Any idea that the laity are simply passive recipients of ideas and practices imposed by the priesthood becomes untenable. Rather the whole field of religious practice has to be viewed as a field of struggle and dispute, as individuals and groups attempt to impose their practices and their understandings on others. And it is through such debate that new forms of religious expression and understanding are created. At the wider level, in this book culture is seen as something which is ever changing, developing and transmuting, the object rather than the tool of analysis.

The next two chapters are concerned with the broad history of the Catholic community in Sri Lanka since the early nineteenth century.

Chapter 2 concentrates on the colonial period, on the efforts of the European missionaries to create a strong sense of common identity amongst Catholics, on their attempts to introduce a specific set of religious practices and on the growing opposition between Catholics and members of other religious groupings in Sri Lanka. The post-Independence period is discussed in chapter 3 with particular stress on the resurgence of Sinhala Buddhist power in Sri Lanka and the impact of Vatican II on relations between priest and laity.

Chapters 4, 5 and 6 are all concerned with Kudagama. The first of these chapters deals with the rise of the shrine and the creation of a traditionalist focus amongst Sinhala Catholics. Chapters 5 and 6 both concentrate on demonic possession and exorcism. In chapter 5 the major theme is the way in which a strong dualistic cosmology is generated at Kudagama through the exorcism process and the ways in which general and particular themes are brought together which bring issues of power and authority to the fore. In chapter 6 a series of individual cases are examined to show how possession and exorcism are used to reinforce relations of domination and subordination.

Up to this point the book is mainly concerned with stressing themes within the Catholic tradition and with what separates Catholics from non-Catholics. The remaining chapters are concerned with what Catholics share with their fellow Sri Lankans, particularly with Sinhala Buddhists. Thus chapter 7 widens the discussion to look at three other Sinhala Catholic shrines. Here the focus is on the holy men at these shrines and the ways in which the construction of holiness displays both Catholic and non-Catholic elements. Chapter 8 deals with the social context in which these new shrines and various new forms of Buddhist religiosity have arisen, and it is argued that these particular forms of religious practice are intimately related to transformations in the political economy of Sri Lanka over the last few decades. In chapter 9 some new forms of religious expression are examined.

# 2

## The colonial Church

### Introduction

Rita was born in 1935. Both her parents were devout Catholics, her father being one of the *annavis* (lay leaders) of Pallansena church, and her mother a member of the Legion of Mary. She was educated in a convent school, many of her teachers being nuns from Europe. During adolescence, she thought of becoming a nun herself, but this wasn't very serious and when she was eighteen her parents arranged her marriage to a very distant relation, also a Catholic, who was in government service.

The world that Rita and her contemporaries grew up in was very largely defined by religion. Each day there was the cycle of prayers signalled by the Angelus bell from the local church. Each week she attended mass on Sunday morning. Through the year she, her family and her neighbours observed the annual cycle of church feasts and fasts. Most years the family went on pilgrimage to Madhu or Talawila. Just as the temporal dimensions of her life were defined by religion, so too were the social dimensions. Most people in Pallansena were Catholic, the few Hindus, Buddhists and Muslims forming an insignificant minority. All her relations and friends were Catholic and she rarely met anyone outside the Catholic community. People like Rita grew up in a self-confident, almost arrogant community, confident in its superiority over non-Catholics in Sri Lanka.

This chapter is concerned with the historical construction of the Catholic world in which Rita and the majority of those who frequent Kudagama grew up. It is concerned with the ways in which under British colonial rule, the Catholic minority in Sri Lanka became conscious of its identity and, under missionary pressure, developed a series of specific practices and beliefs. The picture that emerges is of a claustrophobic, self-satisfied

B

and over-privileged minority. Today that world has gone, probably for ever, but it is out of such a past that the consciousness, assumptions, hopes and dreams of people such as Rita have been generated. It is in terms of the past experience of Catholics in Sri Lanka that the rise of shrines such as Kudagama has to be understood.

## The Catholic community

In the decades leading up to Independence, villages such as Pallansena, Ambakandawila and Vahacotte formed self-enclosed, bounded Catholic units. Each village centred on the church. Around the village stood crosses or *suruvamas*, statues of the saints. As the church in Pallansena was dedicated to *Viksopa Maniyo*, Our Lady of Sorrows, most of these statues depicted the grieving Virgin with the body of Christ in her arms. Immediately to the east of Pallansena and Ambakandawila, and all around Vahacotte, were communities of Buddhists and Muslims, but apart from market relations and, to a lesser extent, dealings with the administration, contact between Catholics and non-Catholics was infrequent. Catholics in Pallansena felt themselves to be an autonomous social entity in Sri Lanka. Buddhists and Hindus were no more than heathens, whilst Muslims were relegated to the religion of the Old Testament, no Jews being available.

This sense of separateness was something that had been deliberately encouraged by the missionaries. The Catholic Church had first arrived in Sri Lanka in the sixteenth century, as what might be called the 'ideological apparatus' of the Portuguese colonialists.[1] By the twentieth century all that was left of Portuguese influence, at least on the west coast, were the names, not just of Catholics but of many Sinhala Buddhists: Perera, Pieris, Fernando, de Silva and so on.[2] People still remembered that their ancestors had been converted by the Portuguese, 'With a sword in one hand and the Bible in the other', but much more salient in their representations of the past were memories of the Dutch who had controlled the coastal areas from the mid-seventeenth to the late eighteenth centuries. These times were remembered as a 'time of trials', a 'period of persecution' of Catholics by the Protestant Dutch (Boudens 1957). In Negombo, a few miles from Pallansena there had even been a minor Catholic revolt against the Dutch (Boudens 1955). What was also remembered was the work of famous Oratorian missionaries from Goa who, despite persecution, continued to enter Sri Lanka during the Dutch period and preach the gospel.[3] In Bolawatte, a short distance to the north, one of the most famous of these Oratorians was buried, and each year people from Pallansena went to the Bolawatte church feast and prayed for his soul. Others went to Vahacotte where once again they remembered and celebrated those times of troubles.

As far as Catholics were concerned, the great shift in their fortunes had come with the establishment of British rule in the last decade of the eighteenth century. This led, first to toleration of the Catholics, and later, to official recognition of the Catholic Church. Once again missionaries were allowed to enter the country freely. In the early years of British rule Oratorian missionaries continued to come from Goa, but their numbers were few,[4] and, if some rather biased reports are to be believed, they lacked 'missionary zeal' (Boudens 1979: 55–6). In 1830, the Portuguese Crown suppressed the Oratory of Goa and Rome reclaimed rights to missionary activity in the East.[5] Goan priests were replaced by European priests and after a certain amount of rivalry between various missionary orders, the Oblates of Mary Immaculate (OMI), an order based in France, became the dominant group working in southern Sri Lanka.[6] The Oblates and other missionary groups were largely responsible for the strong sense of identity which existed among Catholics by the time Sri Lanka achieved Independence in 1948.

**Missionary organisation**

In contrast to Buddhist or Hindu ecclesiastical organisation, one of the features which characterises the Catholic Church is a hierarchy, not just of persons but also of territory. As well as sending priests, Rome also made appointments at higher levels. An Apostolic Vicar was appointed in 1834. In 1850 the island was divided into two vicariates, and in 1893 five dioceses were established with an Achbishop in Colombo. Pallansena and Ambakandawila were in the Colombo diocese, the most populous Sinhala Catholic area, whilst Vahacotte found itself in the Buddhist-dominated Kandy diocese.

More immediately relevant to the laity was the establishment of the parish system. During the Dutch period the Oratorian priests had established themselves in a few bases and from there made forays into Catholic communities. Much of the day-to-day running of local congregations had been left to lay leaders known as *muppus* and *annavis*[7] whose understanding of Catholic teachings was, as far as the European missionaries were concerned, decidedly limited and often heterodox. As the number of missionaries increased, these quasi-autonomous lay leaders were brought under a measure of priestly control. Yet the missionaries' poor knowledge of Sinhala and Tamil often meant that these laymen remained important as mediators between the priests and the laity.

By the middle of the nineteenth century, the mission and parish organisation which has since dominated the local organisation of Catholic Sri Lanka was firmly established. Each mission (*misema*) was the responsibility of one priest. The mission itself usually consisted of a number of parishes each with its own church, the priest either living in one church or moving in an annual cycle around his churches. Each separate congregation was usually under the authority of a *muppu*, and was subdivided into novena groups[8] each led by an *annavi*. Finally, each family was issued with a *pavula pota*, a 'family book'. In this, attendance at the feasts of obligation, confession and the various life cycle rituals of the Church was recorded, along with payment of church dues. Non-payment of dues or failure to attend the prescribed rituals could mean that the whole family was refused the sacraments of the Church.

In constructing the parish and novena organisation, the missionaries worked on the assumption that there were substantial entities such as 'village' and 'caste'. However, during the early nineteenth century such entities were highly fluid, and by making them the basis of parish organisation priests imbued them with a new substantiality. By the twentieth century, village membership in Catholic areas was largely a matter of church membership,[9] and church and novena group membership was often based on caste. Thus Pallansena was a Durava-caste church. The other three churches in the mission were Karava, Goyigama and Potter churches.[10] Right up to the 1970s the priest was expected to move from church to church through the year, even though all were within a mile of each other.[11] Priests encouraged competition between both congregations and novena groups over the scale of expense on church feasts and were scathing in their criticisms of those who avoided such expenditure. Caste boundaries hardened and caste competition intensified.

The result was a tight, hierarchical organisation. The family was only the smallest unit in the totality of the Church, a totality which ultimately focused on Rome. It was an organisation which could and did exercise rigorous control over its members. Contact between Catholics and non-Catholics was actively discouraged. Attendance at Buddhist rituals was banned. Marriages between Catholics and non-Catholics were frowned upon and non-Catholics had to convert. Older people in Pallansena and Vahacotte could remember the penances imposed on miscreants: having to wear a crown of thorns through the mass; having to carry a heavy cross around the church for seven Sundays; in the last resort even being refused a Christian burial.

**Priests and administrators**

Although the British rulers were predominantly Protestant, Catholic missionaries and civil administrators generally got on well. The decision to allow missionaries to enter Sri Lanka in the early nineteenth century was primarily based on the judgement that Catholics would form a group loyal to the colonial rulers. This judgement was broadly correct, and as late as 1935 *The Messenger*, the major Catholic newspaper in Sri Lanka, was proclaiming that 'To a Catholic loyalty was a virtue' (*CM* 3 May 1935). Admittedly there were tensions. In the twentieth century, French missionaries tried to promulgate the cult of Joan of Arc with its anti-English aspects, and there were occasional criticisms that Iberian colonialism was superior to British colonialism because it was Catholic (see, for example, *CM* 3 July 1931), but in general the missionaries viewed colonialism as 'beneficial to society'.

Missionary and administrator needed each other. For the administrators, the missionaries acted as unpaid assistants, settling local disputes not just between Catholics but also between Catholics and non-Catholics. A word from a Government Agent (GA) to a priest was often enough to solve a problem, the power of the missionary being something the administrator frequently envied. In the opposite direction, petitions from villagers were channelled through the priests, and administrators were suspicious of Catholics who bypassed the priest and came direct to them. At lower levels of the administration, it was not uncommon for village headmen also to be lay leaders of the congregation. In Ambakandawila, the *muppu* and the headman was the same person for over fifty years.

In many ways the positions of the priest and the British civil servant were remarkably similar. Both were mediators, the latter between the native and the colonial state; the former both between the villager and the administration and between man and the divine. Both were European; both saw their role as that of carrying civilisation to the natives; both at least in part, justified their position in terms of racial superiority. The GA in his residency and the missionary in his often enormous mission house led very similar styles of life. 'A foreign, an imperial or colonial, aroma hung about most mission stations' (Vidler 1961: 251).

The parallel between the two was recognised by the laity. Priests and GAs were both addressed with the same honorifics and treated to the same degree of respect. In Pallansena as late as the 1940s parishioners would kneel and cross themselves when the priest walked through the village. The hierarchy of the Church whose bishops lived in 'palaces' paralleled the hierarchy of the state, even the ecclesiastical boundaries following the boundaries of the civil provinces. The paternalisms of Church and state reinforced each other to produce a situation in which the laity were represented, and saw themselves, as spiritual and political dependants. To quote Neill writing of another continent at another time, 'the duty of the convert is clear – to trust in the superior wisdom of the white man and so to be conveyed without too much trouble in the safe bark of holy church to the everlasting kingdom in heaven' (Neill 1964: 438).

### Schools and networks

Being a Catholic in colonial Sri Lanka did not just result in spiritual salvation: of much more immediate importance were the practical benefits which could derive from being part of the Catholic community. Education was crucial here.

Returning for a moment to the early years of the nineteenth century, one of the complaints of the laity was that they were losing out to Protestant Sri Lankans in terms of access to English, the language of the rulers (Boudens 1979: 53). Even after the arrival of the European missionaries, the Catholic Church was slow to become involved in education, and in 1860 there were only forty-one Catholic-run schools in the island (Boudens 1979: 93). Nine years later, however, Catholic schools outnumbered Protestant ones.[12] This rapid growth was associated with two factors: a change in government policy towards 'grant-in-aid' schools, and the work of Father (later Bishop) Bonjean.

Until the 1860s, government aid to schools was in practice given either to state schools or to those run by Protestant missions. The Catholic Church strongly objected to this, and the state gave way. From 1869, with the introduction of the denominational system of education, Catholic schools successfully applied for government grants. Given the organisational and technical skills of the Church, it was not long before an extensive network of Catholic schools was set up, largely at the state's expense. In Pallansena, Ambakandawila and Vahacotte, elementary schools were established next to the churches. Besides rigorous religious education, what was for the period a very good basic secular education was also supplied. At higher levels a series of secondary schools was built up, many of the teaching staff being foreign nuns and monks. Although none quite gained the status of elite Anglican schools such as Trinity College and Royal College, the best Catholic schools produced students highly competent in English.

The result was that compared with Buddhists, Muslims or Hindus,

Catholics enjoyed considerable advantages in gaining government and private sector jobs. From places such as Pallansena, the children of small-scale cultivators moved into white collar jobs, the small Catholic minority becoming grossly over-represented in more prestigious occupations. For Catholics in general, their schools became a symbol of their existence as a community and of their 'progressive' attitudes.

The success of Catholics in obtaining powerful and prestigious jobs was not just a matter of their education: it was also a matter of the close-knit network of contacts which developed within the small community. Catholics were expected to help each other. Priests would intercede with successful members of their congregations to obtain posts for young Catholics. Older people in Pallansena talk of how jobs were found for them through what appears to have been a 'mafia'-like structure of contacts based on a common religious identity. Not surprisingly, Catholic success led to resentment from other groups in the island, in particular from the Buddhists.

**Religious conflict in the nineteenth century**
Until the middle of the nineteenth century, relations between Catholics on the one hand, and Buddhists, Hindus and Muslims on the other, were fairly good. The missionaries had their hands full dealing with self-professed Catholics rather than trying to convert Buddhists,[13] but the situation for Protestant missionaries was rather different. Having no self-made constituency they had to make converts. At first they attempted to convert Catholics, but where this failed they turned to followers of other religions. This soon led to conflict, particularly with the Buddhists. From the 1850s onwards the Buddhist reaction became increasingly militant and Buddhist leaders began to confront the missionaries.[14] At first these attacks were directed against the Protestant missions, but by the 1870s Catholics also became subject to attack. As far as the Buddhists were concerned, Catholicism, Methodism, Anglicanism or whatever were simply variants of Christianity and there was little to choose between them. However, the growing material success of the Catholic community further aroused the anger of Buddhist militants. From 1875 onwards there was a series of violent incidents and a number of deaths.[15]

The first of these clashes between Buddhists and Catholics appears to have been in 1875 at Peliyagoda, just north of Colombo. However, the details are confused and caste differences rather than religious conflict may have led to the conflict (Dep 1969: 97). Much more serious was the riot at Kotahena, a suburb of north Colombo, at Easter 1883, when

Catholics attacked a Buddhist procession.[16] This marked the beginning of a series of clashes between religiously defined groups involving all the major religions of the island, the most serious being the 1915 riots between Buddhists and Muslims.[17]

Two things stand out about these clashes, at least from the Catholic side. The first is the importance of space. Catholics (and other religious groups) considered that certain territorial areas 'belonged' to them. Trouble was fomented when members of one religious group invaded the territory of another, usually in procession. Thus one of the last incidents involving Catholics, still remembered in Pallansena, involved a Hindu procession attempting to go past the main Catholic church of Negombo in 1906.[18] These clashes reinforced lay Catholic ideas that they controlled specific territories, and it was around this time that the practice of erecting religious statues and crosses at the boundaries of parishes became widespread. Social identity was made physically manifest in spatial terms.

The second aspect which stands out is the arrogant and confrontational language used by the leaders of the Catholic community. 'Buddhism is a dormant system', announced *The Catholic Messenger*, 'and every effort to rouse it from its deathlike slumber is destined to total failure' (*CM* 20 July 1883). And of the Church,

Nothing can check her progress because she is endowed with a divine vitality and a supernatural power ... because she is THE TRUE RELIGION [*sic*] and truth will always win.                                                    (*CM* 10 September 1909)

Priests appear to have encouraged the violence. The Committee of Enquiry into the Kotahena riot blamed the local priests for organising the Catholic mob, whilst immediately after the riot *The Messenger* claimed that,

However peaceful Catholics may be, they are not people who will stand any nonsense and ... even the protection of the police will not secure impunity to processions insulting Christianity.                          (*CM* 26 June 1883)

These themes – a willingness to use violence to defend Catholic privileges, and a certainty of superiority – recurred over and over again. The result was to reinforce a sense of identity amongst Catholics and to widen the gap between them and members of other religious groups in the country. Missionaries encouraged such developments because the more socially isolated the Catholic laity, the easier it was to control them. Even today in villages such as Pallansena and Vahacotte older Catholics can still remember the days when the Catholic community was so sure that God was on their side that they could engage in such clashes with the Buddhist majority.

**The Church on the defensive**
The confidence of the Catholic Church in Sri Lanka was probably at its height in the years immediately before the First World War. Thereafter, the hierarchy was forced to move onto the defensive. With the introduction of universal suffrage through the Donoughmore constitution of 1931, 'race' and ethnicity became increasingly important as bases for social identity.[19] As Catholics straddled the ethnic divide, it might have been expected that attacks on Catholics would decline. However, this was not to be, for the stress on ethnicity also involved religious identity. To be a 'true' Sinhala was interpreted as also being a Buddhist Sinhala, and Sinhala Catholics became exposed to the criticism that they were not 'really' Sinhalese.

This argument was possibly put forward most strongly by G. P. Malalasekera, the president of the All Ceylon Buddhist Congress (ACBC), and Malalasekera became something of a *bête noire* to missionaries and Catholic laymen involved in public affairs. Even in villages such as Ambakandawila the laity remembered him as an enemy of the Church. As far as Malalasekera and his followers were concerned, Catholics were 'denationalised', following alien customs, being controlled by foreign missionaries and owing their allegiance to a foreign Pope. Furthermore, Malalasekera went on to claim that Catholic Sinhalese were no more than mongrels:[20] 'Any attempt to make a full blooded Sinhalese the follower of any other religion other than his ancestral faith [i.e. Buddhism] would be like grafting something alien to the stem of an old oak' (Malalasekera, quoted in *CM*, 8 March 1940). Either Catholic Sinhalese were traitors to their heritage or they could not have pure Sinhala ancestry.[21]

Such rhetorical attacks had relatively little effect on most of the laity who were firmly locked into their identity as Catholics. On the other hand, the hierarchy and those most involved in public life, saw clearly that Sri Lanka was moving towards greater political autonomy, and that as a small minority Catholics had to reach some sort of accommodation with the dominant Buddhist majority. In *The Messenger*, attacks on Buddhists and Buddhism became much less strident. Rather weak efforts were made to deny the linkage between ethnicity and religious identity. Thus *The Messenger* attempted to claim that,

Religion is not an element of nationality ... The evidence of history goes to show that Buddhism was not the guiding force in the formation and development of Sinhalese national life.                                    (*CM* 27 January 1931)

But it is doubtful whether anyone outside the Catholic community took such claims seriously, and for most of the Catholic laity, being Catholic was a much more important identity than being Sinhalese or Tamil or Burgher.[22]

The argument as to whether Sinhalese Catholics were 'denationalised' was not just a matter of rhetoric: it also concerned power and access to power. The Catholic educational system was crucial here. By the 1930s the Catholics were generally considered to have the best school system in the country, and Church control over these schools was continually attacked by Buddhists and other nationalist groups. It was argued that these schools gave Catholics an unfair advantage; that as they were supported by government grants-in-aid they should be controlled by the state; that they were used as a means of proselytising non-Catholic children who attended them; that they introduced alien customs and values into Sinhalese society.

The debate over the schools was closely linked to a second line of attack: the network of contacts which led to Catholics being over-represented in the civil service, in business and in what little industry there was. Vague claims of a 'Catholic Mafia' were linked to more specific accusations concerning 'Catholic Action'.[23] Buddhist critics claimed that it was a source of information for the hierarchy and a means by which the hierarchy passed on instructions to the laity. The Church continually denied these accusations, but Buddhist suspicions remained, and their unease was only increased by statements such as that in *The Messenger* just before Independence that, 'Catholic Action must find ways and means of helping to form a political elite' (*CM* 8 September 1946).

By this time, the Church in Sri Lanka was caught in a dilemma of its own making. Its very success in creating a self-conscious, autonomous Catholic community and an effective school system had made the community an object of attack. Furthermore, it was an alien organisation: priests and Catholic laity did owe allegiance to Rome. Admittedly the Church could point to the slowly growing number of Sri Lankan priests as symptomatic of its indigenisation, but they were as European in their values and outlook as the missionaries. A few churches were built in a rather peculiar 'neo-Kandyan' architectural style, but this impressed no-one, least of all the laity who viewed European Gothic as the only authentic Catholic architecture.

The more dominant reaction in the Church was to make no compromise with the rising Sinhala Buddhist movement. The Church claimed that it had a right to control the schooling of its members and that the schools had been built with the funds of the Catholic community. If Catholics were over-represented this was the result of their own efforts, and Buddhists should emulate the Catholic example rather than winge about privilege. In the parishes, priests and the laity reaffirmed their exclusivity in the face of attack.

At the same time, the Church became more deeply involved in the electoral process. With the extension of the franchise in the 1930s, the hierarchy and individual priests found their role as champions of the laity and mediators between individuals and the administration being eroded. Instead, they turned to influencing both candidates and the electorate. In the run-up to the 1936 election the Catholic Union circulated all candidates with a questionnaire concerning their attitude towards religious neutrality of the state, the independence of schools, and their position on divorce (*CM* 4 February 1936). Catholics were instructed to vote for those candidates (57 out of 117) who had given 'satisfactory replies'. Older people in Pallansena still remember the priest of the time, a Father Bernard, warning them from the pulpit of the fate that awaited them in the afterlife if they disobeyed the Church's advice. They go on to add that the threats were needless: no one would have considered disobeying the advice of the Church and its ministers.

## Missionary religiosity

So far, I have concentrated on the way in which a specific Catholic identity was generated in colonial Sri Lanka and how this led to tension between the Catholic minority and the Buddhist majority. But the missionaries themselves were more interested in spreading the word of God than in creating a privileged minority, and in their eyes attempts to create a Catholic community in Sri Lanka were only a means towards evangelisation.

The European missionaries of the nineteenth century presented the teachings of the Church as absolute truth. Other religions were gross errors – the work of the devil – and salvation could only be attained through mother Church. Admittedly, the missionaries accepted the pragmatic power and efficacy of what they saw as the 'spells' and 'sorcery' of the indigenous religions, but these were presented as producing only short term benefits. In the long run people who had recourse to them were damned. Between the morality and ethical correctness of Catholicism and the amorality and ethical incorrectness of the indigenous religions there were no shades of grey, only an all-encompassing opposition.

To understand the particular style of Catholic religiosity introduced into Sri Lanka during the nineteenth and twentieth centuries a little has to be said about the European background. Theology does not develop in a social or political vacuum. Rather, it finds its forms and metaphors from its context, the dominant religiosity of an age owing at least as much to political realities as to abstract principles. The missionaries came to Sri Lanka bearing the theological preoccupations of their European, particularly French, background.

The great wave of Catholic missionary activity in the sixteenth century was predicated on a close relationship between state and religion, 'Gallicanism' holding that the Church was dependent on the absolutist state.[24] In eighteenth-century Europe the 'inductive model for understanding divine relations' (Christian 1972: 174) was the model of the state headed by an absolutist ruler. In terms of such a model, religious representations focused on God: other divine beings only figured as mediators between man and God. But with the decline of the absolutist state, the shift towards 'ultramontanism' – the principle that Rome was dominant in spiritual matters – and the growing split between the secular and the spiritual in western Europe, the model for understanding divine relations changed. As the autonomy of the Pope as the 'Vicar of Christ' increased, Christocentric and Mariocentric religiosity became more important (Heyer 1969: 177–83). Furthermore, drawing on arguments first developed by St Thomas Aquinas, the family not only became the dominant metaphor through which divine relations were understood but also, by refraction, became part of the divine order itself. Thus the relationship between Christ and his Church could be figured in terms of parent and child and also in terms of husband and wife (Kselman 1983: 97–102). Similarly the priest could be presented as both father and husband to his congregation. Through a complex series of metaphors, the priest's crucial role was made concrete through implicit ideas concerning the homology of the family and relations within the family with ideas of the divine and relations between man and the divine.[25]

Thus one major theme in missionary activity right up to the middle of the twentieth century was a stress on the family. Strenuous efforts were made to regularise family relations.[26] Life cycle rituals, especially marriage, were of major importance. Those who lived in sin were subject to excommunication, and when they repented were subject to fines and penances. Family life became infused with sanctity and served as the basis for missionary representations of the nature of divinity.

A second major theme was what the missionaries presented as an 'ethicalisation' of religion. As far as they were concerned, the emphasis on the saints which they found in Sri Lanka was part of an 'instrumental' approach to religion, the laity looking for pragmatic benefits rather than spiritual salvation. The missionaries attempted to deepen and improve the inner spiritual life of the laity. They presented mankind ever since Adam as being inherently sinful, salvation being attainable only through purification of the soul, through what William Christian (1972) has called, 'generalised devotions'. Central to this view of salvation was Christ who, through dying on the Cross, absolved us of our sins and held out the promise of salvation. Through confession, through regularly receiving the mass and the other sacraments, people could be purified of their sins and escape the taint of original sin. Throughout the colonial period the missionaries strove to encourage attendance at the mass and various forms of spiritual devotion, particularly the Christocentric cults such as those of the Sacred Heart, the Five Wounds of Christ, the Holy Face and the Blessed Sacrament. They also encouraged a view of suffering as an imitation of Christ: as a path to salvation.

Precisely how the missionaries promulgated these cults remains unclear. Sermons and teaching in schools were undoubtedly important, whilst sodalities and other societies were created in the parishes. As in France, special missions were launched to evangelise particular parishes using specialist clergy (Kselman 1983: 17). In Pallansena and elsewhere there were various groups active in the twentieth century which encouraged devotional activity. Despite some suspicion of externals, missionaries were willing to use some pre-existing forms of religious expression. The most obvious of these were the Easter Passion Plays. These appear to have been introduced by the Portuguese, but they fell into disuse during the Dutch period, and were revived by the missionaries. Instead of actors, huge puppets, often made in India, were used to depict Christ and his disciples. One description of such a drama comes from the diary of the Assistant Government Agent (AGA) who visited the church at Nainamadamma, a few miles to the north of Pallansena, on Palm Sunday 1869. Here he found 'about two thousand people or more', all looking 'as clean and respectable as possible'.

After high mass a [drama] took place on the stage in front [of the church] of Christ's entry into Jerusalem. All the principal figures were puppets worked by strings from below, and some were men dressed in a costume that was never seen before even in the heavens above or in the earth below or in the waters under the stars. Anything more outrageously bad, a stupidly [illegible] could not be conceived. To a good Roman Catholic it was nothing less than blasphemous. To a philosopher the most silly nonsense. How it is tolerated by the priests I cannot conceive. I have had a bad headache all through the day ...                (SLNA 42/47)

Such performances were common throughout the coastal belt from Colombo to Mannar. Even where there were no dramas, as for instance in Vahacotte, a version of the Passion written by Jacob Goncalvez was often read by parishioners during Easter. Elements such as the 'harrowing of hell' on Easter Saturday became minor pantomimes, small boys dressed up as demons running through the streets, stealing from shops and insulting their elders. By the 1930s and 1940s the dramas were beginning to die out. In some places they just faded away; in others the puppets were replaced with human actors, and after a Sinhala Catholic had visited Oberammergau, many of the surviving Easter plays became imitations of the more famous European performance.[27] Pallansena was one of a very few parishes which still put on a performance with puppets in the 1970s.[28]

A third major theme in missionary religion was the cult of the Virgin Mary. Again, the development and propagation of this cult must be seen in terms of processes based in Western Europe, processes which had an important political dimension. In both Europe and Sri Lanka, devotion to Mary had of course been a major theme in popular religiosity prior to the nineteenth century (Peiris 1948), but from the early 1800s onwards, 'Mariolatry' became increasingly important (Pope 1985). The nineteenth century was the great period of the Marian revival, especially in France, and many French missionaries had personal devotions to the Virgin. In 1830 St Catherine Laboure experienced an apparition of the Virgin which was the stimulus for the cult of the Miraculous Medal. In 1849, there was a further apparition at La Salette and in 1858 the even more famous apparition at Lourdes took place.

Christian has suggested that the stress on the Virgin Mary in the nineteenth century was related to the growth of the symbolic importance of the family (Christian 1972: 174), but other factors were also important. Given the renewed Christocentric nature of nineteenth-century Catholic teaching, the role of the Virgin, Christ's mother, necessarily took on a new significance. Furthermore, in the ultramontanist atmosphere of the nineteenth century, the particular religious inclinations of the Pope became increasingly important. Pius IX was cured of epilepsy at the Marian shrine of Loretto (Heyer 1969: 179) and had a strong personal devotion to Mary. The apparition in 1858 at Lourdes when the Virgin announced that she was 'The Immaculate Conception' effectively put the seal on Papal Infallibility and the dogmatic announcement of the immaculate conception which had been made by the Pope without the bishops. Devotion to Mary thus became intimately associated with loyalty to the Pope and the encouragement of Marian devotion by such missionary orders as the OMI (Kselman 1983: 33, 161) and Sylvestrine Benedictines was in part a sign of their loyalty to the universal Church.

Within Sri Lanka, various Marian devotions grew in popularity. Foreign missionaries encouraged the use of the Rosary. As in Europe, May became the 'Month of Mary' and in some parishes such as Pallansena and Vahacotte novenas in her honour were (and still are) held every night throughout May. The various advocations of Mary – Our Lady of Seven Doulours, Our Lady of Mount Carmel, Our Lady of the Snows, Our Lady of Perpetual Succour and so on – all became popular in Catholic areas of Sri Lanka.[29] From the turn of the century onwards, grottos began to be built in imitation of the one at Lourdes. At some of them miraculous cures began to take place which attracted large numbers of pilgrims.

In the twentieth century, the apparitions at Fatima and Garabandal introduced a further dimension to the cult. Whereas in the nineteenth century the cult of the Virgin had been in part an aspect of the Church's battle against 'rationalism' and 'modernism', she was now stressed as the protector of the Church, particularly against communism.[30] In Europe the Church supported such reactionary regimes as Franco's Spain and Mussolini's Italy and supported Christian Democrat parties. In Sri Lanka, when the first left-wing parties appeared in the 1930s, priests such as Father Bernard in Pallansena thundered against the evils of socialism from their pulpits, threatening excommunication against anyone who supported such enemies of the Church. The cult of the Virgin continued to increase in popularity and reached its peak in the years immediately after Independence, of which I shall say more in the next chapter.

## Saints and gods

How far the missionaries were successful in inculcating the laity with the teachings of the Church is unclear. It is probably impossible to know in any detail what Sinhalese Catholics in the early nineteenth century or before believed about the nature of God, the sacraments, the saints or indeed any of the features which are often taken to be central to the Catholic faith. Protestant missionaries were scathing in their comments on Sri Lankan Catholic religiosity at this time.[31] Such comments, given their source, have to be treated with a pinch of salt, but Catholic observers were equally critical. As late as 1844 Bettachini, the first OMI Vicar Apostolic in Jaffna, claimed that, 'children did not know anything about God, paradise, hell, sin, and virtue; they did not know even the sign of the cross' (Saverimuttu 1980: 38–9). But over all, it is extremely difficult to make any hard judgement for, as Boudens remarks, 'not much is known about the concrete religious life of the Christian communities' (Boudens 1979: 107).

Certainly the European missionaries who entered Sri Lanka in increasing numbers during the nineteenth century were highly critical of their Oratorian predecessors. In general there was a feeling that the Oratorians had insisted over much on 'externals' and had given too little attention to inner religiosity. Furthermore, there was criticism of the missionary methods used by the Oratorians, in particular their stress on miracles. Indeed, miracles of various sorts were crucial weapons in the armoury of the eighteenth-century missionaries. Thus in the documents translated by Perniola there are continuing references to miracles of various sorts, in particular the exorcisms of the demonically possessed, demonstrations of the superior power claimed by the Catholic missionaries. At the same time, the Oratorians were seen as dangerously 'sainto-centric'. Boudens describes the Oratorian missionaries as preaching devotion to St Anna before 'making known Jesus Christ' (Boudens 1979: 55–6).

One of the major problems is that most information on this period comes from biased sources, on the one hand either Protestants or European Catholic missionaries intent on criticising the Oratorians, and on the other from Oratorian sources intent on presenting their endeavours in glowing terms. Certainly there was a strong sense of Catholic identity at this time, but what this meant in terms of behaviour or belief is as yet impossible to determine.

In homogeneous Catholic areas where priests were powerful and able to discipline their congregations, the European missionaries were able to establish a measure of orthodoxy at least in terms of externals. Yet even in villages such as Ambakandawila where contacts with non-Catholics were few, villagers continued to attend the Hindu/Buddhist festival at Munesseram near Chilaw throughout the twentieth century even though they denied they went to worship. Furthermore, as far as belief was concerned, some people in all three villages I concentrated on had views which were decidedly heterodox in terms of the teachings of the Church. A fuller discussion of the problems of orthodoxy, heterodoxy and syncretism will be found in chapter 9, but what has to be stressed at this point is that despite the attempts of the priests to create a self-enclosed orthodox world, Sinhala Catholics continued to retain a knowledge of the practices and beliefs of their non-Catholic compatriots. Indeed, the sorts of practices found at modern Catholic shrines depend, as will be shown later, on a rather detailed knowledge of Sinhala Buddhist religious practice. Furthermore, there were some obvious similarities between the religious activities of Sinhala Buddhists and Sinhala Catholics so that Emerson Tennent could claim that,

it is with the least conceivable violence to establish customs, and the slightest apparent disturbance of preconceived ideas, that the Buddhist finds himself at liberty to venture on the transition from his own faith to that of his new advisors.

(Tennent 1850: 95)

Although the saints lost some of their pre-eminence, they continued to play a central role in popular Sinhala Catholic religiosity. Indeed, throughout the nineteenth century the stress placed by the missionaries on the importance of the sacraments and the importance of salvation reinforced a functional division of labour remarkably similar to that in Sinhala Buddhism. This division, as we shall see later, was important in the changes which took place in the late twentieth century amongst Sinhala Catholics.

As is well known, there is a distinction in 'traditional' Sinhala Buddhism between religious activities centred on the Buddha and those centred on the gods (Ames 1964; Gombrich 1971; Obeyesekere 1963, 1966). At the most general level, those activities which focus on the Buddha are concerned with man's salvation. They are concerned with problems of rebirth, either rebirth into a good life in the future or the attainment of *nirvana*. Activities concerning the gods are not concerned with salvation but with the here-and-now. Buddhist gods are called upon to help man in this world and thus health, wealth, fortune and so on are all in the gift of the gods.[32]

This division of labour is also apparent in the traditional view of the relationship between Buddha, gods and space. Buddha is, as it were, unlocated in space. There are the sixteen holy places where Buddha visited Sri Lanka, eight at Anuradhapura and eight spread around the island, but these are not ranked in importance. Rather they express the total relationship of Buddha with Lanka. The gods on the other hand are spatially located. Each of the main gods is traditionally associated with a particular area of the country and each has a central shrine. Minor gods have minor territories which they are also said to 'own' or 'protect' (Gombrich 1971; Obeyesekere 1966). The distinction is also apparent at the level of personnel. Activities centring on the Buddha involve monks (*bhikkhus*). They are celibate, shave their heads and ideally should live apart from the mundane world. The priests associated with the gods are (generally) known as *kapuralas* or *kapumahattayas*. They are married, hirsute and live in the world. They are usually part-timers, and they may become possessed by the gods they serve.

At its most encompassing level, the distinction between 'Buddhism' and the 'Spirit Cults' is the distinction between the 'supra-mundane' and the 'mundane', two rather poor translations of the Sinhala terms, *lokottara* and *laukika* (Stirrat 1984b). The gods, the personnel associated with the gods, the gods' power and the reasons why people go to the gods are all to do with the mundane world. Buddha, the monks, the teachings of the Buddha and the reasons why people go to the Buddha are concerned with the supra-mundane.

Yet whilst these two areas of Sinhala Buddhism can be seen as separate and contrasted, they are also closely related and form one field. The power of the gods depends upon the *varam* (authority) which Buddha gave them. In return for the help received from the gods people transfer *pin* (merit) to them which helps the gods in their own search for *nirvana*, and *pin* is the result of actions done in conformity with the teachings of Buddha. Thus the two systems form one totality each in part dependent on the other. They exist in a complementary relationship even though activities associated with the Buddha are conceived of as morally superior to those associated with the gods. The complementarity of Buddha and the gods is most visibly expressed at *viharas* (temples of Buddha) which are frequently flanked by *devales* (temples of the gods).

In the Catholic practice encouraged by the missionaries, a similar division of labour was apparent by the late nineteenth century. What priests stressed was religious activity centring on God: attending church on Sundays, on feasts of obligation and the life cycle rituals sacramentalised by the Church. In such rituals the saints were of little importance except when used by the priests as exemplars of the good Catholic life. Furthermore, the point of such activities was to gain *galavima* (salvation): the worship of God, attendance at and receiving the sacraments brought no benefits in this life but only in the hereafter.

Yet just as the cult of the gods complemented the cult of Buddha in Sinhala Buddhism, so the cult of the saints complemented the cult of God in Sinhala Catholic practice. Saints continued to be important and people turned to them for help in this world: they were turned to during illness, when there were financial problems, when there was difficulty finding a job. Furthermore, there was a reciprocity between people and saints: vows (*bare*) were made to saints, and once the saint had given what was asked these vows had to be fulfilled. Usually this involved lighting candles or making votive offerings, but it could also involve giving *dane* (alms) 'in the name of the saint' or giving money to the church 'on behalf of the saint'. Furthermore, whilst God was considered to be everywhere, saints were localised and particularised. Thus each parish had its own patron saint who, like a Buddhist god, was said to be the 'owner' (*ayitikaraya*) of the parish and whose job it was to 'protect' (*araksha karanava*) the inhabitants of the parish. At the same time, saints were not just protectors but also had functional specialities. St Anne was the specialist on educational matters, St Anthony for business affairs, lost property and stolen money, and St Sebastian for infectious diseases.

Yet it would be wrong to view the cult of the saints and the cult of God as two separate systems, and again they should be seen in terms of one over-arching framework. First of all, the power of the saints was considered to be the delegated power of God. Thus God had given *varam* to St Anthony to look after business; God had given the patron saints the *varam* to look after parishes. Secondly, the morality of God-centred religiosity was considered to be superior to that centred on the saints.

Of course, there were differences between the role of the gods and the role of the saints, and these should not be ignored. Thus Buddha is dead whilst God is alive, and thus the nature of the saints' power differed from that of the gods. Thirdly, the position of the gods and the saints in terms of salvation was rather different. Whilst the gods were still seeking salvation and depended on the merit they received from people to attain salvation, the saints had already achieved that state. Yet even so, there was a remarkable similarity between the Sinhala Buddhist pantheon and that which emerged in Catholic Sri Lanka. This similarity could, and at times did, lead to identifications being made between gods and saints, and a reluctance on the part of the laity to accept attempts by the missionaries to identify the gods of the Buddhists with the demons of the Catholic tradition.

In practice, the majority of priests tolerated what many saw as idle superstition. Many themselves had particular devotions to individual saints, and they realised that not everything could be remodelled to their ideals immediately. Taking refuge in the notion of a peculiar 'Oriental mentality' which they ascribed to the Sri Lanka laity, they allowed indigenous forms of religiosity a certain amount of autonomy. But as well as accepting the importance of the cult of the saints, missionaries also attempted to use them as means through which 'inner spiritual renewal' could be attained. One of these methods was through the encouragement of pilgrimages.

**Saints and pilgrimage**

As in Buddhist Sri Lanka, pilgrimage had long been a feature of the religious practice of Sinhala Catholics. This continued under British rule, and in the nineteenth century, particular churches became centres of pilgrimage. Most of these were small-scale affairs attracting a thousand or two for the annual feast, providing opportunities for the missionaries to address larger than usual congregations. But two shrines, that of St Anne's at Talawila and that of Our Lady at Madhu, became pre-eminent.[33]

The shrine of St Anne at Talawila stands on the western shore of the Kalpitiya peninsula about eighty-five miles north of Colombo. St Anne's predates the British period. Myths claim that it was founded during Portuguese times and it was definitely of some importance in the latter years of Dutch rule. After the British took over the Maritime Provinces, Talawila grew rapidly in importance. An Oratorian priest built a church which began to attract pilgrims from all over Sri Lanka and even a few from South India.[34] Well into the present century Talawila was the most popular shrine in Sri Lanka.

A slightly less ancient history is claimed for Madhu. The most popular origin myth tells of a statue of Our Lady being taken from Mantota, a town on the coast north of Mannar, into the jungle to escape destruction by the Dutch. In the early British period there seems to have been a minor shrine at Madhu,[35] but it was only in 1870 that the annual pilgrimage to Madhu was formally instituted by Bishop Melizan. From then on it was encouraged by the Church and became progressively more and more important until by the 1920s it was attracting larger crowds than Talawila.

Many people from Pallansena, Ambakandawila and Vahacotte went to both these shrines. Today, older people remember travelling in bullock carts to Madhu, a journey which often took a week in each direction. During the pilgrimage a special language was used, negatives being banned. The grace one obtained from the journey depended on the trials and tribulations of the journey, but at the same time, a refreshing shower of rain was greeted as proof of the Virgin's favour.

For the pilgrims who flocked to these shrines the great attraction was the miraculous powers which both were believed to possess. The earliest detailed description of Talawila, that of W. C. Macready, the AGA for Puttalam in 1867, describes people buried up to their necks in the open sand in front of the church in the hope of miraculous cures. Others were tied to a cross, 'their arms outstretched well above their heads. They were also afflicted in some way or other and looked to St Anna for relief' (AR 1867: 68). A few years later, Father (later Bishop) Joulain described how, 'the speciality of the St Anne pilgrimage is the number of possessed who come to be freed. It would appear that St Anne has a very special power over the devil' (quoted in *CM* 22 August 1948).

Madhu was similarly the scene of searches for miraculous cures (J. P. Lewis 1917: 180). From both Madhu and Talawila, pilgrims took sand home in the belief that when mixed with water it would act as a cure for all ailments, Madhu sand being particularly efficacious against snakebites. At both shrines coconut oil was poured over the crosses which stood in front of the churches, the oil then being taken home for use as medicine. Finally, at the end of the feasts huge amounts of cooked rice were distributed to the pilgrims who treated it as supernaturally charged.

The missionaries were ambivalent about such behaviour. Protestant observers were shocked by what they saw as, 'a pitiable spectacle of superstitious idolatry which is not in any way checked though tacitly recognised by the priests' (SLNA 42/57). Some Catholics brushed off such criticisms. 'If some people believe that a little flogging will do them good there is no great harm in indulging it', was *The Messenger*'s reaction to Protestant criticisms (see *CM* 17 September 1926). Yet it is clear that the priests did not approve of all the 'superstitious idolatry' which went on at Madhu and Talawila. The parish priest at Madhu for example chased away a woman and her relatives who were beating her in the hope of a cure (J. P. Lewis 1917: 180). Macready wrote that at Talawila, 'the priests ... rather discountenance these exhibitions', although 'they are anxious to think that some remarkable cures have taken place at this shrine' (AR 1867: 68).

The missionaries had to accept much that they disapproved of at Madhu and Talawila. The two shrines were major sources of income and to ban such expressions of popular religiosity might have forced lay Catholics into even more unorthodox forms of religious behaviour. As long as the Church could control these shrines, 'popular superstition' was allowed to continue and the shrines were used as a means by which the 'life of faith' of Catholics could be 'deepened and interiorised' (Boudens 1979: 159). Furthermore, both Madhu and Talawila attracted large numbers of non-Catholics and the miracles at these shrines were used in attempts at conversion.

### The role of the priest
What perhaps stands out most strongly in both written records and oral reminiscences of the colonial period is the power and authority of the

missionary priests. On the one hand they mediated between the colonial state and the Catholic laity; on the other between humanity and the divine. The stress on a Christocentric form of Catholicism reinforced their symbolic importance. Priests performed the miracle of the mass and distributed the sacraments. Through the priest grace (*asirvadaya*) flowed to the people. Because of God's grace and the efficacy of the priests, Catholics were able to enjoy not only spiritual but also material benefits. The relative prosperity and material success of the Catholic community was proof of the superiority of Catholicism and the efficacy of the missionaries.

So whilst priests were mediators between humanity and the divine, the means by which good Catholics could enjoy the benefits of God's grace, they were also the cause of Catholic privilege. The laity became dependent on the priest, and whilst priests might see their role as encouraging the laity to follow the good Catholic life, the latter, at least in part, saw their salvation, both spiritual and temporal, as dependent on the way in which the missionaries led their lives.

A crucial aspect of the missionary priest's position and power was his foreignness. He was identified with the superior white rulers of Sri Lanka: priests were the bearers of what the laity understood as a superior religion and culture. As far as the laity was concerned, the missionaries had given up worldly possessions and concerns to come to Sri Lanka. In Pallansena and elsewhere stories abound of how particular priests were the sons of rich and powerful families who had renounced the world to come to Sri Lanka. They had chosen a life of poverty, of renunciation and of suffering, and through that choice had become particularly efficacious vehicles through which God's grace could flow to the laity.

The priests did little to discourage these views and indeed encouraged them. They taught that the welfare of their parishioners was dependent on the priest. They provided models of perfect Catholic behaviour but at the same time encouraged the laity to see themselves as incapable of emulating these ideals. Through stressing the sanctity of family life they encouraged wonder at their own willingness to renounce such a life for something greater. The front that was presented to the laity was one of renunciation: the ideal priest spent his time praying, practising devotions and fasting. Perhaps significantly, the mission houses built in the late nineteenth and early twentieth centuries were mainly two storey buildings. The lower floor was a public area, always bare and spartan. The upper storey, out of sight from the public, was often much more luxurious, and here the missionaries could indulge in less ascetic activities.

## The indigenisation of the priesthood

Since the seventeenth century, the official attitude of Rome has been to encourage the formation of indigenous clergy. In practice this policy was widely ignored until the present century (Aubert 1978: 396). Where there were indigenous priests they remained second-class clerics, and only European missionaries could be granted the title of 'apostolic missionary' (Aubert 1978: 401).[36]

By the early twentieth century, pressure was growing for the more vigorous development of an indigenous clergy throughout the Church. In part this was a practical matter: it was clear that without such a clergy there would be a serious shortage of priests. At the same time it was also recognised, as Vincent Lebbe pointed out in China, that the dependence of the Church on European priests denied the basic tenets of the ultramontanist movement (Aubert 1978: 397–8). In 1919 Pope Benedict XV issued an encyclical in support of indigenous clergy and ordered the creation of regional seminaries under direct control from Rome (Aubert 1978: 401). From the 1920s onwards new ecclesiastical territories were created which were under the full control of the indigenous clergy.

In Sri Lanka, there was strong missionary prejudice against the formation of a local clergy. Doubts were expressed as to the intellectual capabilities of the Sri Lankans, over their commitment to celibacy, and their ability to overcome ties of caste and family or their involvement in local affairs. The first Sri Lankans were ordained during the Portuguese period but none seem to have served in Sri Lanka. Similarly, the first Sri Lankans to become priests during the British period appear to have served abroad. Recognition of the need for a local clergy was one of the factors involved in the Church's support of education and schools in Sri Lanka, but it was only with the creation of the Papal Seminary in Kandy in the 1920s that priests could be educated in Sri Lanka.

Recruited from middle-class backgrounds, removed to the closed world of the seminary and taught by European brothers and priests, these local priests took on the values and attitudes of the missionaries. In terms of their lifestyle, clothing and language, they adopted the models of their European mentors. Like the missionaries, Sri Lankan priests identified Catholicism with the superiority of Western culture in general and saw themselves as a local elite. Yet because they were brown, the indigenous clergy remained second-class priests. It was only in 1939 that Chilaw diocese was created to be staffed by indigenous priests under a local bishop. The first Sri Lankan Archbishop of Colombo only took over just before Independence, whilst as late as the 1960s a number of dioceses in Sri Lanka continued to be led by missionary bishops.

The Catholic laity generally favoured missionary rather than indigenous priests. Partly this was a matter of the colonial presence: because the missionaries were white they had better contacts with the government and were thought to be more effective mediators on behalf of their congregation.[37] More importantly, the laity generally shared the missionaries' prejudice against local priests. Simply because they were locals they were open to accusations of helping their kin or amassing fortunes through corrupt use of Church funds. Indigenous priests could never hope for the same degree of respect or deference which the missionary priests received as of right. Unlike the missionaries, they were seen as men first and priests second.[38]

In practice I suspect that there was little to choose between the missionaries and their local counterparts. Within both categories there were good and bad priests. Some took their duties very seriously and by the standards of the pre-Vatican II Church led impeccable religious lives. Others were much more interested in mundane and worldly affairs. But they were differently placed in relation to the laity. The squabbles of the missionaries were played out in an arena which was at one remove from lay life. The deeds of local priests were much more visible to the small and enclosed Catholic community from which such priests came. Within a society in which it was expected that kin should help each other, it is not surprising that the local priests should have been the frequent targets for accusations, usually false, that they used their positions wrongfully.

The indigenisation of the priesthood had the effect of progressively involving it in more mundane matters. Whilst missionary priests were insulated from such tensions, their social world looking inward to the religious order and outward to Europe, the indigenous priests were not nearly so well insulated from the pressures of local society. Indeed, they were caught in an impossible position. If, in imitation of the missionaries, they denied all ties with family, caste or friends, they exposed themselves to the criticism that they denied their moral obligations. If, on the other hand, they retained such links they were open to the criticism that they were too involved in the world and were not 'true priests'. No matter what they did the local priests were not safe from lay accusations of wrongdoing from which the missionaries were generally immune. And because of these charges, the position of the priesthood began to decline from the pre-eminent position it enjoyed in the late nineteenth century.

# 3

---

# The Church in crisis

## Independence and after

When Independence was granted in 1948 it was greeted by the Church and the Catholic community in an extremely restrained fashion. Admittedly, the Archbishop of Colombo ordered church bells to be rung throughout the island, and a new advocation of the Virgin Mary, 'Our Lady of Lanka', was proclaimed, the shrine at Teewatte being dedicated to her.[1] As far as the hierarchy was concerned, in an independent Sri Lanka, it was clear that the Church would be exposed to attack from the Buddhist majority. As for the laity, the advantages they had enjoyed during colonial rule had made them allies of the colonial power, and most appeared to have been indifferent at best to Independence.

During the first eight years of Independence, Sri Lanka was ruled by the United National Party (UNP). Under UNP rule, the situation of the Church remained much as before: missionaries were still allowed to enter the country at will; the Church retained its schools; Catholics remained a privileged minority. The UNP under Prime Minister D. S. Senanayake attempted to create a secular, Western-oriented capitalist state which implicitly favoured the Catholics of Sri Lanka. But this policy alienated the UNP from the majority of Sinhala Buddhists, and led to their spectacular defeat in the 1956 election.

In this election, the Sri Lanka Freedom Party (SLFP) led by S. W. R. D. Bandaranaike gained a victory which is often seen as being more significant than Independence.[2] The events of 1956 marked a shift towards more populist policies attractive to the Sinhala-Buddhist masses. Sinhala became the official language, Buddhism the *de facto* state religion, foreign policy more left-oriented and non-aligned, whilst various socialist and populist policies were introduced into domestic affairs.[3] Since 1956, no matter which party has been in power, the Sinhala language, the Buddhist religion and (until 1977) the rhetoric of socialism have been the dominant themes in political discourse. In such a context the Church and the Catholic community came under increasing attack, but whilst before Independence the British held the ring, now there were no external agents to protect the Church. The result was a series of traumatic defeats for the Catholic community.

### Pre-Vatican II religion

Even though Sri Lanka was now an independent country, the Church continued to be dominated by Rome. In 1946 the first Sinhala bishop was appointed to the newly created diocese of Chilaw, but European missionaries continued to dominate the local hierarchy. The primary role of the priest remained the spiritual formation of his parishioners and the encouragement of devotions which would enhance the 'inner spirituality' of the laity. There was little direct interest in social matters as such except in so far as they might threaten the Church's ability to further its spiritual mission.

In the immediate post-war world, the major pre-occupation of the Church was the danger of communism. In Europe this led the Church to support Christian Democrat parties where they existed and to invent them where they didn't. Both in Europe and Sri Lanka much of this anti-communist feeling centred on the cult of the Virgin Mary (Christian 1984; Pope 1985). In 1950 there was a visit to Sri Lanka of the 'Pilgrim Virgin', a statue of Our Lady of Fatima, and 10,000 people were present at Ratmalana airport to greet her (*CM* 27 July 1950). From the pulpit and in the Catholic press explicit comments were made linking the apparitions at Fatima with the fight against communism (e.g. *CM* 20 May 1950). Devotion to the Immaculate Heart and recourse to prayer, penance and spiritual reparation were presented as the model of how a good Catholic should act and thus ensure the help of the Virgin in defeating atheistic and materialistic communism. The Pope nominated 1954 as 'The Year of Mary', and a statue of the Virgin was taken on a semi-triumphal tour of Colombo diocese. 1955 was the year of the 'Family Rosary Campaign': 'With the Rosary said in every Catholic home, we shall have no fears for the future' (*CM* 19 February 1955). By June the claim was made that 95 per cent of all Catholics had pledged themselves to the Family Rosary.

In sum, the first decade of Independence saw an intensification of missionary religiosity. A growing proportion of priests might be Sri Lankan and the country might be independent, but forms of religious practice remained focused on the Virgin, the priest, devotions and spirituality. As late as 1962 the *Catholic Messenger* was still writing that,

[The priest] is a mediator between two worlds – the world of God and the world of man – the priest is a man whose goal is to be another Christ, who lives to serve, who has crucified himself so that he too may be lifted up and draw all things to Christ.                                                   (*CM* 1 September 1962)

In such a world Satan had a very real existence:

Satan has convinced a mass of cynical sophisticates that Mary is a sentiment, a slogan, a pious luxury for sentimental fools. And this is his ephemeral victory of our day. But Satan cannot win [for] Mary is the complete antithesis of Satan [and] we are now actually in the greatest Marian age of history.    (*CM* 5 January 1963)

Yet whilst in the past such religious forms were accompanied by various temporal advantages, in this new world the realities of power were rather different.

### Attacks on the Church
In post-Independence Sri Lanka, the Catholic community was attacked from two main directions. First, since the 1930s, left-wing groups had seen the Church as over-wealthy, over-privileged and over-powerful. For them, the existence of Catholics in Sri Lanka was an unfortunate residue of the colonial presence, and the Church was accused of owing allegiance to Rome rather than to the newly independent state of Ceylon. Furthermore, the Church and Catholics in general were seen as 'a creature of Western imperialism' (Wriggins 1960: 332).

Much more important however was the continuing attack from Sinhala Buddhist activists which continued to be orchestrated by the ACBC. The major themes in this onslaught remained as before, but they were made with a new intensity, particularly after 1950. A series of scurrilous pamphlets attacking Catholics and the objects of Catholic devotion was published, whilst a couple of churches were burnt in Buddhist-dominated areas (*CM* 14 August 1954). These attacks culminated in a report produced by a committee of the ACBC which was published on Independence Day 1956, just before the election. The English version of the report was entitled, *The Betrayal of Buddhism*, and consisted of the usual attacks on Catholics and their Church, particular emphasis being placed on schools and the 'alien culture' introduced by the missionaries (Weerawardena 1960: 110–14).

Faced with these attacks, there was little the Church could do. In response to the Left, the Church made vigorous attacks on communist regimes elsewhere in the world. *The Messenger* was full of horror stories concerning the state of religion in Russia, Eastern Europe and China. 'If colonialism was bad, then communism has proved itself much worse' (*CM* 25 April 1955). The hierarchy also tried, unsuccessfully, to forge an alliance with Buddhists on the grounds that communism presented a challenge to all religions. At the same time the Church denied Buddhist claims that Catholics were 'anti-nationalist' and tried to claim there had been a 'Catholic contribution to Independence' (*CM* 30 January 1954).

It is doubtful whether these statements had any effect outside the Catholic community. What they did was reinforce the sense of separateness amongst the Catholics of Sri Lanka. Such feelings were intensified by the attempts of the hierarchy to influence voting. During the 1952 election the Vicar General of Colombo diocese claimed that whilst the Church did not intervene in party politics but only when 'moral law' was involved, to vote for communists was 'against God's law' (*CM* 17 May 1952). More generally, voters were commanded not to support 'those who are hostile to the Church' (Weerawardena 1960: 135). In the run-up to the 1956 election, statements by members of the hierarchy were more muted, but even so, Catholics had a 'moral obligation' not to vote communist (*CM* 7 April 1956).

### The Church defeated

Bandaranaike's victory in the 1956 election marked the end of the Church as an effective force in Sri Lankan political life. Despite a few Pyrrhic victories, within the next five years the Catholic community lost most of its privileges and began to see itself as an embattled and persecuted minority.

Soon after the election, a scandal developed which became a major issue for Catholics involving the republication of a pamphlet entitled, *Kanni Mariyange Hetti* ('Concerning the Virgin Mary') by a *bhikkhu*, Mirissa Panditha Chandajothi. This was the latest in a series of blasphemous pamphlets attacking Christ and the Virgin Mary, and it evoked a bitter Catholic response. Huge rallies were held in Kotahena, Wattala (just north of Colombo) and Negombo demanding its withdrawal (*CM* 29 September 1956, 3 November 1956, 10 November 1956), and the leader of the ACBC was forced to condemn the pamphlet.[4] Such a minor victory may have reinforced Catholic confidence in their power, as perhaps did the publication in 1957 of *The Companion to the Buddhist Commission Report*, a detailed reply to the *Betrayal of Buddhism*.

By the middle of 1957 the government was moving ahead with measures which adversely affected Catholics. Restrictions were placed on Catholic staff working in state hospitals and in the civil service. The Church's ability to own and purchase land was made more complicated (Dornberg 1985: 45). *The Messenger* began to complain of a 'general policy of discrimination against Catholics' (*CM* 13 April 1957) and ran headlines such as, 'Can Christians expect JUSTICE from Government?' (*CM* 12 April 1957). Plans to tax religious bodies, exclude nursing sisters from state hospitals, expel foreign missionaries and nationalise the schools were presented as 'communist' and a danger to all religions. In 1959, a year after the first major outbreak of Sinhala–Tamil violence, *The Messenger* suggested that this year, 'the chosen victims are not the Tamils but the Catholics' (*CM* 25 April 1959). Later in the same year the Archbishop concluded a speech in Negombo attacking plans to nationalise the schools with a statement supposedly made by Negombo Catholics to the Dutch: 'We shall resist unto blood' (*CM* 11 July 1959).

A number of measures were eventually taken which were seen as attacking the Catholic community. Foreign missionaries were either expelled from the country or had to pay a hefty annual visa tax, whilst it became increasingly difficult for new missionaries to enter. Nuns were removed from state hospitals and after the ill-fated coup plot of 1962, which was mainly planned by Catholic officers (Horowitz 1980), Catholics were purged from the armed services and from other sectors of the civil service and the press. Discussions took place as to the possibilities of limiting the number of Catholics in higher education, and in the late sixties Sundays were replaced by *poya* days as the weekly holiday.[5] But by far the most important move was the nationalisation of the Church-controlled schools.

The order vesting all Catholic-owned primary schools in the state without compensation took effect on 1 December 1960.[6] Almost immediately, many of these schools including those in Pallansena, Ambakandawila and Vahacotte were occupied by irate parents in an attempt to prevent the take-over. Priests and bishops were active in encouraging this action. However, faced with the power of the state the clergy soon found themselves in an untenable position, and despite talk of 'parliamentary dictatorship' (*CM* 10 January 1960) and a 'violation of human rights' (*CM* 14 January 1960), the Church had to give way. On 18 January it was announced that,

The entire hierarchy of Ceylon has decided, in the interests of the Church and the State, to appeal to the faithful to withdraw their 'occupation' in order to enable the schools to function in a normal manner.          (*CM* 21 January 1960)

In some confusion, 'Many hundreds kept gathering at Archbishop's House surprised at the latest move' (*CM* 21 January 1960).

Resistance to the schools take-over was not just a matter of the privileges which accrued to Catholics through their educational system: it was much more a matter of identity.[7] For Buddhists the existence of these schools was blatant evidence of the extent of Christian influence in the island, whilst for the Catholics they were 'a substantial part' of their identity (Dornberg 1985: 47). As Paul Casperz, a leading Catholic priest of the period, remarks,

The take-over of schools was violently opposed because it was felt that with the schools would go the last bulwarks of identity of Christians in the nation.

(Casperz 1974: 108)

Another leading priest, Father Balasuriya, wrote of the 'complete bewilderment' of the laity who were 'stunned' by the bishop's surrender (Balasuriya 1975: 11). The same writer described the Catholic community as a 'beaten, splintered, discouraged and vexatious group' after the events of 1960 (Balasuriya 1972: 228).

Even twenty-five years after the event the schools take-over is well remembered throughout Catholic Sri Lanka. In Pallansena and Ambakandawila, stories of who did what, who was active and who kept out of the way, are still told with relish. But what was of particular importance was, first, that Catholics were now only too well aware of their position as a minority in Sri Lanka, and second, that they increasingly felt that the clergy had let them down. Having led them into a battle they could not win, the hierarchy had effectively abandoned its followers. Such was the strength of feeling against school nationalisation that in some places such as Pallansena the sit-in continued for a few days after the bishops had backed down. Bitterness against the priests was widespread for a short time after the surrender, and in a few cases priests appear to have been attacked by their parishioners. The priesthood in general became the object of criticism. Clearly they could not be as good as their predecessors, for now they were failing to protect the Church and the faithful. Whereas previously the laity had been able to enjoy God's favour through their mediation, the take-over of the schools and the other forms of discrimination against Catholics were interpreted as the result of the priests' failure as effective mediators. Such criticisms were only made more extreme with the changes which were introduced into the Sri Lankan Church during the 1960s.

## Vatican II

The councils of Vatican II lasted from 1962 to 1965, and it is perhaps to soon to judge their long-term importance. For most observers, however, they marked a transformation in the stance of the Catholic Church. In Sri Lanka, Vatican II had a major impact on the Catholic community, both priests and laity.

Since the middle of the nineteenth century, if not earlier, the dominant policies of the Church had revolved around its claim to have a monopoly of the truth, its commitment to the idea of a universal, ultramontanist Church, and its determination to fight modernism, secularism and communism. By the 1950s, it was clear to many within and outside the hierarchy that the Church was dangerously out of touch with the twentieth-century world. In Europe 'secularisation' could not be halted simply by denying history. In America the official teaching of the Church was becoming increasingly anachronistic. The majority of Catholics lived outside Europe and America, and here, for instance in Latin America, the contradictions between the stance of the Church and social and political realities were even more marked. The indigenisation of the priesthood throughout the world meant that priests inevitably became more involved with local interests. The increased talk of 'justice', 'freedom' and 'equality' in colonial and post-colonial territories made the monarchical and hierarchical character of Church government increasingly questionable.

In the present context, any consideration of Vatican II as a whole is clearly out of the question. As far as Sri Lanka is concerned, three themes are of particular importance.

The first of these is the change that Vatican II marked in the official attitude of the Church to other religions. From being 'heresies' or 'idle superstition' at best, to 'the work of the devil' at worst, the councils instead encouraged the view that other religions enshrined different ways of approaching God. Even Buddhism and Hinduism were granted a new status in Catholic thought:

In Hinduism men explore the divine mystery and express it both in the limitless riches of myth and the accurately defined insights of philosophy ... Buddhism in its various forms testifies to the essential inadequacy of this changing world. It proposes a way of life by which men can ... attain a state of perfect liberation and reach supreme illumination ... Let Christians ... acknowledge, preserve and encourage the spiritual and moral truths found among non Christians, also their social life and culture.

(*Vatican II*, Nostra Ætate, 28 October 1965, translated in Flannery 1975: 739)

Second, Vatican II instituted major changes in the liturgy of the Church, increasing its relevance for and accessibility to the laity. The most obvious of these changes was the encouragement of local languages in worship. Other features included the priest saying mass facing the congregation and the encouragement of indigenous customs in the liturgy. All these changes marked a retreat from the extremes of ultra-montanism towards more locally orientated Churches. Through such developments, and through acknowledging the status of other religions, Catholics were encouraged to see themselves as members of local cultures and societies rather than as aliens owing allegiance to Rome alone.

Third, and perhaps most important, was the way in which Vatican II redefined the nature of the priesthood and the character of the good Catholic life. Peter Hebblethwaite, writing about disputes after Vatican II, sums up the debate over the nature of the priesthood thus:

One view stresses the 'vertical' element in faith, the relationship to God; and it selects certain persons, institutions, objects which in a privileged way are held to give access to the divine clearly and unmistakeably ... The other view of the sacred refuses to localise it in people, places and things. Its favourite text is John 4 where Christ says that worship in the future will not take place in temples but will be 'worship in spirit and truth' ... Priesthood, for example, ceases to be an attribute of a specialised sacred life but becomes a function which the community needs ... The sacramental, instead of being a sacred rite to be viewed with profound religious awe, parachuted down from on high, becomes the summing up of the high points of human existence.                    (Hebblethwaite 1975: 15–16)

In the pre-Vatican II Church, the priest had been the mediator between man and God, the channel through which grace flowed. In the new vision of the priesthood he became not the mediator but the exemplar. Grace comes not through such sacramental channels but rather through individual action.

### The Church in the 1960s

By the middle of the 1960s, the Sri Lankan priesthood was in a state of some confusion as to its role and what it meant to be a good Catholic in post-colonial Sri Lanka and the world of Vatican II, although most were agreed that the Church could not continue to exist in its present state. Throughout the 1960s leading up to the National Synod in 1968, and continuing in a modified form into the 1970s, various factions developed within the priesthood with the bishops attempting to maintain some sort of consensus.

Immediately after the schools take-over, the hierarchy continued to encourage a 'martyr' ideology within the Catholic community. The troubles of the sixties were represented as a modern parallel to the Dutch persecutions of the Church. Just as the Church had emerged triumphant from that experience, so now it would emerge from the Buddhist persecutions. Partly in response to Vatican II, and partly in response to the local situation, this policy was soon abandoned and the hierarchy began to look for forms of accommodation with the majority community.

The first thing the hierarchy did was disengage the Church from politics. The nationalisation of the schools was accepted as a *fait accompli*. The Church as an institution ceased to issue directives as to how Catholics should vote and announced itself neutral in matters of secular politics. In other words, the hierarchy redrew the boundaries of what it saw as its legitimate area of interest. Furthermore, the hierarchy accepted that Buddhists were the majority community in Sri Lanka and that Catholics could not demand special treatment.

At the same time, the hierarchy encouraged a cultural *rapprochement* with the local situation. Indigenous languages were introduced into the liturgy largely as a result of Vatican II, and by 1970 almost all services were held in one or other of the three local languages: Sinhala, Tamil and English. Work started on producing translations of the Bible suitable for Catholics, but whilst Sinhala and Tamil versions of the New Testament existed by the end of the sixties, the Old Testament took much longer to produce.[8] Besides language, the laity were encouraged to use local names rather than names derived from the calendar of saints. Experiments were made with 'indigenous' forms of prayer and the introduction of 'traditional' elements into the various life cycle rituals of the Church. People were even encouraged to use white, the Buddhist colour of mourning, rather than black.

The process of 'indigenisation' was particularly marked in the context of the annual feasts held in honour of the patron saints. One of the most famous of these feasts was held at Vahacotte in honour of St Anthony. Here, in fulfilment of a vow made in the eighteenth century, Buddhist drummers from a neighbouring village had come to honour the saint. The missionaries of the nineteenth and twentieth centuries had vigorously opposed this custom, but as far as the people of Vahacotte were concerned, the presence of the drummers only demonstrated the superiority of their patron saint over the gods of the Buddhists. In the 1950s, however, the drummers came under pressure from Buddhist activists and stopped attending the feast. Their role was taken over by Catholic villagers, but this still did not satisfy the priest of the time who saw all

C

drumming as Buddhist. In the mid-sixties, however, a new priest was appointed with very different ideas. He viewed drumming not as 'Buddhist' but as 'Sinhalese'. And he went further. He dressed up the *muppus* and the *annavis* in 'traditional' Kandyan costumes and mounted the statue of the saint on an elephant. What he tried to do for a few years was to create a Catholic version of a Buddhist *perahara*, an attempt which did not go down well with the villagers.

The case of Vahacotte is admittedly rather extreme, but throughout Catholic Sri Lanka attempts were made to exclude elements which could be described as 'culturally alien' and introduce 'indigenous' customs. In Pallansena for instance, the priest introduced Kandyan dancing and a *hevisi* band into the church feast and attempted to ban the Western-style brass band which had performed each year.[9] He encouraged people to wear national dress and insisted that the national flag be prominently displayed wherever possible.

Thus just as the hierarchy attempted to redraw the lines between religion and politics, so too priests tried to shift the boundary between culture and religion. What had previously been derided as Buddhist or backward was now encouraged as representing true Sinhala rather than Buddhist culture. This rediscovery of a cultural heritage was only too often an invention of culture, but it did have a certain efficacy in encouraging Catholics to see themselves as part of local society. Indeed, the split between Tamil Catholics and Sinhalese Catholics in the late 1970s and the 1980s was in part the result of this rediscovery of ethnic culture (Stirrat 1984a). The church feast in Pallansena hovered on the edge of a celebration of Sinhala identity – with Catholic overtones.

### The role of the priest

Central to the deliberations of Vatican II had been the question of the role of the priest. By the late sixties, new definitions of what a priest should be were becoming popular in Sri Lanka, and the bishops were encouraging the clergy to move out of their mission houses into the world. Priests were encouraged to involve themselves in the social and economic lives of their parishioners. Spiritual devotion and inner spirituality became less important; social activity more important. Rather than see themselves as *swaminvahanse*, 'lord priest', priests now described themselves as *misema sevaka*, 'servant of the parish'.

At the level of the Church as a whole, one manifestation of this change was in the foundation of new specialised institutions concerned with economic and social 'uplift'. Institutions such as SEDEC (Social and

Economic Development Centre), usually funded by European charities, began to investigate the problems of the laity and set up various development projects. Some of these institutions were concerned with social problems: others with economic development, and they in turn linked up with smaller institutions at a diocesan level.

Individual parish priests also participated in such activities. Either in association with specialist Church institutions, or by themselves, priests set up small-scale development projects throughout Catholic Sri Lanka. Funds which had previously been used to build churches or support spiritual activities were now used to set up small farms for unemployed youths, handloom factories for girls or new co-operatives for impoverished farmers or fishermen. From the pulpit, through less formal contacts and through their own example, priests attempted to change not only their relationship with the laity but the laity's own ideas about what it meant to be a good Catholic. Personal devotions, pilgrimages, attendance at mass, membership of pious societies, were all played down. Social activism, charity work and involvement in community projects were encouraged. Within the priesthood, individuals began to be judged in terms of their success and failure in such activities, not in terms of their congregation's attendance at mass as in the past.

### Divisions within the priesthood
The increased involvement of the priesthood in the mundane world inevitably led to a growing factionalisation within the Church. The development of specialised institutions such as SEDEC meant that less weight was put on parish organisation, and many of the more ambitious (and often the most able) began to see such institutions as the routes to status and power in the Church. Furthermore, instead of isolation in some remote parish, involvement in diocesan or national institutions meant access to scarce assets: trips abroad, further study and so on. During the 1970s, tensions grew between the parish priests on the one hand and clergy in the specialised institutions on the other. The latter viewed the former as backward and reactionary, 'rural hicks', whilst the parish clergy viewed those involved in the institutions as a favoured minority insulated from the real problems of the parishes.

At the same time, even though the Church as a whole had retreated from involvement in politics, individual priests became more involved in political matters. By the end of the 1960s the majority of priests were Sri Lankan. Many had relations or friends involved in political activities and, not surprisingly, had their individual political preferences. Given the

ways in which MPs had become major economic patrons,[10] any priest
who entertained ambitions for development projects in his parish had to
become involved in the political process. The result was that within the
priesthood divisions emerged in terms of political alignments, different
sets of priests supporting different parties or factions within parties.
Priests became active in elections and began to hold appointments in
state-controlled organisations such as co-operatives. At the same time,
this affected not only the allocation of resources to particular parishes but
also appointments within the Church.[11]

The political linkages of the clergy were most clear at the extremes. For
some priests, the reforms of Vatican II and the way in which these had
been implemented in Sri Lanka had not gone far enough.[12] They viewed
the bishops as reactionaries intent on minimising change and on maintaining the economic and social *status quo*. More radical interpreters of
Vatican II began to appear in the late sixties and, amongst other things,
argued against clerical celibacy at the National Synod of 1968.[13] A few
priests appear to have supported the 1971 Insurgency, but many more
were vociferous in their criticisms of the manner in which the government
dealt with the insurgents and with the Church's failure to condemn
government excesses. Individuals such as Paul Casperz and Tissa Balasuriya set up centres which became foci for criticism of both the Church and
the government.

In general, such radicals received little support from the bishops except
for Leo Nanayakkara, Bishop of Badulla.[14] Although never very numerous, these radical priests were well organised and highly articulate
Western-educated intellectuals whose aim was to produce a 'contextual
theology' relevant to the particular situation in which Catholics found
themselves in Sri Lanka.[15] They criticised the Church for failing to fight
oppression and poverty and compromising itself with the forces of neo-
colonialism and capitalism. For them, 'human liberation' and 'spiritual
liberation' were inextricably linked and the Church was falsely separating
the sacred and the profane.

Whilst the most prominent leaders of the radical movement had been
educated abroad and were not involved in parish work, their influence
was felt most strongly amongst younger priests educated in Sri Lanka and
taking charge of their first parishes around 1970. They found their
position particularly difficult. On the one hand they were limited by their
bishops as to how far they could go. On the other hand they found that
the administration of a large parish left them little time to engage in social
and economic activities, let alone radicalising a generally hostile congre-

gation. Many of these young priests, especially in the large Catholic communities of Chilaw and Colombo dioceses, became increasingly frustrated. Some tried to move out of parish work; others sought transfers to the diocese of Badulla, whilst still others left the priesthood. Such departures caused problems of morale and numbers throughout the seventies.

Not surprisingly radical priests allied themselves with left-wing political parties. Drawing on both Christian and Marxist traditions, some priests became active in political affairs and their statements, reported with glee in the press, were a continuing source of embarrassment to the hierarchy. Each time, one or other of the bishops had to restate the Church's position on political involvement: that as individuals, priests had the same rights to political views as anyone else, but that as an institution, the Church was neutral.

Yet if one section of the priesthood thought that the bishops were not going far enough, another section thought that they had gone much too far. For them, both Vatican II and developments peculiar to the Sri Lankan Church were moves away from 'true' Catholicism. They were uneasy about attempts to indigenise the rituals of the Church, they saw attempts to produce vernacular translations of the Bible as little more than blasphemous, and in a general way they maintained a loyalty to the older forms of Catholic practice.

However, what worried them more than anything else was the way in which the role of the priest was being redefined. One priest, in his sixties by the time I met him, remarked that it was true that Christ had said, 'Love God, love thy neighbour.' 'But today', he went on, 'everyone, especially the priests, reverse this and forget to love God.' He went on to use the old analogy of the Cross. 'The vertical', he said, pointing upwards, 'symbolises the love of God. The horizontal symbolises love of neighbours. If you take away the vertical the Cross falls down.' Another priest put it even more strongly:

There are plenty of social workers around, but not enough priests. A priest's job is to bring God to his people: that is his first priority rather than social work. Priests should be holy. They should be in the church or the mission house praying and exemplifying the spiritual life rather than rushing around and involving themselves in the secular world.

Most of these priests kept a very low profile. In the atmosphere of the post-Vatican II Church in Sri Lanka they felt themselves under pressure from the modernists, but one or two were outspoken in their resistance to change and continued to attack the hierarchy and other priests.

Perhaps the most outspoken of these critics was an old Italian priest,

Father Pio Paolicci, OSB, who had come to Sri Lanka around 1930 as a missionary and had remained in the island ever since. By the early seventies he had retired from parish work but was still very active, spending most of his time orchestrating the conservative response to the reforms in the Church. It was strongly rumoured, particularly amongst the radicals, that Father Paolicci received funds from some of the more conservative bishops.[16] What was not a matter of rumour was his connection with 'The Association of the Faith of the Fathers', a suitably ambiguous title for a rather shadowy lay organisation opposed to change. He was also editor of two monthly journals, *The Rock*, an English-language periodical founded in 1969, and *Haktiya*, the equivalent Sinhala journal. Both promulgated an extreme theological, political and social conservatism. Needless to say, Father Paolicci and his associates supported the relatively right-wing UNP, although with reservations.

Father Paolicci saw himself as fighting 'modernism' in the Church. In print he likened the reforms of Vatican II to the Arian heresy, writing of the 'apostasy of the bishops' and the infiltration of the Church by 'men bent on her destruction'. His journals consisted of a series of attacks, often reprinted from European and American sources, on all sorts of 'modernism', plus reports of miracles and apparitions of the Virgin Mary throughout the world. He rejected the theory of evolution because it implied the rejection of the doctrine of Original Sin. Communism and socialism were branded as atheistic. The film, 'Jesus Christ, Superstar', which was on show in Colombo in the seventies, was dismissed as 'blasphemous, heretical and sacrilegious' because it depicted Christ as subject to human passions. Nuns and priests who became involved in social work were held up to ridicule, nuns for 'cutting their skirts short'; priests for wearing trousers rather than the traditional cassock, and for using 'mini-skirted girls and young nuns as acolytes'. In his speech he was even more extreme. His most bitter comments were reserved for those he called 'pariah priests', priests such as the Bishop of Badulla whom he saw as a Marxist revolutionary.[17] Other bishops and priests he branded as 'cowards' whilst he described the National Seminary at Ampitiya as a 'hotbed of heresy' where priests were taught existentialism and Marxism. Rather grudgingly he would admit that there were some good priests in Sri Lanka, but these were few and far between and mostly restricted to the older generation.

### Relations between priests and the laity

Not surprisingly, by the end of the 1960s a large proportion of the laity was somewhat confused as to what it meant to be a Catholic and what they should expect from their priests. A decade or so before, they had been a relatively privileged and self-confident minority. For over a century they had been told that the Church had a special relationship with the divine, a relationship which guaranteed the success of the Church and a privileged position for its followers. Now the Church had been defeated by the Buddhist majority. Catholics saw themselves losing their privileges and began to feel themselves a persecuted minority. For a similar period of time, the Church had claimed a monopoly of the truth, and that it alone could provide the correct, timeless and unchanging teaching about the divine and man's relationship with the divine. Yet now priests were openly arguing about what that truth might be. Many were abandoning all that had been taught as true in the past. Much of what the laity had once been taught was branded by the Church as, at best, irrelevant, and at worst, just plain wrong. Where once prayer, penance and devotion were held up as virtues, now it was social work. Once Buddhists had been presented as the enemy, but now they were to be treated as friends. What had once been derided as 'Buddhist' was now held up as 'Sinhala culture'. What had been condemned as 'communism' was now encouraged as 'social responsibility'.

The speed of this radical break with the past led to large sections of the Catholic population entering a somewhat anomic state. Given the way in which the priests had been central to pre-Vatican II religiosity in Sri Lanka, it is also not surprising that one reaction to this crisis was to criticise the priesthood. Given the priests' claim to mediate between man and the divine, then the eclipse of the Catholic community was surely their responsibility. In the past priests had been effective as mediators and as a result the Catholic community and individual Catholics had prospered both materially and spiritually. Now they were failing, and the reason for that failure was easy to discover: priests were forgetting their true vocation, denying true Catholicism and becoming too involved in the world.

Of course there have always been strains of anti-clericalism in Sri Lanka as in any Catholic community. Individual priests became involved in disputes with their parishioners who then sent petitions to the bishops demanding the priest's replacement. Despite continuous exhortations, there were always some Catholics who refused to go to church. Occasionally whole groups of families would leave the Church as a result of a clash with the priest, often over the *renda*, the dues claimed by the Church.[18] Talking to older Catholics, it appears that there has always been a degree of cynicism over certain of the teachings of the Church, particularly the doctrine of purgatory. Yet both priests and laity in the sixties and seventies saw the past as a time when the position of the priest had been much more secure. Priests talked of the time when they had been treated with much greater respect, even fear, by the laity. And the laity agreed. 'Priests were like kings in those days', one old man told me. 'When they passed we would kneel down and ask for their blessing. Now we don't kneel and just ask them, *koheda yanne* (where are you going), just as we would ask any man.' Whilst the laity recognised that the respect shown to priests of the past was in part a simple recognition of their power, they also saw it as something those priests had deserved.

Sex loomed large in the laity's critique of modern priests. Whilst in the past priests had kept to the mission house, worn a cassock and shunned the company of women, they were now moving out into the world, and it was widely held that many priests were engaged in illicit sexual activities. For one thing, the statements of some priests against clerical celibacy led to lay suspicions. Secondly, the move in some dioceses for priests to shed their cassocks when 'off duty' gave rise to rumours that priests were 'passing' as laymen and having affairs. Thirdly, the involvement of priests in social work brought them into greater contact with women, and relationships of friendship or even of pastoral care could be, and often were, interpreted as having a sexual component. Frequently, as in the case of one parish priest a few miles from Pallansena, a priest would be referred to as a *kukulu swami*, a 'cockerel priest', and accused of having or attempting to have liaisons with unmarried girls and more mature women. In the seventies there were a number of incidents in which priests were physically attacked by members of their congregations on suspicion of having women in their mission houses overnight. In the two incidents which I know about in any detail, the women were the priests' sisters. But the demand on the part of the laity was not simply that a priest should be celibate but that he should be above suspicion. On the one hand, not to be celibate was to be impure and thus imperfect as a priest. On the other hand, to use his position as a priest to gain sexual favours was to make a mockery of his role.[19]

The second area of criticism of contemporary priests was that they were abusing their position by using church funds for their own purposes and for the benefit of their relations. In part this was related to the indigenisation of the clergy and the increasing predominance of secular priests in the Sri Lankan Church.[20] However, the reforms in the Church had forced, or at least encouraged, priests to become more involved in economic affairs, and once they did so they were open to the accusation of being more interested in money than in spiritual activities. The priest in Pallansena in the early seventies, by no means a radical, set up a number of small-scale development projects. In the village he was jokingly referred to as 'Martin *mudalali*', 'Martin the trader', rather than as 'Martin *swami*', 'Martin the priest'. Not only was he accused of giving his economic activities more time than his spiritual life, but also of diverting profits made from a small farm he ran to his sister and her children.

On a more general level, the Church as a whole was accused of becoming a 'business'. In Pallansena and elsewhere complaints were made that funds and property given to the Church for religious purposes were being misused. Thus in one of the churches controlled by Father Martin, ten acres of land had been given to the Church in the 1930s to support religious activities. The parishioners were incensed when Father Martin used the funds to set up a small co-operative farm to employ some of the unemployed youth in the parish rather than have the church buildings redecorated. In Ambakandawila, the parish priest used church funds to help a group of the poorest fishermen in the village. Again this was vigorously opposed by other members of the church, mainly richer fishermen, who stopped paying the *renda* in protest against what they saw as a misuse of funds.

In this context, much of the conflict centred on expenditure at church feasts. In the late sixties and seventies, the Church made considerable efforts to cut down on the elaborate and expensive ways in which these feasts, particularly those in honour of the patron saints, were celebrated. Rather than spend money on novenas, the congregation was encouraged to give the money to the priest for use in charitable work. Rather than engage in individual acts of charity, parishioners were asked to give the money to the priest for distribution through his own charities. In Pallansena there was widespread resentment of Father Martin's activities to control the annual feast, and his efforts were resisted whenever possible.

Similar sorts of objections were raised to the involvement of priests in political activities. Whilst in the past the Church had pursued a political line which benefited both the Church and its adherents, and individual priests had acted as mediators between their parishioners and the state, priests were now taking part as individuals in party political activities. In the 1970 election priests spoke on the election platforms of both main parties. Others were active in a less public fashion. In some cases individual priests became important patrons controlling access to significant resources, and whilst sections of the laity were only too willing to take advantage of such patronage, this by no means meant that they approved of the priest's involvement in such activities.

The most extreme criticisms were reserved for the most radical priests, those who became closely involved with left-wing political movements. Despite the retreat of the Church from formal political activities, the sympathies of the majority of the laity remained with the UNP, and they still remembered the older anti-communist stance of the Church. Now some priests were actively espousing what had been anathema only a few years before, and they found little support amongst the laity. In Pallansena such priests were treated with contempt and bewilderment: how could a man be both a priest and a communist? Elsewhere, radical priests found it extremely difficult to deal with increasingly recalcitrant congregations.[21]

Finally, there was the matter of the indigenisation of rituals and relations with Buddhists. Matters such as the use of local languages and the adoption of local names led to some grumbles but were usually accepted fairly readily. What was much more difficult for the laity to accept was the Church's attempt to introduce local customs into the liturgy and into church rituals, to indigenise church architecture and to build up closer relations with Buddhists. The problem here was that in general the laity did not accept the distinctions now being made between culture and religion. For them, Gothic architecture was Catholic, not European. The ritual forms of the Church were not culturally alien but part of the Catholic heritage. Attempts to introduce *hevisi* bands and Kandyan dancers were seen as Buddhist infiltration or pandering to the Buddhist majority. Thus in Pallansena, Father Martin had to compromise: besides his *hevisi* band there was also an old-fashioned brass band. The former was described as 'Martin's band'; the latter as 'our band'.

The laity also objected to various attempts to improve relations with the Buddhists. Priests began to appear on platforms with *bhikkhus*; *bhikkhus* began to be invited to Catholic events. In some cases Catholic priests helped Buddhists find plots on which to build temples in Catholic areas. Substantial sections of the laity saw such behaviour as incomprehensible: as a denial of all that the Church had stood for, and of all that they had been taught by the missionaries over the last century and a half.[22]

### The reaction of the laity
Although such criticisms of the Church and the priesthood were widespread throughout the Catholic community by the late 1960s, the degree

and extent to which they were held varied. Feelings of distrust and antagonism towards the priests were held most strongly amongst the middle classes and those who depended upon wages and salaries: places like Pallansena and the sprawling suburbs and commuter towns north of Colombo. In more isolated villages such as the small Catholic fishing communities along the northwest coast, the degree of antagonism towards the Church was less marked. Whilst individual priests might be criticised there was relatively little direct criticism of the Church as a whole in such areas. Criticism of the Church and of the reforms of Vatican II was most strongly expressed amongst those groups who had gained most out of the Catholic schools system and the Catholic networks in business and government employment.

Perhaps the most visible expression of the laity's resistance to change was the spread of *suruvamas*, public statues of the saints, throughout the Catholic belt. Such public religious furniture has been a feature of Catholic Sri Lanka since the late nineteenth century when it was introduced by the missionaries as a public display of what they considered Catholic territory.[23] By the sixties, however, most priests were discouraging the building of such statues partly because they considered them a waste of money, and partly because they could cause resentment amongst Buddhists.

From about 1968 there was a boom in the construction of *suruvamas*. With increasing frequency individuals or groups erected statues of the Virgin, St Anthony and other patron saints along the roads and at road junctions throughout Catholic Sri Lanka. The construction of these statues was undertaken entirely by the laity, often in direct opposition to the wishes of the priests. It was a deliberate effort to reaffirm Catholic identity and mark off what was considered to be Catholic space in the face of what the laity saw as an attempt by Buddhists to impose their hegemony on the whole of Sri Lanka. Thus in Chilaw a statue of Our Lady of Mount Carmel appeared one night at the main road junction of the town because of rumours that the Chilaw Buddhist Association was about to place a Buddha statue there. In Pallansena, six *suruvamas* were put up between 1970 and 1974, all in very public spots, and most concentrated on the east of the parish abutting Buddhist-dominated areas. Two of these statues were of St Sebastian, the warrior saint, whilst three were of the Virgin. But whilst the patron of Pallansena was Our Lady of Sorrows, the image that was chosen was not of Our Lady cradling the dying Christ but of the Virgin trampling the serpent under her foot.[24]

The priests opposed the proliferation of these statues partly on grounds of cost, but also because they feared it would exacerbate relations with the Buddhist majority. At the same time, the erection of these statues often posed a threat to the priests. Around some of the *suruvamas* various independent cults grew up. Groups of devotees, particularly women, began to gather around particular statues and, led by a lay person, formed weekly, or in some cases, daily prayer groups outside the control of the priest. In a few cases such statues became imbued with supernatural power, foci for vow-making. Around others, small chapels were built in which not only prayer meetings were held but also annual feasts celebrated. One such chapel, dedicated to St Sebastian, grew up about three miles south of Pallansena in the neighbouring parish, and led to a confrontation between the priest and its devotees. The latter invited the priest to celebrate the feast at the shrine. At first he refused, but later he was cajoled into attending. The priest then demanded rights over the offerings made here, and this provoked an angry reaction from those who had built and looked after the shrine. 'The only time you ever see a priest is when he comes to empty the collection box', was the comment of one lady who lived next to it. 'That's the trouble with all the priests these days.'

Attempts to escape from the formal Church were not restricted to these new *suruvamas*: what might be called, 'religious privatisation' was also evident in other ways. Many Catholics began to cut down their attendance at mass, coming to church only for the life-cycle rituals and the feasts of obligation. They ceased to view the priests with the respect they once enjoyed, denied their authority to determine what good Catholics should or should not do, and began to practise their own private devotions at home, in the local church, or in private chapels. In the main these devotions were based on forms introduced by the missionaries. Often they involved the rosary or other Mariocentric cults. At times, as with Gabriel, my landlord in Pallansena, they consisted of a complicated series of devotions, different prayers for different days of the week and, he claimed, different months.

For such people, priests became increasingly irrelevant. Devotions ceased to be an adjunct but an alternative to church attendance. Individuals experimented with their own forms of religiosity, either using prayers they had learnt from the missionaries in their childhood, learning prayers from other like-minded people, or even making up their own. Priests might object to such activities, but there was little they could do. Their authority had dissolved; their effective power was at an end. Through such private activities individuals attempted to regain contact with the divine, contact which had been hitherto mediated through the priests.

A further alternative was to seek out 'traditionalist' priests, those who remained faithful to the older order. From Pallansena individuals and families began to visit another parish, about fifteen miles away, where the elderly priest still spoke out against communism and Buddhism, and criticised the newer forms of the priesthood. Others turned to even more extreme shrines which held out the promise of an even more direct contact with the divine. It is with these shrines and with individuals' searches for grace through these shrines that the rest of this book is concerned.

# 4

## The rise of Kudagama

**Introduction**

The most famous of these new shrines is that of Our Lady of Lourdes in a village called Kudagama. This and the next two chapters are all primarily concerned with this shrine, with its rise to fame and with the sort of religiosity which the shrine represents. It must be remembered, however, that Kudagama is not representative in any simple sense of Sinhala Catholicism as a whole: many Sinhala Catholics, both lay and clergy, reject what goes on there. Furthermore, in one crucial respect it is also unrepresentative of the other new shrines which have developed in Sri Lanka. Kudagama centres around a priest in holy orders whilst the other new shrines are focused on laymen who claim a particular charism. Yet Kudagama is in many ways the model for these other shrines, and it was by far the most popular of all the holy places which developed in Sri Lanka in the 1970s.

This chapter describes the rise of Kudagama, the sort of rituals which take place there, how the sacred is constructed at the shrine, and the relation between this shrine and the wider Catholic Church and community in Sri Lanka. The next two chapters are concerned with the symbolic analysis of behaviour at Kudagama, particularly with the ways in which suffering is understood and elaborated. In many ways the story of Kudagama is a story of how a rather odd young man, Camillus Jayamanne, became for many Catholics the most powerful priest in the island, and of how a quiet backwater of Sinhala Catholicism became, depending on one's taste, the most holy place in Sri Lanka, a centre of regressive superstition, or a dangerous threat to the unity and teachings of the Church. At the same time it is a story of how sections of the laity rejected the reforms in the Church and affirmed their commitment to what they saw as true Catholicism.

**Father Camillus Jayamanne**

Camillus Jayamanne was born in the late 1930s, the son of schoolteachers who had left the coast and settled down in the inland town of Polgahawela. Here there was a small Catholic community and Camillus attended a Church-run school. Whilst still a boy he decided to become a priest and despite his parents' misgivings, for he was an only child, he attended the junior seminary in Galle. From there he went on to the Papal Seminary at Ampitiya near Kandy, but the seminary was transferred to Poonah in India where he continued his studies. He appears to have led a somewhat chequered career as a seminarian, oscillating between extremes of piety and pleasure seeking, and at one time there was talk of him being asked to leave the seminary.[1] Finally he was ordained and returned to the Galle diocese where he worked as assistant to a number of priests, never staying in one parish for very long. According to one priest, he had a nervous breakdown and seriously considered leaving the priesthood, but he remained in the robes. By the late sixties he was displaying tendencies which only became fully developed when he came to Kudagama: his strong opposition to the reforms in the Church, his great devotion to the Virgin Mary, and his interest in healing.

There was nothing particularly unusual about Father Jayamanne's devotion to the Virgin. Many priests in Sri Lanka have a personal devotion to the Virgin, and all treat her with the honour to which she is entitled. But Father Jayamanne's devotion was strikingly emotional and more than one priest indicated to me that the bishop considered his excesses 'unhealthy'. Similarly healing, especially the exorcism of evil spirits, had been a part of the traditional priest's activities. By the early seventies most priests considered that beliefs in demons were dangerously backward, and whilst there was still one priest appointed as 'exorcist' in each diocese, the clergy generally saw possession as a psychological rather than a spiritual problem. Father Jayamanne claims that it was around 1968 that he began to realise his vocation to heal. He began to pray over people, discovered that their ailments were caused by evil demons, and was able to cure them. And just as his superiors were disturbed by his emotional excesses, so too were they worried by his interest in spiritual healing. On one occasion his superior reported him to the bishop for insubordination: he was healing people in their homes without the permission of the parish priest. As another priest put it, 'Wherever Camillus went there were demons and exorcisms. He always wanted to go and bless people.'

Given Father Jayamanne's behaviour, the bishop seems to have doubted whether he should be given a parish of his own. In 1971–2 when the diocese was being reorganised and his peers given their first charges, Father Jayamanne found himself overlooked. The story is told that he began to persecute the bishop. He 'sat in' at the bishop's house demanding his own parish. Each night he would walk up and down on the verandah outside the bishop's bedroom praying aloud continually. Eventually, presumably worn down by lack of sleep, the bishop gave way. Up until then Kudagama had been administered from the neighbouring village of Hewadiwella, but it was now made a separate parish and given to Father Jayamanne. Not only was this the smallest parish in the diocese but also the most remote from Galle. The bishop may have felt that this was a suitable place to get rid of an embarrassment – but he was wrong.

### The village of Kudagama
Kudagama consists of around 400 families and lies in the most northerly corner of Sabaragamuva Province between the Low Country plains and the Kandyan interior. The area is one of the most beautiful in Sri Lanka. Between the monotonous flat lands of the coconut triangle and the high mountains of the Kandyan provinces, the area between Kurunegala and Kegalle is one of hills and valleys, the hills covered in rubber trees, patches of forest and the gardens around the village houses, whilst paddy lands occupy the valley floors. Kudagama is particularly beautiful with fine views across the Low Country as well as up through the valleys into the hills, very different from the coastal area where most Sinhalese Catholics live.

As I shall show later, the beauty of the area figures prominently in the mythic construction of the shrine, as does the history of the village. It is claimed, as is the case with so many Sinhala villages, that Kudagama was founded 'in the days of the kings' before the British arrived in Sri Lanka.[2] Most of the inhabitants belong to the Batgama or Padu caste, a large and relatively low status group whose traditional role was to carry the palanquins of the king and his ministers and act as general bearers when so required by the state.[3] Whilst in general caste was not an important factor in conversion to Catholicism, in Kudagama and two or three adjacent villages conversion to various brands of Christianity was very much a caste matter.

The first missionaries to take an interest in this area were probably Anglicans who began to convert local Buddhists in the 1880s. They were quickly followed by the Salvation Army and then by the Catholic Church, whilst in recent years Seventh Day Adventists have become active. Today there is a bewildering variety of religions in Kudagama, members of the same household often belonging to two or more religions and frequently changing their religious affiliation. One aspect of the presence of various groups of missionaries was competition over education. The result is that many villagers have become teachers in various parts of Sri Lanka whilst others have used their contacts to gain positions in private firms and public-sector organisations.

Catholics built their first church in Kudagama around 1910. After the First World War the Church bought a huge rock known as Kehelgala ('Banana Rock') with money reportedly donated by Low Country Catholics. A small church was built here, but it was soon replaced by a larger one built with funds from pious Low Country Catholics. The church was dedicated to Our Lady of Lourdes and behind it a grotto was constructed where masses were held during the annual feast. Finally, a Way of the Cross was laid out, each station marked with a cross and culminating in a Calvary scene consisting of life-size concrete statuary.

Being in Sabaragamuva Province, Kudagama was part of the Galle diocese which until recently was largely staffed with Jesuit missionaries. Only rarely was there a resident priest in Kudagama, the parish being administered from Hewadiwella. Even so, a fine mission house was built and at times priests were resident, one of whom was called Father Yakonis (or Iannaccone), an Italian Jesuit from Naples. Somehow he had come into possession of a thorn said to be a relic of Christ's Crown of Thorns and accompanied, it is claimed, by an authenticating certificate from Rome which unfortunately was lost.[4] When Father Yakonis left Sri Lanka the Thorn stayed behind. Priests who succeeded him did not consider the Thorn a true relic and it remained hidden in the mission house. But all this was to change with the appointment of Father Jayamanne to the parish.

**Father Jayamanne at Kudagama**
When he arrived in Kudagama in 1972, Father Jayamanne found a quiet, almost moribund, parish. There were around forty or fifty households with Catholic members, but few attended church. For the first time Father Jayamanne was free to do what he wanted and he immediately instituted a number of devotions. He first concentrated on the recitation of the rosary in each Catholic household in the parish. For this he went around the houses each day encouraging, exhorting and, according to some, threatening. Secondly, he introduced the Way of the Cross each Friday night. Finally, on Saturdays he held weekly novenas in honour of Our Lady of Lourdes.

At this stage, it appears that all Father Jayamanne was trying to do was reassert the pre-Vatican II style of religiosity, particularly its stress on devotion to the Virgin Mary, and it is doubtful whether he had any glimmering of what Kudagama was to become. Also, it is not clear how popular his reforms were in the parish. But soon after his arrival he came across the Thorn hidden in a cupboard in the Mission House. At first the Thorn was simply used as an object of veneration, 'given what it was due' in Father Jayamanne's words. However, a few months after taking up his charge, two young men from the village were brought to him suffering from demonic possession. They had been taken to Madhu and Talawila but the demons had remained. Other priests had refused to accept the reality of their possession whilst *kattadiyas* (Buddhist exorcists) had been unsuccessful in curing them. So the young men were brought to Father Jayamanne and he blessed them with the Thorn. According to Father Jayamanne they were immediately healed. He realised the power of the Thorn and so began to use it to bless other people, not just those who were possessed but those who were suffering from physical and mental ailments. They too were cured.

After this, the fame of Father Jayamanne and Kudagama spread rapidly. At first people came just from the villages around, but then pilgrims started coming from towns such as Kurunegala and Kandy, and finally from the Catholic heartlands along the coast. Father Jayamanne claims that within six months of his arrival people were coming from all over the island. At first, the popularity of the shrine appears to have been greatest amongst poorer working-class Catholics, particularly from urban areas, but by 1974 Kudagama was attracting pilgrims from all social backgrounds with, if anything, the middle classes being over-represented.[5] Most were seeking cures, particularly for demonic possession, and this was (and is) what Kudagama became most famous for. Others came for other sorts of help: to get jobs, to pass exams, to solve family problems. Others came simply to worship at a holy place.

The rapid growth of the shrine was associated with a widening of the focus of attention. At first, all that was important was the miraculous Thorn in which divine power was held to reside. But very quickly both Father Jayamanne and the place of Kudagama were considered to be imbued with the divine.

As I have already mentioned, Father Jayamanne was opposed to the reforms in the Church long before he came to Kudagama. But once in charge of his own parish, he was able to indulge his own particular style of religiosity and became an extremely pious priest. Each weekend he fasted from Friday to Sunday and at other times of the week followed a very ascetic lifestyle. As he walked around the shrine his lips constantly moved in prayer, and he was never without his rosary. He steadfastly refused to become involved in the 'social works' favoured by other priests and followed a life of prayer and meditation. To the faithful who thronged to Kudagama, Father Jayamanne epitomised the qualities of an old time priest and stories developed which imbued him with the same sort of power as the Thorn. Thus it was claimed that he enjoyed the favour of the Virgin Mary. She had first been attracted to him because of his piety. When he had been experiencing problems with the hierarchy and considered leaving the Church, it was she who appeared to him and persuaded him to stay in the robes in order to carry out her will. It was the Virgin who had arranged for him to come to Kudagama and find the Thorn. After he came to Kudagama she still appeared to him in dreams and told him what to do, and she had also arranged for him to receive a small miraculous statue of her which, it was claimed, he even took to bed with him!

Similarly, the place itself began to be seen as divinely chosen by the Virgin Mary. Once more, it was no accident that the Thorn and Father Jayamanne had been directed to this particular spot, for the Virgin herself had chosen it. Partly this was a result of its beauty, for the Virgin always chooses beautiful places, as at Lourdes. Similarly, just as she had chosen to appear to a lowly shepherdess at Lourdes, so she chose a low-caste village as the site of her shrine in Sri Lanka, for to the Virgin all are equally her children.

So relic, priest and place were all united to form one complex imbued with divine power. Through them the divine was made manifest and the power of the divine could be tapped by the laity, not just for purposes of healing but for many other purposes. Kudagama had become a sacred place, a *siddhastanaya*, to which pilgrims came in increasing numbers.

By 1974, Kudagama was attracting over 2,000 pilgrims every week, with even larger numbers on the first Friday of each month[6] and on Marian feast days. The shrine was probably at the peak of its popularity in the mid-seventies, and although the number of pilgrims has since declined, it still attracts a sizeable crowd each weekend. The weekly ritual cycle instituted by Father Jayamanne for the good of his parishioners now became rituals for all, and some inhabitants of Kudagama began to complain that they had lost their parish church to outsiders.[7] Indeed, although a 'parish council' (*dayaka mandalaya*) continued to exist, an informal group of outsiders began to emerge who took over much of the day-to-day running of the shrine. They made themselves responsible for such matters as decorating the altars and organising the cleaning of the shrine. Rich devotees donated such items as a bell tower, marble slabs to pave the grotto, and a galvanised roof to cover the grotto area. From the donations of poorer pilgrims new buildings were erected to house visitors and a new confessional was constructed by the grotto to cater for the crowds. But as the popularity of the shrine grew, problems in its management also increased. Central to these was that of differentiating between the 'sacred' and the 'profane': of maintaining the power of the shrine by maintaining its sacredness.

### The organisation of space

One of the major themes in the lay critique of ecclesiastical reforms was that the distinction between the sacred (*suddha*) and the profane (*laukika*) was being eroded, and that this undercut the ability of the laity to tap the power of the divine. Such criticisms were particularly directed against the priesthood, and Father Jayamanne by his behaviour and his statements provided an example of a priest who remained true, as far as the faithful were concerned, to the traditions of Catholicism. But such charges were also directed against the great pilgrimage centres of Catholicism in Sri Lanka. One of the criticisms of Madhu and Talawila voiced over and over again by the pilgrims at Kudagama was that they were little more than carnivals; that they were no longer sacred because the hierarchy was failing to insist on proper behaviour at the shrines, and that as a result the miracles of the past no longer took place there. They had ceased to be channels of grace. On the other hand, so they claimed, Kudagama was very different. Here the sacred and the profane were kept apart and here grace could be attained. And what was particularly important in this context was the use of space and controls over behaviour within spatially defined limits.

When I first knew Kudagama in 1974, it was approaching the height of its popularity. The first sign that one was approaching the shrine was not particularly edifying. It consisted of the boutiques and hotels catering for the physical needs of the pilgrims along the road at the foot of Kehelgala. The largest of the hotels was the 'Victor Rest' owned by a successful entrepreneur from Kegalle who had rented a large block of land near the entrance to the church grounds. Over a hundred people could be fed here at any one time, and over forty rooms – little more than partitioned cubicles – were available for the visitors. This was only the largest of about thirty boutiques which supplied food, drink and lodging for the pilgrims. Others specialised in religious bric-a-brac: statues, pictures, rosaries, scapulars, candles and olive oil. They lay in rows along the boundaries of church property on land owned by villagers, some of whom had become very prosperous from the pilgrim trade.

These commercial establishments formed the frame within which the shrine existed (see figure 1). They not only met the physical needs of the pilgrims; they were also a crucial element in the symbolic construction of the shrine. Here was the world of the market place, of materialism, of profit. Many pilgrims complained loud and long about prices at the shrine; about the rapacious profiteers who ran the boutiques.[8] As they traded for only two or three days a week, it was not surprising that prices

Figure 1    Plan of Kudagama

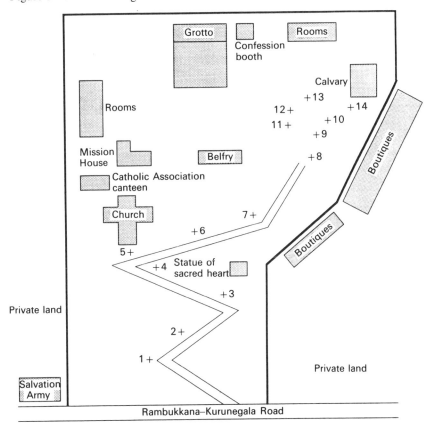

Key: Stations of Cross +

were relatively high in the private boutiques. But it was striking how few of the pilgrims used the Catholic Association canteen and shop situated within church grounds where prices were lower and the profits accrued to church organisations. Moving to and fro across the line which separated the sacred area of the shrine from the secular world around only reinforced people's awareness of the rule-bound nature of the sacred. Within the boundaries of the church land, people were expected to act with a decorum that was absent outside. Drinking and sex were banned. Trading was not allowed, except in the Catholic Association canteen, and of items such as candles and prayer books.

Policing within the sacred area was done in a number of ways. Given Father Jayamanne's other-worldly preoccupations, he could have little direct involvement except to make appeals for decorous behaviour from the pulpit. But his *golayo*, his informal group of helpers, both young men and a few young women, did have a more direct impact. Dressed in blue T-shirts with 'Our Lady of Lourdes, Kudagama' written on the back in English, they patrolled the shrine and scolded malefactors. On a less formal level, public opinion prevented people from smoking or drinking or generally behaving in an offensive fashion within the limits of the sacred area. Around the grotto itself were notices exhorting both prayer and seemly behaviour, and reminding the pilgrims to remember where they were.

It is tempting to see at least some aspects of this profane/sacred distinction in terms of Turner's well-known distinction between 'communitas' and 'societas'.[9] For Turner, 'societas' is the world of normal society, 'a structured, differentiated and often hierarchical system of politico-legal-economic positions with many types of evaluation separating man in terms of "more" and "less"' (Turner 1969: 82). He goes on to claim that in all societies there is a strain towards its opposite: towards 'a relational quality of full unmediated communication, even communion, between definite and determinative entities' (Turner and Turner 1978: 250). He calls this 'communitas'. He argues that in peasant societies the search for communitas takes the form of pilgrimage, and that in pilgrimage centres communitas rather than societas rules supreme.

For many of the pilgrims who turned up at Kudagama week after week, what was important was something akin to what Turner labels 'communitas'. They contrasted the shrine where all were 'brothers in Christ' with the divisions of normal society. Here, they said, caste and class were unimportant: all were as one, and the claim was made that everyone mingled as equals at the shrine. Even the low caste status of the villagers in Kudagama was seen as evidence of this equality before Christ. This sense of oneness was equated with Kudagama's status as a 'sacred place', a *siddhastanaya*. In part it was what marked it off from the older pilgrimage centres of the Sinhala Catholics for at those, it was claimed, there was no mixing. Yet at the same time, there was a tension inherent in such claims for the sacred status of the shrine. For whilst in part it depended upon a lack of organisation, at the same time it required organisation to maintain the purity (*suddha*) of the shrine. This was partly supplied by Father Jayamanne's 'disciples' who acted as informal police, preventing behaviour which they considered unseemly or threatening to the purity of Kudagama. Furthermore, there was an increasing tendency for what was defined as proper behaviour to approximate to the ideals of middle class urban pilgrims rather than poorer urban and rural visitors. Thus views on the 'oneness' of pilgrims at Kudagama tended to be voiced by the rich; the poor saw things slightly differently and occasionally rebelled against what they saw as the sacred being hijacked by the middle class.

Yet if on the one hand space was organised in terms of a sharp distinction between the profane and the sacred, on the other there was an alternative structuring of space which depended not upon an opposition of the sacred and the profane, but upon the absoluteness of the sacred. In this context, the movement towards the sacred started when the pilgrims left home to travel to Kudagama. The journey itself partook of the sacred and as the pilgrims approached the shrine so they came closer and closer to the sacred. Moving up the hill towards the church and the shrine was only the final stage in this journey. Thus behaviour became more and more restrained, more and more sanctified, until the absolute was approached in the form of the Thorn, Father Jayamanne or both.

This aspect of the sacred was most evident in those who were possessed, a topic which will be discussed in more detail in the next chapter. Here, all that needs to be mentioned is that demons which could remain hidden within their victims even within the boundaries of the shrine at Kudagama were forced to show themselves when brought face to face with the priest or the relic. One pilgrim put it to me like this: 'In everyday life all is confused. But the sacred is pure; there is no confusion.' Thus approaching the sacred was not simply a matter of slipping from one side of a polar divide to another: it was also a matter of moving progressively from a world full of ambiguity to one where such ambiguities dissolved and where, as we shall see later, everything stood out starkly in black and white.

## The weekly rituals

Just as space was imbued with meaning, so too was time. Once a person left home to travel to Kudagama he or she was on a pilgrimage (*vandana gamana*), and whatever happened on the journey took on new significance within that context. Thus overcrowded buses, lack of water, loss of belongings, all became part of the suffering which made the pilgrimage valid. On the other hand, a convenient empty bus or a well-timed shower of rain were viewed as the boons which adhered to the true pilgrim. Chance ceased to be a valid mode of understanding events: each random happening was given meaning within the framework of the pilgrimage process. At the shrine itself time was broken up by an oscillation between ritual and non-ritual time, yet once again there was a sense in which this distinction between the sacred and the profane overlay a progression towards the sacred, in this case the 'Thorn blessing' which for most pilgrims formed the culminating event in the weekly pilgrimage.

The rituals at Kudagama followed much the same pattern throughout the seventies (see table 1). They were broadly based on forms of devotion which were introduced by the missionaries in the nineteenth century, but with various additions, and performed with an intensity which might even have shocked the missionaries.

The Way of the Cross (*pada namaskaraya*) consists of fourteen meditations and prayers on various stages of Christ's Passion. It can be a purely private affair, but in Sri Lanka it normally takes place either before pictorial representations of the Passion hung in churches, or in the open air before a series of crosses or statues marking the various stations. Prior to Vatican II it was a favourite form of devotion encouraged by priests. The Way of the Cross is a dramatic reliving of Christ's Passion accentuating the theme that Christ died for the sins of mankind. Thus in the prayer at the first station we hear,

My adorable Christ, it was not Pilate; no, it was my sins that condemned thee to die,

And at the third station,

My beloved Christ, it is not the weight of the Cross but of my sins that has made thee suffer so much pain.

Yet the Way of the Cross is also importantly concerned with the Virgin Mary. Each of the stations ends with a short prayer to the Virgin such as that at the second station:

Table 1. *The weekly rituals at Kudagama*

| | |
|---|---|
| Friday evening | |
| | Way of the Cross |
| | Holy Mass |
| | Holy Hour |
| | Benediction |
| Saturday | |
| | Holy Mass |
| | Novena to the Blessed Virgin Mary |
| | Blessings |
| Sunday | |
| | Holy Mass |

Oh, how sad and sore distressed, was that mother highly blest of the sole-begotten one,

Or this one at the tenth station,

Holy Mother! Pierce me through, in my heart each wound renew of my Saviour crucified.

And of course the Virgin Mary receives special attention at the fourth station where she meets Christ on his way to Calvary, and at the thirteenth station where Christ is taken down from the Cross.[10]

At Kudagama in the seventies the Way of the Cross was held every Friday, in the open air, and marked the beginning of the series of weekend rituals.[11] Although billed for 6.30 in the evening, it almost never started before 7.00 or after. Visually, it was perhaps the most dramatic of all the rituals at Kudagama, and a fitting introduction to the shrine for the new arrivals. Each of the participants carried a lit candle, and followed Father Jayamanne from station to station. At each of these the priest led the people in the appropriate responses; at some, particularly those associated with the Virgin, he delivered a sermon on an aspect of Christ's Passion: of how he died for our sins, of how we are responsible for his death, of the need to emulate Christ's life. Between the stations he led the crowd in hymns honouring the Virgin. Throughout the procession Father Jayamanne presented an image of extreme piety, almost in tears, his voice quivering with emotion.

The sight of hundreds of people holding candles, praying, singing hymns and slowly moving up the hillside after the priest, was a very impressive spectacle, made even more so by the behaviour of the possessed. As soon as the prayers began, some collapsed in fits. As the rituals progressed more and more fell into trances. Some rolled up the hill in front of the priest; others tried to run away into the village. Some howled, others wailed, still others tried to tear their clothes off. All the time some yelled abuse at Father Jayamanne whilst others screamed in agony. The scene could be very eery and rather frightening.

The Way of the Cross culminated in mass celebrated at an altar in front of the statues of the Calvary scene. The mass itself was much like any other Mass in Catholic Sri Lanka except for two things. First, the cries and shouts of the possessed continued in counterpoint to the ritual, reaching a peak during the moment of transubstantiation and again when the host was held aloft for all to adore. Second, before the host was distributed, Father Jayamanne announced that it was for Catholics only, and went on to list those who could not receive it: Buddhists, Hindus, Muslims and non-Catholic Christians. As the host was distributed, so more people collapsed in fits. By around 9.00 p.m. the mass was over. The congregation sang a hymn in honour of the Virgin, the possessed writhed and screamed, and the first stage of the weekend rituals was over.

There was then an interval of an hour or so for the people to have their supper, whilst some of Father Jayamanne's helpers decorated the altar in the grotto with flowers and a statue of Our Lady. Pre-recorded hymns sung by Father Jayamanne were played over the loudspeakers, and some time after 10.00 p.m. he would emerge from the Mission House carefully carrying another small statue of the Virgin which it was claimed had miraculous powers. This he placed on the altar before leading the congregation in a Holy Hour consisting of a communal telling of the rosary interspersed with hymns and prayers in honour of the Virgin. Fewer people attended Holy Hour than took part in the Way of the Cross. People came and went and even the possessed were fairly quiet during this period.

Holy Hour finished soon after 11.00 p.m., when Father Jayamanne went to the Mission House to collect a wafer which he brought out to be placed in a monstrance on the altar. As he used this to bless the crowd, the tempo again quickened, the possessed once more collapsing and shouting abuse at the priest. The crowd was larger than it had been for Holy Hour, but by this stage people were tiring and many had already gone to sleep. However, after the benediction came individual blessings. A long line of people formed in front of the grotto and were let into the inner enclosure one by one. Here Father Jayamanne, with helpers on each side, blessed people individually. Should an individual possessed by demons try to attack the priest, they would be forcibly restrained by his helpers. As the people filed through, about one in ten would collapse whilst others would start trembling, signs of minor demonic attack.

By 1.00 a.m. or 2.00 a.m. the rituals of the day were over. The altar was cleared; the monstrance and the loudspeakers removed. Father Jayamanne retired with his helpers to the Mission House. Most people went to sleep but a few of the faithful would remain praying in the grotto or the church for the whole night, their arms outstretched in imitation of the crucified Christ.

The Saturday rituals began with mass, scheduled to start at 9.00 a.m. Before that, a priest heard confessions. If possible, outside priests were cajoled to take part, but if none were available Father Jayamanne heard them himself. The problem was that if he heard confession himself he was overwhelmed by the faithful and the mass could be delayed indefinitely. As it was, the mass frequently did not start until after 10.00 a.m.

The Saturday mass was held in the grotto. A cross and a picture of the Miraculous Face of Jesus were placed on the altar, already decorated with flowers. Loudspeakers and taped music were used as on the night before. The mass followed the standard pattern, and once again the possessed collapsed or yelled insults at Father Jayamanne, the Virgin Mary and Christ. It was usually over soon after 11.00 a.m. and the altar was cleared. There was then either a break for lunch, or there would be another novena in honour of the Virgin led by one or other of the priest's helpers.

During the lunch interval, two 40-gallon drums standing by the grotto were filled with water and a queue began to form of people clutching bottles or plastic containers. Around 2.30 p.m. Father Jayamanne would re-appear from the Mission House carrying the statue of the Virgin which he had used the previous night. Once again he blessed the crowd with the statue, with holy water, and with prayers in Latin. Usually there were four separate blessings: for oil, for salt, for medicine and king coconuts, and finally for medallions and rosaries. In practice all these objects along with passports, photographs, job applications and house plans were held up by the faithful each time there was a blessing or when Father Jayamanne liberally sprinkled holy water over the crowd. During the blessings, corks were removed from bottles, lids from tins, and packets of salt and medicine were opened 'to let the blessings in'. Finally, Father Jayamanne blessed the whole crowd with the statue of the Virgin, particularly mentioning the sick (which included the demonically possessed).

The priest then moved over to the drums of water and prayed in Latin over each. He made the sign of the Cross over the water and then immersed the statue of the Virgin. Whilst Father Jayamanne returned to the Mission House, two of his helpers doled the water out to the queue of pilgrims who took it home. In the meantime, another queue was forming in the grotto, this time for the high point of the whole ritual sequence: the Thorn blessing.

Around 4.00 p.m. Father Jayamanne came in a small procession from the Mission House carrying the Thorn. He went to the grotto, placed the Thorn on the altar, and gave a short prayer in honour of the relic and its association with the crucified Christ. Then, one by one, individuals came forward, and knelt before him. Closely watched by his helpers, Father Jayamanne pressed the block of glass containing the Thorn against each person's forehead and asked for God's protection.[12] At this point many people collapsed, some because of demons, others overwhelmed with emotion at being in such close contact with a relic of the crucifixion. Many of those already known to be possessed were dragged screaming and wailing to receive the blessing and had to be held down by the priest's helpers. After all had received the Thorn blessing, Father Jayamanne blessed the crowd and the rituals of Saturday were at an end.

The major rituals over, most of the pilgrims started their journeys home. A few pilgrims stayed over until mass on Sunday, but compared with the crowds and the emotional tension of the previous two days, Sunday was very quiet. By midday, the last of the visitors had left, the boutiques were shut down and all that was left were a few semi-permanent residents at the shrine, either too poor or too ill to return to their homes.

### Old-time religion

Not surprisingly, the popularity of Kudagama amongst the laity soon attracted the attention of the more traditionally-minded members of the clergy. One of the first outsiders to become involved in the shrine was a Franciscan monk called Brother Gerard, who was a teacher in Ja Ela, a predominantly Catholic town on the coast. He began to visit the shrine on a weekly basis and act as Father Jayamanne's general helper. He also began to organise buses to bring the pilgrims from the coast to the shrine. After him, various priests also began to visit the shrine and would help Father Jayamanne when the crowds were at their greatest, particularly at the times of the Marian feasts. One of the most frequent visitors to Kudagama in the early seventies was Father Paolicci, and for a time at least he was one of the shrine's most active proponents.

For Father Paolicci, Kudagama was evidence that the reforms in the Church and the modern-day teachings of the Church were wrong. He was particularly interested in demons and demonic possession which for him provided visible and audible proof of the existence of the demonic, and he railed against modernist priests who denied its existence. He took great delight in addressing the demons in Italian – and claimed that they answered him in the same language! His age, and his nationality, gave him a certain status with the pilgrims who would listen to him with respect as he denounced the clergy for their 'Arianism' and various other heresies. Throughout 1974 and 1975 he publicised Kudagama in his two journals, *The Rock* and *Haktiya*, each issue bearing photographs and stories of the shrine on their front covers. Readers were exhorted to visit Kudagama and witness the miracles taking place there, whilst lurid stories told of what happened to those who failed to believe.

Sometime in 1975 Father Paolicci fell out with Father Jayamanne. What their quarrel was about remains a mystery, but what is striking is how all Father Jayamanne's clerical helpers seem to have had quarrels with him and stopped visiting the shrine. It appears that in all cases the problem centred around the claims that were being made for Father Jayamanne by his followers, claims which he did little to discourage. What they were claiming for him were powers over and beyond those which any other priest could hope to attain and such a status was resented by other priests no matter how 'traditionally' orientated they might be.

One of the features of the stories concerning Kudagama which Father Paolicci published was the way in which the shrine was placed in an international context. Most of the articles in his journals were reprinted from foreign journals and concerned European shrines such as Fatima, Garabandal and Lourdes, along with attacks on radical elements within the Church. Foreign literature also began to circulate at Kudagama such as *Michael Fighting*, an extreme North American publication which presented itself as the guardian of true Catholicism.

Kudagama thus became not just a local phenomenon but began to be viewed by the pilgrims as the local manifestation of a world-wide movement. At the same time politics became more important. Whilst the identification of Kudagama as the Sri Lankan equivalent of Lourdes put the stress on miracles of healing and the immaculate conception of the Virgin Mary, the parallels drawn with Garabandal and Fatima stressed a view of the Virgin as the champion of religion against the dangers of communism. Radicals in the Church were now identified with atheistic Marxists, and the miracles of healing seen as ways by which the Virgin was displaying her power and recovering people from irreligion. As one old man put it to me, 'What the miracles are all about is the Virgin saying, "Oyi. Look I'm here." But really what is important is defeating atheism.'

Here there are clear parallels with Christian's discussion of apparitions of the Virgin in Western Europe which shows the link with the Cold War and anti-communism (Christian 1984). Given that in the early seventies the ruling party in Sri Lanka was the leftward-leaning Sri Lanka Freedom Party, it is not surprising that Kudagama became something of a rallying point for anti-government Catholics.

In line with this international context, attempts were made at Kudagama to revive various international devotionalist movements. Thus the Blue Army, an organisation based at Fatima in Portugal which encouraged devotion to the Virgin Mary and the rosary, and which also had a strong anti-Marxist element, was active at the shrine in the early seventies. In 1975 this was replaced by the 'Family Rosary Crusade', a movement which again originated outside Sri Lanka. Members had to promise to say the rosary daily with their families, attend church regularly, and celebrate the major Marian feasts. In return they received a certificate to hang on their wall, and most insisted that Father Jayamanne bless it before they returned home. Within six months over 4,000 families had signed up.

Through such processes, the faithful at Kudagama felt themselves part of a world-wide movement, not members of a small and rather marginal minority within a minority of Sri Lankans. Through publications received at Kudagama, through gossip and stories told at the shrine, through experiencing the rituals and witnessing the miracles of curing, they developed a sense of belonging to a world-wide network of like-minded Catholics who rejected the reforms of the post-Vatican II Church. To borrow Benedict Anderson's phrase, they became part of an 'Imagined Community' which spanned the world (Anderson 1983). And also their confidence grew. If they could witness such miracles of curing at Kudagama, then they could have confidence in the power of the Virgin in the future. For phrases such as 'Blue Army' were for many not simply metaphors: there really was an army, and the battles were to come, culminating in Armageddon when the Virgin Mary would lead her followers in the final victory over evil. Some of the faithful even believed that the war was to start at Kudagama, and stories circulated of a huge ghostly blue rosary being seen hovering over the shrine.

### The reaction of the hierarchy

Kudagama generated a range of responses amongst the clergy. Amongst the more radical priests, Kudagama was a throwback, a reversion to an older style of Catholicism which was now seen as hopelessly superstitious. But as far as they were concerned, there was no real danger in it: such behaviour would simply fade away with the education of the laity in 'correct' ways of thinking and behaving. The sort of religiosity apparent at Kudagama was doomed to disappear. A more frequent reaction was to attack Kudagama and Father Jayamanne and to attempt to dissuade people from visiting the shrine. From the pulpit sermons denouncing Kudagama became a frequent occurrence, and some priests threatened to stop giving the sacraments to those in their congregations who frequented Kudagama. Such threats had little impact.

Amongst the bishops, reactions to the shrine were also mixed. The person who had to deal with the problem was Father Jayamanne's bishop, the Bishop of Galle. He was not amongst the most radical of the bishops, and if left to himself might well have simply left Kudagama alone. But he was under pressure from other bishops who were more radically inclined and felt more threatened by the shrine. Indeed, the vast majority of pilgrims at Kudagama came from the dioceses of Colombo and Chilaw rather than from Galle. The problem the Bishop of Galle faced was how precisely he should react to the rise of Kudagama, and in this he was hampered by the distance of the shrine from Galle, one of the factors which had first led him to send Father Jayamanne to the parish. If on the one hand he did nothing, then it would look as if he approved of Father Jayamanne's behaviour. But if he was too heavy handed, then he risked turning Father Jayamanne into a martyr and alienating even more of the laity. Furthermore, it was very difficult to prove that Father Jayamanne was behaving in a manner which would justify disciplining him. Technically speaking everything he did and said was orthodox: even when exorcising demons he was careful to say it was a 'blessing of the sick' which all priests can perform, and not an 'exorcism' for which the priest has to obtain a licence from his bishop. Priests were sent to the shrine, but could gather little evidence to use against Father Jayamanne. The grandiose claims for his powers were made by his followers, not by the priest himself.

Various possibilities were canvassed, the most popular being to send Father Jayamanne abroad for 'further training'.[13] Another was to transfer him to a parish closer to the seat of his bishop and hope that this would dilute the power of the shrine and priest. Father Jayamanne let it be known that he would refuse to be moved, and the bishop retreated for fear of making him a martyr.

There were, however, two points at which the Bishop of Galle could attempt to control the growth of the shrine. The first was the status of the Thorn. Given that it had no accompanying certificate, it was extremely doubtful whether it was a true relic, and the bishop ordered Father Jayamanne to stop using it as such. Father Jayamanne obeyed the order and the Thorn was returned to the cupboard in the Mission House. But almost immediately, he obtained another relic, this time a piece of the True Cross, duly certified from Rome.[14] Instead of using the Thorn to bless the pilgrims, he began to use this new relic although many of the pilgrims continued to refer to it as a Thorn. But by this stage it didn't really matter, for by now Father Jayamanne was as important a source of power as the relic.

Secondly, there were problems over the administration of the shrine. With increasing numbers of pilgrims coming to the shrine, the income of Kudagama church was rapidly increasing from various forms of offerings. The financial growth of the shrine faced Father Jayamanne with something of a dilemma. Much of his fame depended on his 'other-worldliness'; his refusal to become involved with the profane world as did so many of the priests whom his followers were criticising. Yet not to keep control over the finances of the church exposed him to the accusation that funds were being misappropriated by his followers. By the second half of the seventies rumours were common that the offerings of the faithful were being appropriated by some of Father Jayamanne's *golayo* and the bishop took this opportunity to appoint a priest from the nearby parish of Rambukkana to act as administrator of the shrine. This priest took no part in the rituals of Kudagama: he simply collected the money from the offering boxes, paid the bills of the shrine and kept the accounts. He also ensured that basic facilities for the pilgrims were available at the shrine and presumably also kept a general eye on what was taking place there. The growing surplus was remitted to the bishop.[15] Whilst at first many of the faithful resented this interference from above, they soon began to view it rather differently. Whilst the bishop may have seen his actions as a reimposition of his control over the shrine, for the faithful it amounted to a recognition by the hierarchy of the importance of the shrine and the status of Father Jayamanne.

The introduction of an administrator at Kudagama brought it into line with other shrines such as Madhu and Talawila where there is a similar division of duties between an officiating priest and a priest who looks after more mundane matters. It also marked the first stage in the effective recognition by the Bishop of Galle that Kudagama was not simply a church with a somewhat odd incumbent but rather a pilgrimage centre. By the late seventies the bishop began to attend the occasional feast at Kudagama, effectively giving his imprimatur to what was going on there.

Rather than make a martyr of Father Jayamanne the shrine was co-opted into the mainstream of diocesan life, for despite problems with the style of religiosity expressed at Kudagama, the decision appears to have been taken that it was safer to integrate the shrine into the Church rather than force it and its followers into secession. After all, Kudagama was at least run by a priest, unlike other shrines which centred around members of the laity.

# 5

## Demonic possession and the battle against evil

### The centrality of demonic possession

All that I was told about Kudagama when I first heard of it in 1974 was
that hundreds of demonically possessed people were going there every
week to be cured. Throughout the seventies and eighties, the first thing
that anyone would say about the shrine was that it was famous for the
treatment of the demonically possessed. Those who supported the shrine
saw the treatment of the possessed as proof of the sacredness of the shrine
whilst those who were opposed to such forms of religiosity saw the
incidence of possession as evidence that the shrine was founded on a
major error concerning the nature of religion, and that it was no more
than a manifestation of 'superstition'.

In a very real sense the legitimacy of the shrine and the claims made by
and for Father Jayamanne depended upon curing the demonically possessed. The ranting, raving, screaming, rolling in the mud and speaking in
strange tongues of the demonically possessed were taken as proof that the
shrine was a sacred place, a hierophany, where divine power was imma-
nent. Because of this, devotees came for other reasons: for jobs, for
health, for money, for legal assistance or just for divine grace. The shrine
of Kudagama grew on the backs of the demonically possessed and
depended upon them for its existence. Only as long as shrines such as
Kudagama could provide a visible and audible display of the battle
between the forces of good and evil could they prosper, but shrines
declined as soon as they failed to supply such visible proof. Thus for the
devotees at Kudagama, the older shrines of Madhu and Talawila were
obviously no longer sacred as there were no exorcisms there.

In this chapter I am concerned with the symbolic structure of possession at Kudagama. One theme concerns the way in which the individual

experience of possession was placed within a greater totality. For both the possessed and others, possession and exorcism only made sense and became meaningful and manageable through situating the experience of possession within a generalising and totalising context. What happened at an individual level and what happened at the cosmic level were presented as one and the same. This relates to the second theme of this chapter: the relationship between good and evil and the contrast between two aspects of the supra-mundane – good sacred and bad sacred. I shall argue that this contrast is central to the symbolic construction of demonic possession at Kudagama and that it is used to infuse meaning into what would otherwise be mundane and even meaningless events and experiences. But first a little has to be said about demonic possession and exorcism in the Sinala Catholic tradition.

### Possession and exorcism in Catholic Sri Lanka

Even though the incidence of demonic possession and the popularity of exorcism have increased in recent years amongst Sinhala Catholics, there is nothing new about such activities. Throughout the Portuguese and Dutch periods the ability of priests and others to exorcise the demonically possessed was a central feature in the evangelical activities of the missionary Church. Thus Perniola's three volumes of documents covering the Dutch period are replete with stories of the exorcism of the possessed. In some cases this involved the use of the rite of exorcism whilst in others the command of the priest was sufficient. To take just a couple of cases at random from the early eighteenth century, Father Jacob Goncalvez is reported to have exorcised four men in Colombo.

Of these, three had been charmed; the fourth had been deprived of the use of hands, feet, and tongue, and was lying on a couch, unable to speak and get up. With a mere command of his voice, the Father commanded the evil spirits to go and thus freed those four men ...                                    (Perniola 1983: 331–2)

In another case, Father Francisco Goncalvez was approached by three women when he was at mass. One of these women was a Christian although 'the two others were pagans, but ready to become Christians if they could be freed from the devil. God our Lord was pleased to show his power. This is not anything singular, but very ordinary and frequent in every district where our missionaries work' (Perniola 1983: 393).

But priests were not the only exorcists active in the Sinhala Catholic tradition. As has already been mentioned, the scarcity of priests during the Dutch period coupled with the vicissitudes of life under Dutch rule led to laymen known as *muppus* and *annavis* being extremely important in the day-to-day organisation of Catholic communities. These laymen relied on books of prayers supposedly written by Jacob Goncalvez in the early eighteenth century and used these prayers for various pragmatic purposes including exorcism. Although these lay exorcists came under increasing pressure in the nineteenth and twentieth centuries from the priesthood, they have continued to exist and continue to exorcise the demonically possessed. I will have more to say about these men and the character of the prayers they use in chapter 7.

Although exorcisms by eighteenth century missionaries appear to have been public affairs, in the nineteenth century they became more and more private, priests becoming increasingly loath to turn individual exorcisms into public spectacles. Similarly, the work of lay exorcists was, if not totally private, at least carried out in the domestic arena. In contrast, exorcisms at Kudagama were and are public events.

**A case from Kudagama**

I have studied literally hundreds of cases of demonic possession at Kudagama. On any one day there could be forty or fifty *leda* (patients) present at the shrine, some very serious cases, others very minor. In some instances, individuals were still afflicted with demons years after they had first come to the shrine whilst in others the possession ended as soon as it was discovered. Each case is unique, each individual following or being made to follow his or her own path through the possession process. Yet at the same time there is a general pattern to possession at Kudagama, and the easiest way to approach this general pattern is through examining one particular case and using it as a springboard for an elucidation of the symbolism involved. The case I shall focus on here involves a family I got to know fairly well. I met them on their second visit to the shrine and followed through their experience from the first inkling that they were being attacked by demons to their final deliverance.

When I met her in the late seventies, Mary was about forty years old. She worked as a teacher in Dehiwala, a suburb of Colombo, whilst her husband John was a clerk in the Ceylon Insurance Corporation. They were relatively well-off and had two teenage children, both attending school. Mary had been suffering from arthritis for a number of years and, despite visiting both Western and ayurvedic physicians, her condition had steadily deteriorated. Although John rarely went to church, Mary was a regular attender at Sunday mass in her local church. She first heard of Kudagama from friends at church who told her of the miraculous cures that took place at the shrine. Mary mentioned the shrine to John but he dismissed it as a load of nonsense. Later John told me that he had not believed in demons and possession, and had thought that shrines such as Kudagama were simply means of making money out of the gullible. Mary was less dismissive and she persuaded him to go with her to Kudagama. So one week they went on one of the special buses which ran on the first Friday of each month from Dehiwala direct to Kudagama.

On their first visit to Kudagama nothing extraordinary happened. They attended all the rituals, John under protest. They watched the possessed screaming and writhing, and after a while even John began to suspect that there might be something in the stories of demonic possession. They tried to receive the Thorn blessing from Father Jayamanne but the crowd was too large and so they went home. During the next week, Mary began to feel her arthritis improving and wondered if this had anything to do with their visit to Kudagama. John was sceptical but they decided to go again even though there was no direct bus and they had to make the long and arduous journey through Colombo and Kurunegala. On this visit they managed to receive the Thorn blessing. And, much to their amazement, when Mary was blessed she collapsed.

After the Thorn blessing was over and Mary had recovered consciousness, John and some of their friends took her to see Father Jayamanne. Looking into her eyes, he decided that she was possessed, and he blessed her by putting his hand on her forehead. Once more Mary collapsed, writhing on the floor of the Mission House, screaming and sobbing. Father Jayamanne announced that this was clearly a case of demonic possession. He blessed two scapulars and gave them to John, saying that he and Mary should wear them all the time. Father Jayamanne also blessed them and their rosaries, instructing them to say the rosary every night and to return to Kudagama next week.

At this stage, all that Mary and John knew was that she was the victim of a demonic attack. They didn't know who the demon was, why it had attacked her, how long it had been possessing her, or how dangerous the attack was. Clearly it was a serious case, for the demon had remained hidden until Mary had received the Thorn blessing. So they took Father Jayamanne's advice and before returning home booked a room for the next weekend in one of the boutiques – where I met them for the first time. Once back in Dehiwala they talked about what had happened. Mary remembered that on their first visit she had felt faint during the Way of the Cross but had put it down to tiredness after the journey. Now she realised that it was the first sign of being possessed. John's misgivings about the shrine and the existence of demons had dissolved. He began to wonder if the financial problems he had been experiencing in building their new house might also be the result of demonic attack. They both wore their scapulars continually and each night recited the rosary in front of the altar in their house, but whilst they were at home nothing extraordinary happened.

The next week, Mary and John returned to Kudagama, this time taking their two children as well. Knowing that she might collapse, Mary had brought her oldest clothes and changed into them before the Way of the Cross began. Almost as soon as it started she collapsed. She rolled on the ground, grunting like a pig and trying to eat the dirt on the road. As the ritual proceeded she rolled up the hill grunting all the time and only regained consciousness once the mass was over. People standing around told John that she must be possessed by *peretayo*, for only they would act in such a dirty fashion. They also said that if it was just a matter of *peretayo*, then it wasn't very serious: they would soon depart.

The whole night Mary, John, their children and a few friends prayed in the grotto, asking the Virgin Mary for her help. Throughout the night Mary remained conscious, but during the novena the next day she collapsed again. This time, however, she didn't roll on the ground or eat dirt. Instead a demon calling himself Kataragama announced that he was possessing her and that the *peretayo* who had possessed her the night before were simply his servants. Kataragama started laughing at Mary's friends and her family. In a voice which was much lower than Mary's usual voice he spoke through her: 'I have possessed this woman for years. You can't make me go. I am too powerful for that.' And, still in Mary's body, he stood up, arms above the head, and began to abuse the Virgin Mary and Father Jayamanne, claiming that he had more power than either of them and that, if he wanted to, he could kill the priest. Furthermore, he announced that not only Mary but the whole family was subject to him. John realised that his fears over financial matters were fully justified: they too were the result of demonic attack.

Kataragama went and Mary lost consciousness. She soon recovered without any knowledge of what had happened, but the others told her. Later that day she collapsed again during another ritual, and once more Kataragama announced his presence. Encouraged by some of the regular attenders at the shrine with whom he had become friendly, John began to question the demon, asking where it had come from, why it had attacked them and when it was going to leave. At first Kataragama just laughed at him, but then one of the bystanders forced the demon to drink water which Father Jayamanne had blessed with the miraculous statue of the Virgin. Then Kataragama began to talk. He claimed that he had possessed Mary for over twenty years and that he had been given 'permission' (*varam*), by the Virgin Mary to do so. The man who had poured the blessed water down Mary's throat lost his temper and slapped her around the face, telling the demon not to lie as the Virgin would never allow such a thing. After a little while Kataragama changed his story; he said that he had been sent by a *kattadiya*, a sorcerer. And then he left Mary.

During the rest of the day John, his children and a few friends prayed over Mary. On the advice of regular attenders at the shrine they hung all their rosaries around her neck, rubbed oil blessed by Father Jayamanne into her hair and made her drink what appeared to be gallons of blessed water. She collapsed when the Thorn blessing began, even though she was nowhere near Father Jayamanne. Kataragama announced that he wasn't going to be blessed by that 'dog' (*balla*), in priest's robes holding a bit of wood (i.e. the piece of the cross). John and some of his friends dragged Mary towards Father Jayamanne, but the nearer they got the more violent she became and some of Father Jayamanne's helpers had to assist. From yelling abuse and screaming defiance Kataragama started to shout with fear. 'I am burning, I am burning (*Mama puchanava, mama puchanava*). I can't go. I am tied. Don't do it.' And when Father Jayamanne held the piece of the cross to her forehead Mary collapsed, sobbing and wailing.

Afterwards, once Mary had recovered, John tried to take her to see Father Jayamanne but the priest was too busy, or so his helpers told him. One of the helpers gave John some salt and water blessed by the priest. John was told to make Mary drink the water and use the salt in her food. Before they left the shrine, John and Mary made a vow to the Virgin Mary promising that they would return on twelve first Saturdays if she was cured.

Back in Dehiwala, John and Mary spent much of the week discussing what had happened at Kudagama. Mary could remember nothing of the times when she had been in a trance and Kataragama had spoken through her, so John recounted the details of the sessions. The next week they returned to Kudagama. Again, Mary collapsed during the Way of the Cross, and again there was a violent struggle to bring her close enough to Father Jayamanne to receive the blessing. This visit was more successful than the last, for after the novena Kataragama announced that he wanted to leave but that he couldn't because he was 'tied' (*bandila*) by a sorcerer who had sent him. John, helped by one of the regular attenders, cross-questioned the demon, threatening Kataragama with further blessings from the priest and with objects blessed by the priest. The demons wailed and shouted, begging for mercy. Eventually Kataragama explained that a sorcerer who was now dead had sent him. He went on to recount how the sorcerer had been employed by one of Mary's co-students at Training College who had been jealous of her. After more threats, Kataragama agreed to leave Mary and announced the time and place: the next Saturday at mid-day on Calvary.

When they returned to Dehiwala, Mary tried to remember what had happened all those years before at College. She vaguely remembered another student who had acted strangely and appeared unfriendly towards her. Mary decided that this woman must have been the sorcerer's client.

The next weekend they returned to Kudagama but this time, when Mary fell into a trance, Kataragama didn't shout insults at the Virgin and Father Jayamanne: instead he sang hymns praising the Virgin and knelt before the priest worshipping him. At 11.30 on the Saturday morning Mary fell into a trance whilst praying in the grotto. Kataragama announced his presence and started wailing and sobbing. Then he 'danced', as he put it, in honour of the Virgin Mary. He begged her forgiveness and compassion, fell to the ground and began to roll up the hill from the grotto to the Calvary. John and some friends followed behind reciting the rosary whilst a crowd of onlookers watched attentively. When they reached the Calvary, Kataragama climbed the rocks on which the cross stood and wrapped Mary's body around the shaft of the cross. Finally, yelling, 'I am going, I am going' (*mama yanava, mama yanava*), Kataragama left his victim with a long piercing scream. Mary collapsed into the arms of her husband and was carried away to the room they had rented in one of the boutiques.

Later that day, Mary and her family all received the blessing with the True Cross from Father Jayamanne. None of them showed any signs of being possessed. Afterwards they managed to meet Father Jayamanne in the Mission House and told him their story. He looked at them closely, blessed them with his hands against their heads, and pronounced them free of demonic influence. He gave them a short lecture on the importance of the rosary and of regular worship, and then Mary, John and the children went home to Dehiwala.

At least once a month for the next year they came to Kudagama in fulfilment of their vow to the Virgin. After that they came every two or three months, and whenever they felt that they needed divine help they made a vow to the Virgin at Kudagama. They encouraged others to visit the shrine and some, like Mary, found that they were possessed. John became one of the more knowledgeable of the regulars at the shrine. He started helping others deal with possession, giving advice and controlling the possessed. As he said, his family had been relatively lucky. In some cases demons hang on for ages, and as one is expelled so another takes its place. Or alternatively, a demon expelled from one member of a family then moves into another family member. But in Mary's case there had been no complications and the cure had been totally successful. Her arthritis had steadily improved and their financial crisis passed. Before they moved into their new house they had the plans blessed by Father Jayamanne.

### Evil and the demonic

To anyone even vaguely familiar with Sri Lankan ethnography, perhaps the most striking feature of this story is the identity of the major demon involved. Amongst Sinhala Buddhists, Kataragama is presently the most powerful and popular of all the gods, his rise and qualities being described in detail by Obeyesekere (1977; see also Gombrich and Obeyesekere 1988). Admittedly, even in Sinhala Buddhist contexts there is some ambiguity over his godly status: he is occasionally described as a demon (Gombrich and Obeyesekere 1988: 34). But at Kudagama, Kataragama is unambiguously described as a *yaka* or demon. More generally, all the gods of the Buddhist and Hindu pantheons are seen as demons. To fully appreciate this, we need to look in a little detail at the ways in which this transformation has been achieved.

In the Sinhala Buddhist tradition, there is no great divide between gods and demons. Demons can become gods: gods can become demons. Some beings, such as Huniyam, can partake of both god-like and demonic characteristics.[1] There is a gradation of relative benevolence and malevolence associated with a similar gradation of moral authority, the benevolent enjoying moral and ethical superiority over the malevolent. As described by Obeyesekere (1966) as well as other writers (for example Gombrich 1971; Kapferer 1983), this structure is articulated in terms of the concept of *varam*, variously translated as 'delegated authority' or 'warrant'. This articulation can work in two ways. First, authority is seen as being delegated down through a pyramidal hierarchical organisation: from Buddha through the greater gods to lesser gods and finally to demons. Alternatively, *varam* can be conceptualised as being granted directly by Buddha to all classes of beings both demonic and godly. But in both cases what is crucial is that demonic beings are inferior to and under the control of superior beings. Demons may possess people but they can do so only under the ultimate control of superior beings. This was the thrust of Kataragama's claim, when he possessed Mary, that he had *varam* from the Virgin. In a very Sinhala Buddhist idiom he was accepting her superiority but at the same time asserting the legitimacy of his attack on Mary.

As Southwold (1985) has pointed out, in such a context there is no concept of ultimate or 'radical' evil. Rather, the structure works in terms of relativity: oppositions of good and bad, benevolence and malevolence, are never absolute except in so far as there is an absolute good – in this case the Buddha. Indeed, in the context of a system based on ideas of *karma* and rebirth, any concept of absolutely evil beings is impossible. Such a picture of moral gradation is anathema in terms of the Catholic tradition. Here there is a rigorous and absolute distinction between good and evil which allows for no gradations. Rather, good and evil exist as two radical opposites, and there can be no system in which power is delegated from relatively good to relatively evil beings.

In the nineteenth century and earlier, the missionaries were eager to persuade the laity that the demonic did not just include the demons of the Buddhist and Hindu traditions but also their gods. Thus what they saw as the worship of Buddha, Pattini, Vishnu and so on were all presented as 'devil worship' and opposed to true religion. Interaction with such beings at any level was seen as being outside religion or opposed to religion. Anything else was superstition at best, demonolatry at worst, and only Catholicism was religion.[2] As I indicated in chapter 2, strenuous efforts were made to separate Catholics from non-Catholics, to prevent Catholics from visiting non-Catholic shrines or using non-Catholic specialists. Miscreants were subject to penances, public shaming, fines and even excommunication.

Yet such efforts met with only limited success. Whilst lay people were willing to accept that the lower levels of the Sinhala Buddhist pantheon were indeed demons under the rule of Satan, they were much less willing to do so with the gods. In some cases gods were identified with the saints (see below, chapter 9) or, more frequently it seems, they were placed in a separate but parallel category to the saints of the Church. Until the last few decades, it was very rare for people to be possessed by the Buddhist gods. The beings that possessed Catholics were in most cases the same demons as those which attacked their Buddhist neighbours. More generally, until such shrines as Kudagama began to develop, demonic possession appears to have been less common than now amongst Sinhala Catholics. It did occur, but if one was a good Catholic then one wasn't bothered by demons. Furthermore, ideas about the demonic were fuzzy and unstressed. Even today in areas where shrines such as Kudagama are not popular, such as Ambakandawila, demons are not very important and claims of demonic possession often treated with marked scepticism (see chapter 8).

### The demonic at Kudagama

In contrast, the regular attenders at shrines such as Kudagama were and are fascinated by the demonic. At Kudagama, demons have a very real existence, as real an existence as people or animals or objects. The nature of the demonic is a continual topic of conversation at the shrine. Newcomers such as John and Mary who arrive knowing little or nothing about the demons quickly learn their names and habits. Furthermore, during the fits and trances of the possessed, more knowledge of the demons is generated. The world of the demons is continually being reshaped and reformed in its details. New demons are discovered; new aspects of their being are made plain. Yet at an overall level certain contours of the cosmos remain constant, in particular the essentially dualistic framework of the Catholic tradition which is made manifest in the continual cosmic battle between the forces of good and evil.

Most of the devotees at Kudagama see evil and the demonic in ways which would have gladdened the hearts of the nineteenth-century missionaries. Satan, having become too proud, challenged God's power and was expelled from heaven by the Archangel Michael. The fall of Satan is explicitly linked with the fall of man. By giving Adam and Eve free will (*nidahas kamatta*) God opened up the possibility for humanity to do evil. Satan, in the form of a serpent, took advantage of this and tempted Eve in the Garden of Eden, a sin which led to the second expulsion, this time of Adam and Eve from Eden into the world of suffering. Evil and suffering are thus linked together and both are associated with sexual knowledge and the role of the first woman, a theme which continually recurs in ideas surrounding demonic attack and possession and which forms an added dimension to the general association made in Sri Lanka between women, sexuality and demons.

However, the fall of Satan and the stories concerning Adam and Eve are revisited and transformed in the myths surrounding Christ and the Virgin Mary. Christ, like Adam, was tempted by Satan but rejected these temptations and through his sacrifice made possible the redemption of humanity from the taint of original sin. Mary, often referred to as the 'second Eve', is untainted by original sin because she is herself immaculately conceived and because of her immaculate conception of Christ. Not surprisingly a frequent iconographic representation of the Virgin shows her trampling the serpent under her feet. When I asked about this representation and why a Marian shrine such as Kudagama was so associated with the fight against the demonic, I was continually referred to Genesis 3.15: 'And I will put enmity between thee and the woman, and between thy seed and her seed; they shall bruise thy head and thou shalt bruise their heel.'

The mythic structure of Catholicism at Kudagama is thus based upon a series of paired oppositions: God and Satan; Christ and Adam; the Virgin Mary and Eve; good and evil. Just as Kudagama depends upon the existence of the demonic, so Eve who introduced evil into the world, and the Virgin Mary who leads the battle against evil, are mutually dependent. Some of the pilgrims at Kudagama argue that because God is omnipotent and omniscient he knew that the Virgin Mary would exist when he created Eve: the Virgin Mary was already 'in his mind'. Thus good and evil are not independent autonomous states. Neither exist except in opposition to the other. But what distinguishes this from the Buddhist situation is that, whilst the latter is characterised by relativity, the Catholic conceptualisation denies relativity to replace it with a complementary opposition of two absolute states.

On the one hand, this set of ideas about the relationship between good and evil provides the underlying rationale for all the rituals at Kudagama. The Way of the Cross and the rite of the mass celebrate Christ's redemptive sacrifice. The glorification of the Virgin Mary celebrates her rejection of and victory over evil. In a niche high in the wall of the grotto is a statue of the Archangel Michael, his sword raised as he battles with Satan. On a microcosmic level, the greater battle between the forces of good and evil is being played out at Kudagama. At the same time, within this supernatural framework all other supernatural beings can be given a place. Thus besides the Virgin Mary and the angels there are also the saints of the Catholic Church who can help humanity in its battle against evil, although at Kudagama, where the Virgin rules supreme, there is relatively little stress on such saints.

Within the pantheon of 'good', all power derives from God. The power of the Virgin is ultimately God's power; so too is the power of Father Jayamanne. All are working as God's servants in the fight against evil. But as is so often the case, there is relatively little elaboration of the good: what is elaborated is the pantheon of evil.[3]

In general, all evil beings are described as *yaka*, 'demons'. The aim of this demonic pantheon is to attack the teachings of Christ and to entice humanity away from God's path. This they do by causing suffering, which lessens people's faith in God, or by encouraging them to commit evil. One of the long-running debates at Kudagama is whether or not demons attack the good. The traditional view in Catholic Sri Lanka, and one that was encouraged by the missionaries, is that evil attracts evil. If one is a good Catholic then one has nothing to fear from demons. Not surprisingly this is an unpopular argument at Kudagama, particularly amongst those who have themselves been attacked by demons. They argue that as evil people are already allies of Satan, there is no point in the demons attacking them but rather they attack the good. Others claim that it doesn't matter: that demons attack the good and the bad indiscriminately. What all agree on is that demons try to destroy all that is good in people, try to inflict suffering and try to lessen faith in God.[4]

The pantheon of evil at Kudagama presents a structured re-sorting of beings from both the Catholic and the Sinhala Buddhist traditions. All demons are thought to be under the control of Satan who is frequently described as the *lokka* or 'boss' of the demons. Immediately below Satan come the 'fallen angels' who accompanied Satan on his expulsion from heaven. No-one knows much about them, not even their names, and although they can attack people there is little stress on them at Kudagama. Like the angels they were never human beings, and what is striking at Kudagama is that all the beings who are important, both good and evil, were or are humans. Thus the stress in Kudagama demonology is on humans who led evil lives and thus fell under Satan's power.

The lowest level of these beings are known as *peretayo* or *mala peretayo*. They derive from the Sinhala Buddhist tradition and still bear marks of their origin. They are the spirits of the recent dead who were 'too attached' to the world to leave. *Peretayo* and *mala peretayo* are greedy and avaricious and people possessed by *peretayo* roll in the mud, eat filth or steadily lose weight although appearing to eat enormous quantities of food. Frequently *peretayo* are described as being so filthy and disgusting as not to warrant the title of *yaka*. Sometimes, as amongst the Buddhists, they are thought to be the spirits of recently dead ancestors, but more often their origins are unknown. Basically they are nasty little things but not very dangerous although they can cause trouble when they act *en masse*.[5]

Just as Satan stands opposed to God and the 'fallen angels' to the angels, so the *peretayo* and *mala peretayo* are opposed to the 'good dead'.

The latter are those who die in their beds with a clear conscience having made their final confession, received the last sacrament and arranged their affairs. The 'bad dead' are those who die by accident or alone, who do not receive the last sacrament, whose consciences are not clear and whose affairs are in disarray. Whilst the 'good dead' go to heaven (or more often purgatory), the 'bad dead' are doomed to wander the earth as *peretayo*.

Immediately above the *peretayo* in power, if not in morality, come the traditional evil beings of Sinhala Buddhists. These demons have names, specific qualities and temperaments, and favourite categories of victims. The three most common are Maha Sohona, Riri Yakka and Kalu Kumara.[6] Maha Sohona is the 'great graveyard demon'. He is said to attack people at night by hitting them between the shoulders. When he possesses victims they become boisterous and rather violent. Kalu Kumara, the 'black prince', likes young girls whilst his female counterpart Mohini has a penchant for young men. They are both somewhat lascivious and when they possess people their victims become, and I quote, 'very sexy'. Riri Yakka likes blood. This demon tends to afflict menstruating women or women who have had miscarriages. Those attacked by Riri Yakka become anaemic, pale and listless. All these demons, like the demons mentioned below, have particular *lakunu* or 'signs' by which they can be identified. Such signs may be the way they behave, the way they carry their hands or even their smell! These demons are considered to be much more difficult to expel than *peretayo* but they do have less filthy habits.

Finally, between the demons of the Sinhala Buddhist tradition and the 'fallen angels' of the Catholic tradition come the gods of the Buddhists and the Hindus, beings such as Kataragama, Iswara (Shiva), Saman and Pattini. At Kudagama these beings are viewed unambiguously as demons. Again, they have specific characteristics and even though none have distinctive specialities such as a taste for blood, they each express themselves in particular ways through their victims. Thus Iswara tends to insist that those he possesses take their clothes off. Visnu tends to be 'very tough'. Kataragama is often aggressive and flirtatious. Their characteristics as Buddhist or Hindu gods can be recognised through their new garb as Catholic demons, and it is considered that they have 'pretensions' to godly status. In contrast to the filthy *peretayo* who eat dirt, or even beings such as Riri Yakka who drinks blood, these demons are relatively restrained and less boisterous. They tend to tell the truth when questioned and are thus often asked about the future.[7] Because they want to be treated as gods, so people say, they act in a respectable fashion. Because of their relatively high status they are the most difficult of demons to expel, and the most long-drawn-out and elaborate exorcisms involve such demons. Frequently they hide behind other small demons, and an exorcism often involves moving up through a hierarchy of evil from the *peretayo* through the demons of the Sinhala Buddhists until these powerful demons are isolated (see Kapferer 1983).

To sum up, at Kudagama the demonic consists not just of the demons of the Catholic tradition and of the Buddhist and Hindu traditions but also all the gods of the Hindus and Buddhists.[8] There is no ambiguity as there is elsewhere in Catholic Sri Lanka. Secondly, if one excludes Satan and the 'fallen angels', all the evil beings were once human and became demons through choosing to become evil. Indeed, what stands out in the Kudagama cosmos is that all the relevant beings, both saints and demons, were once human. The world of good and evil is thus a world that is ultimately under human control and the relative balance of good and evil is the result of human choices. It is not a world ruled by abstract spiritual or material forces.

### Demons and sorcerers

Devotees at Kudagama are in broad agreement with other Sinhala Catholics and their Buddhist counterparts as to how demons attack their victims.[9] Demons can attack of their own volition but more commonly they are sent by *kattadiyas*, 'sorcerers', to attack particular named individuals or households. In the former case the attack is usually talked of in terms of the *balma* or 'glance' of the demon. Such attacks can be completely random, the demon acting in a totally capricious fashion, but certain categories of people are more at risk from the 'glance' of a demon at certain times and in certain places. Women, particularly young and unmarried women, are most prone particularly when they are suffering from a state of mind known as *tanikama* which can be translated as 'aloneness' but which has a much greater emotional intensity than the English word might suggest. People in general, but women in particular, are especially prone to demonic attack on *kembura davas*, days of the week which are associated with certain Buddhist gods, and at *samayam velava*, the four times of day – dawn, dusk, midday and midnight – when the demons are most active. When women are menstruating and when they are cooking *telkama* (food cooked in oil) they are in danger because demons are very fond of oil and blood. Of course, if a young unmarried woman is foolish enough to be cooking oil cakes at dusk on *kembura davas* when she is menstruating she is really asking for trouble![10]

The other way in which demons can attack people is through *huniyam*, 'sorcery', in which clients employ sorcerers to attack specific victims. Again certain categories of people, particularly women, are most at risk at certain times and in certain states. At Kudagama there was much disagreement over the details of how sorcery worked, and to show too great a familiarity with it was to risk being accused of having been involved with sorcerers. However, there were certain common themes in comments about sorcery.

The best sorcerers are said to be either Malayalis or Buddhist monks, *bhikkhus*, and it is generally denied that there are Catholic sorcerers, although it was admitted that Catholics do have recourse to sorcerers.[11] In a few cases it is said that sorcerers have gained their powers through pacts with demons, but more generally it is thought that their skills are learnt from other sorcerers. Techniques of sorcery involve the use of spells and the manipulation of objects, human ash appearing to be the most popular. Sorcerers work for clients and through their technical knowledge are able to 'tie' (*bandinava*) or force the demons to do their will. Sorcery can be used to gain material advantage and many fortunes are said to have been made in this way. But, say the faithful at Kudagama, such riches will do their owners little good. They will die a dreadful death and end up as *peretayo*. This type of sorcery is talked about at Kudagama but is much less important than two other sorts. The first is sorcery concerned with love, in which charms are used by a sorcerer on behalf of his client to gain the favours of his or her beloved. The second is sorcery employed to cause harm to others, either to a person or their property. People, things and animals can all be the victims of this sort of attack: on occasion even cars have been brought to Kudagama because of demonic attack.

Usually sorcery attacks are thought of as being directed against households rather than individuals. A distinction is often made between attacks which are 'outside the body', *angata eliyen*, and those which are 'inside the body', *angata atulen*, but the two forms may be combined. The former sort of sorcery is less serious because it does not involve an internal attack on the victim. Rather it consists of spells and rituals and leads to such misfortunes as shortages of money, legal cases, quarrels in the family or problems with jobs. The second type of *huniyam* is more serious in that it involves the ingestion of charmed substances or the use of various sorts of image of the victim resulting in illness. Thus charmed food is given to the victim or pins (like the Thorn relic, also known as *katuva*) are inserted into an image of the victim. At Kudagama, by the cross in the grotto, there are piles of such pins which have been removed from the bodies of their victims. Potentially this sort of sorcery can result in the death of the victim.

Such details are, however, somewhat esoteric and most people have only a shadowy idea of how sorcery works. Rather, they know that demons can attack people either on their own volition or through the work of sorcerers. Precisely what sort of sorcery is involved is not important for, as we shall see, the treatment of all cases of demonic attack is much the same.

Two features of sorcery are worth stressing at this point. The first is that at Kudagama most cases of demonic possession involve accusations of sorcery. This stands in contrast with more 'traditional' forms of possession where the caprice of the demons is more important. In other words, at Kudagama possession is the result of human action. Secondly, just as the demons are locked into a structured opposition to the saints, so too are the sorcerers with Father Jayamanne. Thus there is a series of stories which narrate the priest's struggles with different sorcerers, the most famous being a certain monk known as Kondadeniya Hamuduruvo. He was said to be a particularly evil sorcerer whose knowledge of sorcery was unrivalled in all Sri Lanka. When he wanted to catch a train he simply made it stop in front of him. When he wanted a new car it simply materialised at his command. Besides working for clients and killing his victims, this priestly sorcerer was said to particularly relish attacking Catholics. However, Father Jayamanne kept on exorcising the demons Kondadeniya Hamuduruvo was using, and so the sorcerer launched a number of demonic attacks on Father Jayamanne. The latter sent messages to the monk telling him to desist but these were ignored. In the end Father Jayamanne sent the demons back to the sorcerer and the monk died.[12] This indeed is a frequent claim made about the fate of sorcerers. In some versions exorcised demons have no choice but to return and attack the sorcerer; in others the exorcist may force them to. Sorcery is a dangerous business, and no wonder it is said to be expensive, for the risks are high.

### The drama of exorcism

Paradigmatically, the structure of the cosmos and the structure of exorcism consist of a series of oppositions between good and evil. This is not surprising: after all, Catholic thought in particular and Western thought in general, has always had a tendency towards such a dualism. Perhaps more than any other feature this marks a major distinction

Table 2. *Good and evil in the drama of exorcism*

| Good | Evil |
| --- | --- |
| God | Satan |
| Angels | 'Fallen angels' |
| Virgin Mary | Buddhist and Hindu gods |
| and | and |
| saints | 'traditional' demons |

between the Catholic tradition on the one hand and the Buddhist and Hindu traditions on the other, with the latter stressing graduality, continuity and relativity. At Kudagama and the other new shrines of the Sinhala Catholics, such relativity is shunned. Rather there is a strict set of mutually opposed yet mutually interdependent categories.

This set of oppositions is in turn related to two sets of human operators. On the one hand are priests such as Father Jayamanne and the 'holy men' described in chapter 7. On the other are the sorcerers who manipulate the demons. The picture that emerges is of two hierarchies in conflict with one another, with humanity as the battleground. This dualistic framework is all-embracing and without room for finer shades of morality. Buddhism and Hinduism are firmly placed on the evil side of the duality and Buddhist monks along with Hindu priests become little more than sorcerers. At the same time, the mundane world of humanity and the non-mundane world of good and evil exist side by side, the latter being used to inform the former and infuse meaning into what might otherwise be meaningless incidents and events.

Yet as I have already mentioned, this is a cosmos in which human beings and human volition are firmly in control. Not only were the most active of the supernatural beings once humans who owe their present position to their actions in this world, but their efficacy depends upon human actions in the here-and-now. Even the Virgin is powerless if the faithful do not call on her. This is a cosmos in which human choice rather than divine fiat rules supreme and in which the demonic is not just the cause of evil and suffering but is also a manifestation of human evil. If people were good, if they led moral lives, if they heeded the word of God, then there would be no evil in the world. Ultimately, demons are a manifestation of human frailty rather than its cause. What shrines such as Kudagama do is dissolve the inherent ambiguity of everyday life. As the sacred is approached, whether it be the form of the shrine itself, Father

Jayamanne, the relics or the supernatural statues, evil is distilled out of the inherent ambiguities and shades of grey which make up normal mundane life and the 'true' cosmic opposition between good and evil is made clear.

But to return to exorcisms, if what is stressed paradigmatically is this white/black, good/bad contrast which is continually replayed in the ritual process, exorcism utilises this opposition syntagmatically to build up a structured process through which the confusion of everyday life is dissolved. Furthermore, by the use of cosmic symbols, individual experience is made meaningful as the microcosmic expression of macrocosmic forces. The significance of symbols shifts as one moves from the level of the possessed individual to that of the cosmos as a whole. In this shift meanings and significations are created, raised and presented at individual, family, national, international and cosmic levels. Thus Mary's experience of demonic affliction can be viewed as homologous with the experience of Catholics in Sri Lanka, of Catholics in the world, and of the true religion in the cosmos. Mary is possessed by Kataragama, seen by Catholics as a Buddhist god. Sinhalese Catholics are afflicted by the Buddhist majority in Sri Lanka. Catholics throughout the world are under threat from communism. True religion is always under threat from Satan.

Mary's case is fairly typical of those who come to Kudagama seeking relief from suffering. Before she came she had, so she claims, no idea that her problems were demonically inspired. It was only after she had come to Kudagama and seen others rolling in the mud, with demons screaming abuse through their victims, that she began to suspect her own possession before receiving proof of it. Furthermore, what started out as one form of suffering – in her case arthritis, but it could have been any form of illness or misfortune – was widened to include all those other incidents and experiences, not only her own but those of her family, which involved various degrees of suffering. Her husband's financial problems, her children's dismal performance at school, the quarrels with the neighbours, all became wrapped up in one bundle in which a particular incident or experience was seen as a moment in a wider context. This tendency to conflate all problems, and all types of suffering under one heading is common at Kudagama. Rather than view bodily health, financial problems, family tensions and so on as separate and distinguishable realms explainable in different ways and to be dealt with through different techniques, the dominant logic at Kudagama is to see them all as different manifestations of the same underlying cause or causes. Disparate events and experiences are conflated and totalised through the all-embracing dualistic structure of the Kudagama cosmos.

Thus on the one hand there is a movement from the individual to the general, a generalisation of experience and bulking of individual incidents of misfortune. At the same time there is also another movement which involves a shift from seeking the causes of misfortune in terms of some generalised explanation such as suffering being part of life or the result of past sins about which nothing can be done, to a particular and specifiable set of demonic forces which can be dealt with in a practical fashion. Indeed, one of the great attractions of Kudagama is the way in which it encourages both this bulking of misfortune and specification of precise cause, making clear what was previously hidden. Thus once Mary had discovered that she was possessed, the demons could not remain hidden in the confused moral world of everyday life. The physical movement into the sacred shrine and the contact with the sacred in that shrine generated a clarity of thought and an understanding of her position which was previously absent. As John put it, 'Our eyes were opened. We now understood what was happening.'

At first only the minor demons showed themselves. The *peretayo*, being the weakest of the demonic host, were least able to resist the power of the shrine and Father Jayamanne, and they were soon forced to flee. They were only the 'messenger boys', the servants of the more powerful demons, and as they left so Kataragama, eventually forced out of the shadows, made his appearance. Here, the most powerful god of the Sinhala Buddhists was depicted as a demon, and what followed was a war of attrition. Kataragama, proud and arrogant, announced his presence and his power. He dismissed the Virgin Mary and Father Jayamanne as powerless in comparison with him. He presented his attack on Mary as his own decision: no-one tells him what to do. The god of the Sinhala Buddhists thus proclaimed his superiority and his claim to paramountcy.

Slowly over the weeks that followed, Kataragama was forced to retreat. He gave up his claims to autonomy. Although everyone knows that the Virgin doesn't give *varam* to demons, he showed his stupidity and his inferiority by claiming to have her *varam*. Then he started to suffer. He claimed that he was burning: he wailed and shouted in fear. The demon who claimed to be a god was being made to pay the price for his presumption. And his powerlessness became even clearer. It turned out that he had no autonomy and that even though he wanted to leave Mary he couldn't because he had been bound by a sorcerer. The great god of the Buddhists was shown to be nothing more than a servant of humans.

Kataragama, now a pathetic and powerless being, was made to dance in honour of the Virgin. Being a demon he couldn't even pray properly: all he could do was dance. Finally he left, returning to hell and eternal damnation.

Each time a person is exorcised at Kudagama, the truth of the dualistic version of the cosmos is once more shown to be true. Exorcism provides proof not only of the claims made for the shrine but also of a particular view of the cosmos. No matter what the situation of Catholics in Sri Lanka today, in the end they are bound to win because they have God on their side and they have made the right moral choice. At Kudagama individual experience of pain and misfortune is made congruent with what many Catholics see as the travails of their community in the country as a whole. Thus the public humiliations of Kataragama and the other gods which the exorcisms involve are in some ways an expression of what can only be called a political fantasy: the recovery of past privilege by the Catholics of Sri Lanka. The obvious parallel here is with exorcism in the early Church which, according to Peter Brown, 'amounted to a definite recognition by the demons who bore the names of the gods of the superior *potentia* [of Christianity]' (Brown 1981: 109–10). But whereas Brown is referring to the Church on the ascendant, in Sri Lanka Catholics are on the defensive.

In chapter 3, I mentioned a scurrilous anti-Catholic pamphlet entitled, *Kanni Mariyange Hetti*, 'Concerning the Virgin Mary', which caused a major scandal in the 1950s. At Kudagama, it is claimed that the Buddhist priest who wrote this booklet comes from a nearby village, and that one of the reasons the Virgin chose Kudagama was because of its proximity to her enemy. Furthermore, it is claimed that all his relations have died terribly and that he is now very old, incurably ill and in continual pain. But the Virgin will not let him die until he admits his folly and begs forgiveness. Such is the power of the Virgin.

## Conclusion

Clearly in many ways Father Jayamanne is the successor to his eighteenth-century forerunners, the miracle-working Oratorian missionaries from Goa. Reading their accounts of successful exorcisms (not to mention a stream of other miracles) one is struck how similar themes emerge: the importance of sorcery, the importance of the drama of exorcism, the importance of exorcism as a visible and audible demonstration of the superior power of the divine.

In a sense, such parallels are to be expected, for the contexts of post-Independence Sri Lanka and eighteenth-century Sri Lanka are in some ways rather similar – as far as Sinhala Catholics are concerned. Just as the Oratorians were faced with opposition from both the Dutch Protestants and the Buddhists of the Kandyan kingdom, so today's Catholics are facing the demands of the resurgent Buddhist majority. Miracles and exorcisms are once more the means to assert a privileged access to the power of the divine.

Yet to mention such continuities is not to deny that there are major differences between the eighteenth century and the late twentieth century. The decline in the importance of miracles and exorcisms amongst Catholics during the nineteenth and twentieth centuries was not just the result of a changing set of power relations intersecting on the Sinhala Catholic community. The ambivalence with which the Oblate missionaries viewed the exorcisms at Madhu and Talawila was in part the result of a change in the nature of the priesthood and the rise of a more 'enlightened' and 'rationalistic' clergy, changes which have accelerated in the years since Vatican II. If in the eighteenth century exorcisms were in part public displays of power by priests, by the twentieth century the few priestly exorcisms which did take place were held in private. By the 1970s priests such as Father Jayamanne were in a small minority, engaged in a form of religiosity seen by most Catholic priests in Sri Lanka as dangerously anachronistic.

# 6

## Suffering and sacrifice

### Introduction

In the last chapter I was concerned with one particular case of demonic possession at Kadugama, showing how individual experience was interpreted in terms of an overarching set of oppositions which made individual experience homologous with the experience of the Catholic community in Sri Lanka. Yet this one case does not exhaust the possible paths involved in demonic possession. Rather, there are a whole series of ways through which people become – or are seen as becoming – possessed. I shall argue that central to many of the cases of possession at Kudagama are problems of power and authority both within and between households. Demonic possession in this context is largely concerned with the reimposition of authority within the domestic unit. That these attempts to reinforce authority are largely successful only reinforces the less realistic hope that Catholics in Sri Lanka will recover their lost position in the country.

At the same time however, there is another and complementary theme running through this chapter. Suffering and affliction are not necessarily bad things, states of being which have to be avoided. They can be viewed as penance, not just for the sins of the afflicted but also for the sins of others. Once more, authority is crucial for most of those who glorify suffering are those who in one way or another are free of customary forms of subordination. From this angle suffering becomes akin to martyrdom, and the present travails of the Catholic community can be viewed as a penance for past sins or a form of martyrdom which promises future salvation.

### Motivated possession

At the most basic level, the idea of demonic possession is simplicity itself: a demon attacks its victim either of its own volition or at the behest of a sorcerer, the demon then causing its victim suffering. 'Being possessed', a state of being referred to in Sinhala as *yaksha dosaya* or *avesa*, less frequently by *arude*, does not necessarily imply that the possessed person acts in a strange way or even that he or she knows they are possessed. As in the case discussed in the last chapter, people can be possessed for years without knowing it, and it is only in certain situations that the demon chooses or is forced to show itself. Whether or not a person really is possessed thus becomes a matter of interpretation, and frequently there are arguments as to whether for instance, an illness or a piece of odd behaviour, is a symptom of demonic attack or nothing more than a physical illness or personal quirk. Only when the demon does show itself, when it takes over the persona of the possessed person, can there be any certainty over the matter. The appearance of the demon usually involves the victim collapsing, and thus it was common for people at Kudagama to talk of the victim 'falling', the fall marking the onset of the demonic presence. Thereafter, when the victim speaks, it is the demon speaking. When the victim is slapped it is the demon who experiences the pain. During such interludes, usually referred to as *distiya* or *mayam*, the afflicted person is considered to have no awareness of what is going on, and after they recover they have no memories of what the demon did or said through their bodies nor of what happened to them.

Only in a few cases do people know that they are possessed before they come to Kudagama or any of the other new shrines of the Sinhala Catholics. These are people who have 'fallen' or collapsed whilst at their local church, whilst saying prayers or in a very few cases whilst going about their daily lives. In those cases where there is a certainty of possession, the demons have spoken through their victims before they have been brought to the shrine. An example of such a case is Maria.

**Case 1: Maria**
Maria is the wife of a minor government bureaucrat living in north Colombo. When I first met her in 1978 she was in her late thirties with two teenage children. As far as I could gather, relations between Maria and her husband were poor because of what she saw as his heavy drinking. She claimed that she had always been a devout Catholic and recited the rosary every night. One evening when she picked up her rosary she began to feel giddy. She started praying but immediately lost consciousness. After she recovered, her daughter told her that she had been screaming and that the demon Maha Sohona had spoken through her. When her husband came home they discussed the incident and realised that she had probably been possessed for months. She had been eating very little, felt very listless and complained of pains in the joints, and as her husband told me later, she had lost all interest in her home, even in the family accounts! So the whole family came to Kudagama where it transpired

that Maha Sohona had entered her when she had been cooking *kavum*, oil cakes. After four visits to the shrine the demon left.

Cases such as Maria's are rare. Both she and her family had decided that she was possessed before she came to Kudagama. More commonly, possession might be suspected before coming to the shrine, but only at Kudagama is certainty arrived at.

### Case 2: Sharmani

When I met Sharmani she was in her early twenties, unmarried and without a job. Her father was a teacher in a Colombo suburb and according to Sharmani, was rather strict with his children. Her mother wanted to come to Kudagama partly to make a vow on behalf of Sharmani's elder brother who was trying to get a job in the Middle East. Sharmani claims that as soon as she arrived at Kudagama she 'felt strange'. Then during the Friday mass she collapsed. All her family said that they had no suspicion she was possessed before that moment. When they started questioning the demon, however, they found that Sharmani was the victim of sorcery, the result of a land dispute her family was having with a neighbour.

In both these cases it could be argued that the subjects were instrumental in deciding, either consciously or unconsciously, to become possessed. Everyone concerned stressed that they were completely taken aback to discover that the women were the victims of demonic attack. In both cases it could be argued that there were good motivational reasons for the women to become possessed. Maria felt herself ignored by her husband. By becoming possessed she did at least regain his attentions, at least for a time.[1] In Sharmani's case, she was possessed by, amongst others, Kalu Kumara, the 'Black Prince' whom Obeyesekere has described as the 'Black Eros' of the Sinhalese (Obeyesekere 1981: 31). Whilst possessed by Kalu Kumara Sharmani could and did engage in lascivious dancing and flirting with boys. She could enjoy all the outward signs of sexuality denied to her in her home life.

Yet such cases in which the possessed subject alone appears to have been decisive in becoming possessed are relatively rare. There is always the possibility that other members of the family suspected or even encouraged the subject to be possessed. In both cases, once possession had been diagnosed, previous incidents were seen retrospectively as results of that possession. Thus it was claimed that Sharmani hadn't been able to sleep and had suffered from nightmares before she came to Kudagama, but it is not clear whether her family saw these as symptoms of possession before they came to the shrine. Much more commonly, possession is suspected before proof is available.

**Case 3: Neil**
Neil lived in Pallansena across the road from Elizabeth. He was twenty years old when I met him in 1975. When he left school he had been apprenticed in a factory about ten miles away but he didn't like it and came home. He tried a few other jobs but none went well and he ended up just hanging around the house being bored. He complained of always being tired and of having no appetite. Neil and his mother, an extremely pious Catholic, began to suspect possession. Neil's eldest sister had visited Kudagama, and told her mother about it. So she decided to take Neil to the shrine. As soon as they arrived Neil started acting oddly. Then, during the Way of the Cross, he collapsed. According to his mother, he began 'foaming at the mouth'. They met Father Jayamanne who told them Neil was suffering from a very serious demonic attack. The demons were questioned and it transpired that the attack was the result of his mother's sister's husband's jealousy. Such was the seriousness of the attack that even ten years later Neil had not completely recovered and was unemployed.

In this case, both Neil and his family, particularly his mother, suspected possession before they came to Kudagama, and the trip to the shrine was made primarily to discover whether or not these suspicions were correct. Because of their suspicions, Neil's behaviour at the shrine was not unexpected. For both Neil and his family, the diagnosis of possession provided a welcome rationale for his behaviour and a justification for years of idleness thereafter.[2]

**Regularising possession**
Each demon acts in a distinctive, formalised way. Kataragama behaves differently from Maha Sohona; Riri Yakka from Mohini and so on. They walk and stand differently, the ways in which their victims hold their hands are different. These differences are evidence to the onlookers of the existence of different demons and are interpreted as spontaneous products of the demonic presence. Yet if one watches what actually goes on at Kudagama, it is clear that spontaneity is not encouraged and that ways of behaving when demonically possessed are highly stereotyped.

Even in cases where the subjects already consider themselves to be possessed, they still have to learn the forms of behaviour which are considered to be appropriate at the shrine. When Neil arrived at Kudagama, he behaved in his own idiosyncratic way: he lay rigid on the ground. This is not what the demonically possessed are expected to do, and so his behaviour was modified to fit expectations. Father Jayamanne's helpers (*golayo*) were crucial in this process. When Neil lay rigid, they grabbed him, slapped him around the face and told the demons inside him to behave properly. At first he lay speechless, but demons are expected to talk; and so he was bullied and harried with rituals, with objects and with

prayers until the demon spoke. Similarly, Maria's behaviour was modified once she came to Kudagama. At first she simply flailed around in a
random fashion, but once again the *golayo* moved in and began to control
her behaviour. Her arms were tied and she was held down until she began
to act in an appropriate fashion. When the demons spoke through her
they were corrected: 'Don't lie', they would be told. 'We know Maha
Sohona and he doesn't say things like that.'

At Kudagama even in cases of possession which appear to be internally
generated, the behaviour of the possessed is channelled in certain directions. Indeed, part of the drama of the shrine lies precisely in this discipline. The strength of the shrine and the existence of the demonic are
made visible through the domestication of random jerks or fits of paraly-
sis. Such a process of regularisation not only generates the correct forms
of dramatic behaviour but also demonstrates the power of Father Jayamanne. By domesticating the demons, by making them behave in the
correct way, by forcing them to go through the various stages of exorcism
from admitting their presence to the final screams of terror before they
leave their victims, the authority of Father Jayamanne and his helpers is
given audible and visual form.

Of course there are people whose behaviour is never fully regularised;
whose behaviour does not approximate to the 'properly possessed'. There
are always a few people who are so seriously psychologically disturbed
that they are unable to find space to express themselves within the
confines of the drama created at Kudagama. In the literature on Sinhala
Buddhists, cases are mentioned where exorcists have given up and advised
that the patient be taken to the mental hospital (for example Obeyesekere
1981: 101–2). So too at Kudagama, where Father Jayamanne will at times
pronounce that the patient is not suffering from demonic attack but from
mental illness arising from natural causes.

More generally, the therapeutic powers of Catholic shrines such as
Kudagama are limited compared with the situations Obeyesekere describes. One important point of contrast between possession in the Catholic context and possession in the Sinhala Buddhist context is that in the
latter there is a continuum between the divine and the demonic, between
good and evil. Thus in the Sinhala Buddhist context certain beings shift to
and fro between the status of gods and demons, good and bad. As
Obeyesekere has documented, bad possession, possession by demons, can
be turned into good possession, possession by gods,[3] individuals at first
afflicted by demons later becoming shamans of the gods. In the Catholic
context with its overwhelming and totalistic duality, there is no possibility

of such a transformation. A demon is a demon, and can never be transformed into a deity. Thus as a therapeutic process, demonic possession in the Catholic context holds out fewer possibilities than it does among the Buddhists. It is perhaps not surprising that several of the women who Obeyesekere describes as 'priestesses of the gods' were originally Catholic (Obeyesekere 1981). Staying within the Catholic context they could not resolve their problems through possession: they had to leave Catholicism behind them. For Catholics it's a matter of exorcism or nothing, and thus there are a few individuals who I met at Kudagama in 1974 who were still there ten years later, suffering from demonic attack.

### Learning to be possessed

So far, I have discussed cases in which the prime mover, as it were, is the possessed person. Maria knew she was possessed before she came to the shrine. Neither Neil nor Sharmani was reluctant to be possessed: they both took on the role as soon as they arrived at Kudagama. Yet more frequently it is not the possessed person who initiates the process but other people who are able to exert power and influence over them.

#### Case 4: Mallini

Mallini was in her early twenties in 1977. She was unmarried and unemployed, the daughter of a minor clerk. Her parents began to suspect that she was the victim of a demonic attack after she had experienced a string of minor illnesses and began to gaze vacantly into space, refusing to help around the house. Mallini later said that she had thought she was just bored, staying at home with nothing to do. Despite her protestations, her parents brought Mallini to Kudagama. Nothing much happened, but after a couple of visits to the shrine she began to have 'bad dreams'. She refused to describe them to me, although she did say that she saw *yaka* in them. Mallini began to think that she might be possessed. On the family's next visit to Kudagama, they managed to gain an audience with Father Jayamanne and he told them that the girl was definitely possessed. Mallini collapsed when she received the Thorn blessing. Kalu Kumara announced that he was possessing her, and on questioning it was discovered that he had been sent by a jealous neighbour. Thereafter Mallini had regular fits at the shrine. It took eight more visits before the demon finally left her.

The majority of cases of demonic possession at Kudagama approximate to Mallini's case and show a similar pattern of development. First there is some sort of abnormal behaviour – abnormal that is, to others. The subject begins to act oddly in one way or another. This may involve eating all the time or not eating at all; it may involve sleeping all the time or not sleeping at all; it may involve listlessness or hyperactivity; it may involve falling in love with the wrong person or refusing an eminently suitable marriage partner. It can involve losing a job or failing exams. Secondly, there are suspicions of possession. Almost any sort of abnormal, inauspicious or unfortunate behaviour or experience can give rise to suspicions of demonic attack. Thirdly, the subject is taken to Kudagama where, if she shares these suspicions with her parents, possession is soon verified. If she does not, the process of verification can take longer. Father Jayamanne is central to this process of verification. He may, and occasionally does, decide that a person is not really possessed but simply reacting to the emotional atmosphere of the shrine. Such decisions are rare and much more frequently he diagnoses possession. Finally, the subject 'falls' and the demon announces its presence.

The subject's behaviour is then modified and controlled to approximate to ideas of how the possessed should behave. In the majority of cases the demonically possessed have to learn how to behave appropriately. They learn how to fall, what to say, how to hold their hands, how to behave when a particular demon is possessing them. At first, the possessed seem clumsy as they imitate the other possessed people they see at the shrine. Slowly their behaviour becomes more slick, more dramatic, their performance improving as they become familiar with the behaviour of others. And they are actively encouraged in this process. People who are brought to Kudagama on suspicion of being possessed are exposed to extreme forms of pressure. They are forced to attend all the rituals; they are made to say prayers, sing hymns, tell their rosaries. They have holy water poured over them and are also forced to drink it. They are rubbed with holy oil and made to eat blessed salt. They are brought before Father Jayamanne who has the power to say whether or not they are possessed. A demon afflicting a person who behaves in an odd way will be told to behave properly, not to 'play around'. Furthermore, the possession career is expected to follow a set pattern: the possessed roll up the hill during the Way of the Cross; they scream during the mass; they yell abuse at Father Jayamanne. Not to go through all these stages before the final scene at Calvary is to invite suspicion that the demon has not really left.

Certain key figures are closely involved in this process of learning to be possessed. The subject's close relations, usually parents but also spouses and elder siblings are often the first to suspect possession; they are the ones who bring the subject to the shrine. Secondly, there are the people at the shrine, both the other possessed and the non-possessed. The former do more than provide models for behaviour; they often accuse other people of being possessed. Thus a demon will suddenly point to a young girl: 'Ah! I am there too. She is mine and I will kill her.' Amongst the non-possessed, Father Jayamanne's *golayo* are sources of advice and information, and worried parents consult them over their problems. Lastly, there is the priest himself, the final arbitrator of possession. Given the pressure on the subject, from parents, from demons, from other people at the shrine, and from the priest, there is little that can be done to resist this diagnosis. Once defined as possessed there the subject has little alternative but to go through the rituals of the shrine.

### Case 5: Francina

Francina was yet another young woman from a village north of Negombo. She had failed her exams and her parents suspected sorcery so they took her to Kudagama. At first nothing happened but then Father Jayamanne diagnosed possession and so she was forced to go through all the rituals of the shrine. Eventually she fell, rolled on the ground and Maha Sohona announced his presence. He denied that sorcery had been involved and claimed he had attacked her one evening as she was walking home. After she had crawled to the cross the demon left her and she was cured.

I only met Francina a number of years after this event when she laughingly told me that it was all an act and that she had pretended to be possessed because of her parents' insistence. Not surprisingly she had become bored with the whole business, and so she had watched the other people at the shrine whom she considered to be really possessed and then mimicked them to quieten her parents. Even then, despite her parents' pressure, she continued to deny that sorcery was involved because, so she told me, she couldn't think of a likely culprit!

Francina's case throws up all sorts of fascinating problems about authenticity. Years after the event she claims it was all an act, but it is impossible to know how she felt about it at the time. Significantly, she did not deny the reality of possession in others; it was only her own diagnosis that she doubted. For any individual, the boundary between being possessed and pretending to be possessed is indistinct and impossible to determine. 'Faking' possession, however, does not threaten the reality of the phenomenon. In most cases of possession at Kudagama, people improve their performance over time and this goes with an increased awareness and acceptance that they really are possessed. And this is recognised by the faithful at the shrine who also see it as a learning process, although for them the demons rather than the possessed are the pupils.

## Volition and authority

A recurring theme in the majority of cases of possession at Kudagama is that of volition. Demonic possession causes illness, misfortune and so on, but over and over again it is the responsibility of the subject for their own actions which is at stake. Neil may well have been using demonic possession for his own ends in persuading others in his family that it was not his responsibility that he couldn't hold down a job. Much more frequently the possessed person learns at Kudagama that what they thought were their own desires or behaviour are not really their responsibility. In some cases they learn that the responsible agent was simply a malevolent demon; in others that it was a sorcerer. Thus a young girl will learn through the process of being exorcised that her wish to marry a particular man was only the result of his sorcery. She is denied the reality of her own desires and loses any vestige of autonomy. Responsibility for actions and desires is shifted from the subject on to the others, both demonic and human.

This theme of responsibility appears in both the exorcism process and in the choice of demons. During the process of possession and exorcism, the subject is persuaded, forced or taught, that demonic forces have over-ridden his or her own desires. The whole process of possession involves the externalisation of the subject's volition, its substantialisation in demonic form and its eventual expulsion. At the same time, during trances the possessed person frequently acts out in an exaggerated fashion the behaviour which first generated suspicions of sorcery. Victims of love sorcery tend to be possessed by demons such as Mohini and Kalu Kumara which allow them to act out their sexual passions. Those whose possession is first suspected as the result of violent and erratic behaviour tend to be possessed by violent and erratic demons. Thus particular forms of behaviour or particular forms of desire are objectified in the demonic. Such exaggerated and often caricatured behaviour is linked with the blasphemous insults hurled by the demons at Father Jayamanne and the Virgin Mary. Mohini dances in a lascivious fashion during the mass, flirting outrageously with Kalu Kumara. Maha Sohona indulges in violent play during the novenas.

Put in different terms, most cases of demonic possession at Kudagama are concerned in one way or another with issues of control. By raising questions over volition, and by representing the subject's wishes as those of the demon, exorcism involves the reassertion of the correct moral order, which is the moral order of those who seek to maintain control over others. What is involved in the process of possession and exorcism are disputes over control, usually parents' control over children. Any sort of behaviour which threatens the authority of parents can be represented as demonic possession: the problem is to persuade the children that they are possessed. More generally, possession is something which those who find their authority under question can use as a means of reasserting control over uppity underlings: parents over children, men over women, the old over the young. Masked in terms of a moral discourse, with the demons being represented as amoral and evil, possession is centrally concerned with power, particularly power relations within the family.

## Imposing control

Issues of authority appear most clearly in cases where children are involved in conflict with their parents, most commonly over marriage. Here, the possession process becomes a scene of battle between the child and his or her parents, with the demonic a part of the parental armoury.

### Case 6: Ranjan

Ranjan was twenty-five in 1979, the second son of a lower middle class family who owned a small coconut estate. Ranjan was something of a Walter Mitty character: he was a mechanic of sorts but had dreams of greater things – perhaps his own business. Somehow, he had met and fallen in love with a girl who lived about fifteen miles away, and told his parents he wanted to marry her. His parents were aghast: although he earned little, his money was crucial to the household. Furthermore, his sister, a couple of years younger than him, was still unmarried, and they still had to amass a suitable dowry for her. Finally, the girl Ranjan had chosen was of the Potter caste, and Ranjan's family claimed to be Goyigama. His parents immediately suspected sorcery, and they first visited a local 'prayer man'.[4] Ranjan was not impressed and described all this talk of sorcery as *boru*, 'lies'. However, he agreed to accompany his parents to Kudagama, and within a couple of weeks he 'fell'. It transpired that he was the victim of sorcery, that his girlfriend's parents had used sorcery to entrap him. After a few more weeks the demon was expelled and Ranjan broke off relations with his girlfriend. His sister was married off within the year, and Ranjan married a distant relative chosen by his parents a couple of years later.

Such cases are only a minority of those which are brought to Kudagama, but they do highlight the common processes of possession. Once more, suspicions of sorcery are sparked off by abnormal behaviour, abnormal as seen by Ranjan's parents. The subject is then brought to Kudagama and becomes possessed, Ranjan's own desires becoming represented as demonic. Finally the demon leaves, Ranjan forgets his love and from then on fulfils his parents' wishes.

Not always, however, are things so simple.

**Case 7: Nelun**

In 1977 Nelun was about twenty years old. Both her parents were teachers in a north Colombo suburb. At school she had failed her exams and had been 'simply existing' (*nikan innava*) for a couple of years. Then she had told her parents that she wanted to marry a boy who lived a couple of streets away. Her parents strenuously objected on the grounds that the boy's family was not good enough for their daughter: his father was a carter. Nelun insisted and her parents and elder brother began to suspect that she was the victim of love sorcery. So they brought her to Kudagama. Nelun didn't fall during any of the rituals, not even the Thorn blessing, but even so Father Jayamanne pronounced that she was possessed by demons. Every week Nelun was brought to the shrine and forced to go through all the rituals, made to drink pints of holy water and repeatedly exposed to all the sacred paraphernalia of the shrine. Even so, she continued to deny that she was possessed and didn't fall. In the end she managed to give her mother the slip, ran off with her lover and married him. As far as her family were concerned, this was the final proof that she was possessed, the victim of ensorcellment. Not only had she married an extremely unsuitable suitor but she had also disobeyed her parents, a further proof of possession. Sometimes the demons win.

## Categories of gender and age

Demons do not attack people randomly. As the examples discussed above indicate, demonic possession is most common amongst young women. Indeed, statistically, young women are even more likely to be possessed than these examples show. At Kudagama, between 80 per cent and 90 per cent of those considered to be possessed are female, and of these around 70 per cent are aged between 15 and 25. Young unmarried women are those most likely to be the victims of demonic attack whilst adult married men are those least likely to be the focus of demonic attention.

Such a predominance of young women amongst the possessed is not limited to Catholic Sri Lanka: the same picture appears to be true for Buddhist and Hindu Sri Lanka as well (Kapferer 1983; Obeyesekere 1981; Pfaffenberger 1982). On a wider front, elsewhere in the world it would seem that women rather than men tend to be the most likely victims of unwelcome possession by malevolent beings. This gender asymmetry has of course inspired a large and ever-growing literature on possession, frequently relating it to sexual frustration owing to an increased age of marriage or to 'rituals of rebellion', and I will make no effort here to cover the field.[5] Instead, I shall focus on the two major contributions from writers concentrating on the Sri Lankan data.

Perhaps the most ambitious attempt to analyse the predominance of women amongst the demonically possessed in Sri Lanka is Kapferer's *A Celebration of Demons*, particularly chapter 5. Kapferer, in an argument very similar to one I previously advanced (Stirrat 1977), criticises earlier writers such as Lewis (1971), Obeyesekere (1970b, 1975b) and Wilson (1967) who approached possession in terms of the motivations, conscious or unconscious, of the possessed themselves.[6] Rather, claims Kapferer, the major factor which leads to women rather than men being subject to demonic attack is, 'the typifications or cultural constraints which men have of women and women have of themselves' (Kapferer 1983: 100). He argues that because women are more involved with polluting activities such as birth, menstruation and death, they are more attractive to demons. He then goes on to relate pollution and women to what he sees as the relationship between nature and culture in Sinahala Buddhist culture and argues that women are the 'weak points in structure' (1983: 106), mediating between nature and culture and becoming the 'symbolic vehicles for the manifestation of disorder in the world around them' (1983: 107). Much of Kapferer's extremely complex argument is ultimately not persuasive.[7] However, his stress on the ways in which women are 'prefigured ... as being vulnerable to demonic attack' (1983: 101) is important. Because women are defined as vulnerable, therefore they are more likely to be attacked by demons.

At Kudagama, many of the reasons given why women rather than men are the victims of demonic possession are similar to those reported by Kapferer. The most common explanation is that women are inherently 'weaker' than men. For some, this weakness is seen in physical terms: because men are physically stronger they are better equipped to resist demonic attack. Other people stress the opposition between 'emotion' and 'intellect'. Women are said to be more emotional than men, more easily frightened and thus more easily attacked by demons. In this context, the Sinhala concept of *killa* is often invoked. *Killa*, usually glossed as 'pollution', is associated with childbirth, with menstruation and with death, and as Kapferer and others have pointed out, is both extremely attractive to demons and is a source of female weakness. In this context, it relates to a figuration of women as being a source of disorder and a threat to the social order. Women are the cause of the break-up of households; women cause conflict between men; women are a dangerous force which has to be controlled by men (see for instance Stirrat 1989).

At Kudagama the more theologically minded place these pan-Sinhala notions about the nature of women within a Catholic context and understand the propensity of women to demonic attack within a particular recension of the Catholic tradition.[8] In the last chapter I pointed out how the origins of evil and the power of the demonic were related to the story of the Garden of Eden. What is crucially significant in the present context is that evil entered the world through Eve. The weakness of the first woman was to give way to the temptations of the serpent, and the weakness of present-day women in relation to the demonic is both the result and at times a replication of that original sin. Eve's sin gave rise to the discovery of sexual difference, to childbirth and menstruation, and also to death. The various sources of *killa* are thus enmeshed in a complex syndrome which links women, sexuality, the demonic and death.[9] Furthermore, what went wrong in Eden, so it is said, was that Adam failed to keep Eve under control. First he allowed her to be tempted; secondly he gave way to her temptation. Thus if women as a whole are more likely than men to be possessed by demons, uncontrolled women are even more likely to be subject to demonic attack. Thus, it is claimed, young unmarried women are those most commonly possessed at Kudagama.

Yet there are clearly limitations in simply viewing the predominance of women amongst the possessed as the result of a particular set of cultural categories which constrain thought and behaviour in a strait-jacket of 'custom'. Such an approach reifies 'culture' in a dangerous way and sets it apart from the people who 'live': culture, if it exists, does not exist as a timeless abstract construct but is rather created, recreated, produced and modified in and by the lives of people themselves.

It is precisely the problem of the creation of culture which dominates the other major work on possession in Sri Lanka, Obeyesekere's *Medusa's Hair*. Obeyesekere begins by questioning the validity of one of the distinctions which underlies Kapferer's argument: the distinction between 'public' and 'private' symbols. Rather, argues Obeyesekere, there is a class of symbols which he calls 'personal', which have both 'public' and 'private' significance. His denial of the 'public/private' distinction is only part of a more general attack on the distinction between the social and the cultural on the one hand and the psychological and individual on the other. In Obeyesekere's account, culture is the creation of individuals, themselves the creation of culture, which is in a continual process of reproduction and transformation. In this process particular individuals are of crucial importance for they are the producers of private symbols which become collectively shared and thus have a cultural significance. In charting the genesis of these symbols, Obeyesekere turns to the personal histories of the individuals involved, in particular their family relationships. Thus in *Medusa's Hair*, phenomena such as demonic possession are to be understood neither in terms simply of the individual psyche nor in terms of cultural categories but in terms of the complex interplay between the processes labelled by these terms.

At Kudagama, the approaches advanced by both Kapferer and Obeyesekere find support. Overall, there is a sense in which women, particularly young women, are defined as more likely to be possessed and therefore are possessed. At the same time, there are cases where demonic possession can be related to internal psychic conflicts and these are often extremely important in that they frequently provide the most dramatic performances at the shrine. It is through these performances that new knowledge of the demonic is created. Admittedly, there is nothing at Kudagama to rival the instances of 'culture creation' reported by Obeyesekere, but it does take place on a lesser scale. Thus Maria named demons that no one had ever heard of before. They were added to the pantheon of evil. Similarly, demons which spoke through Neil described ways of performing sorcery which were new. And more generally, demons are used to foretell the future.

But what I hope is striking about most of the cases I have described at Kudagama is that they cannot be seen either in terms of inner psychic conflicts alone, or simply in terms of the symbolic construction of femininity. Rather, they take place in the context of a nexus of social relations in which power and authority are being asserted and redefined, relations which may extend beyond the immediate family of the possessed person and encompass other households as well. Demonic possession at Kudagama is primarily concerned with attempts to impose power over others, particularly young women, *not* with attempts to challenge the power of those in authority or as an expression of internal psychic conflicts. Just as the overall demonology of the faithful at Kudagama has to be seen in terms of Catholic/Buddhist confrontation in Sri Lanka as a whole, so too the individual experiences of possession have to be seen in the context of personal confrontations between individuals in domestic and local contexts. Rather than see demonic possession as being the problem which has to be solved, as most academic analysts do, at Kudagama in the majority of cases possession is the answer to a whole series of problems. Once parents have persuaded their errant daughter that she is possessed, control has been reimposed. And this is why those cases where control is at issue are so important: they can succeed in a way that so many others can not. Given the limited therapeutic potential of Kudagama, and given the failure of the shrine to deal with serious instances of physical abnormality, those cases in which control is reasserted are extremely important in regenerating the fame and efficacy of Kudagama.

More generally, what stands out in these cases is the importance of process and practice: it is people acting in certain sets of relationships who provide instances of demonic possession, not culture acting in itself. Within such a context, opposing 'symbols' to 'reality', an implicit distinction in Kapferer's argument, is to miss the point and to create a false dichotomy. For symbols and reality are not separable. The faithful at Kudagama are, to use Don Cupitt's term, 'naive theological realists' for whom demons have as real an existence as the workings of international capitalism (Cupitt 1980: 67). Thus each case of possession is both proof of the existence of the demons and the basis on which future cases of possession are constructed. Furthermore, the experience of the possession process affects other experiences and alters social relations. Possession is part of practice – in the widest sense – and thus it ceases to be symbolic of anything but is part of 'reality'. Nowhere is this more so than in situations where a person becomes possessed as the result of processes which do not directly affect them.

### The possessed as victim

In the cases I have discussed the behaviour of the person who becomes defined as possessed has been central: illness, odd behaviour, personal misfortune, irresponsible sexual attraction and so on have provoked the suspicion of possession. But there is also a sizeable minority of cases where suspicions of demonic attack are aroused not by the behaviour of any individual but by the general unfortunate experience of the whole household.

#### Case 8: Jacintha

Jacintha's father, Antony, was a schoolteacher who also dabbled in a little trading on the side. His trading activities suffered a series of setbacks with the result that the household fell into grave financial difficulties. Antony began to suspect sorcery and so he took his family to Kudagama. He managed to meet Father Jayamanne who said that he didn't think they were being attacked by demons, but Antony's suspicions were only heightened by what he saw and heard at the shrine. He began to insist that the family said the rosary every night. The next week they came to Kudagama again and once more managed to see the priest. This time he decided that they were subject to demonic attack and that Jacintha was possessed by a demon. She was then treated to the whole panoply of the sacred at Kudagama and 'fell'. It turned out, as Antony had suspected, that they were the victims of sorcery from a neighbour.

In this case, as far as I could tell, there was nothing about Jacintha's behaviour which prompted these suspicions of demonic attack. It was instead the overall situation of the household which led to such fears. Jacintha was the one singled out as the possessed because, as Kapferer

would put it, she was 'culturally prefigured' as prone to demonic possession. But once possessed, this state of being altered her conception of
herself. Much of her past became understandable in these new terms: her
minor problems at school, her occasional illnesses, all were now interpreted as symptoms of possession. More significantly, cases like this
changed not only the life of the possessed person but also altered those of
their families and relations with other families.

In Jacintha's case, as in many others, sorcery was suspected. Indeed, a
crucial part of exorcism is the attempt to identify the source of the demon,
and demons who deny that they were sent by sorcerers are only grudgingly believed. In chapter 8 I shall examine in some detail the nature of
sorcery and sorcery accusations, but it should be noted here that sorcerers
do exist in Sri Lanka, and that Catholics as well as Buddhists use their
services. At Kudagama visible evidence of sorcerers' activities is on show.
In the grotto by the statue of the crucified Christ there is a pile of charms
which people have found in their gardens or houses. These may be
inscribed copper sheets, they may be written on paper and put in copper
tubes, or they may consist of noxious substances such as ash from human
cremations.

As with other aspects of the possession process, the questioning of
demons tends to follow a standard pattern. The demon is threatened and
cajoled to tell who sent it. If a demon denies that sorcery is involved, the
questioning goes on until the questioners, usually the close relations of the
possessed person, are satisfied. Here in a shortened form is the questioning of Jacintha by her father.

Antony: Who sent you?
Jacintha: No one.
Antony: Don't lie. [Slaps her.]
Jacintha: No one.
Antony: [Slaps her again.] Don't lie. [Makes her drink some blessed water.]
We know you have been sent. Tell us.
Jacintha: I can't say. I don't know.
Antony: Tell us. Was it X (X was a distant relation)?
Jacintha: No. I can't say. The sorcerer has bound me. I cannot say.
Antony: You'll tell. [Pours blessed water over her head. Jacintha screams
and claims that she is being burnt.] If you don't tell you'll burn
more.
Jacintha: [Starts crying.] It was Y (her father's younger brother).
Antony: Don't lie. He wouldn't do a thing like that. He's a good man. Tell
us the truth.
Jacintha: [Cries again, then starts to wail.] It was Z (another relation). He
sent me.

Antony discusses this with his wife. They can't decide whether or not the demon is lying so they start the questioning again.

Antony:    Tell the truth. [Hangs a medallion of the Virgin Mary around her neck. Jacintha starts crying again.] Don't lie. Was it A (a neighbour) that sent you?

Jacintha:  [Starts crying again.] No. It wasn't A.

Antony:    Don't lie or we will pour more holy water over you.

Jacintha:  [Her crying has turned to weeping.] Yes. It was him. He went to a sorcerer in Colombo. He paid the sorcerer. He did it. [She wails and cries and then collapses.]

Once more, what stands out in this instance is the importance of authority. The choice of the sorcerer is a matter for negotiation between the possessed person and her interlocutors, and the result is a choice which suits not just her but her parents as well. In some cases, there are suspicions that a particular named individual is responsible for the sorcery even before the person 'falls'. In others, such as Jacintha's case, there appears to be no prior choice of the culprit, his identity emerging during the course of the exorcism. If the demon chooses an unlikely source for the sorcery then it is accused of lying: either the demon comes up with a suitable perpetrator or, as in Jacintha's case, a suitable person is suggested to the demon. And just as in other cases of possession, the responsibility for actions or desires is shifted from the demonically possessed onto the demon, so through sorcery, responsibility is shifted onto other people. In Antony's case his economic problems could have been seen, at least in part, as the result of his own mismanagement. Yet through the possession of his daughter he discovered that his problems were not his responsibility but rather the result of malevolent activities by a neighbour.

What this case also shows is the way in which demonic possession has to be seen not just as a manifestation of women's subordinate role but also as a means by which that subordination is reproduced. Jacintha became, or was persuaded that she was possessed as the result of the experiences of her household in general and her father in particular. She, it appears, had done nothing to focus suspicion on herself except to be a young unmarried woman. But precisely because she was the 'weakest' member of the household, the most likely to be possessed, she was the person her parents most expected to be possessed. Through becoming possessed, through conniving in her parents' definition of the situation, not only Jacintha but others are reminded of her subordinate and vulnerable status. Demonic possession is not just a manifestation of the subordinate role of women: it is also a means through which such subordination is produced.

## Suffering as sacrifice

Let me very briefly summarise my argument concerning possession. First, I have argued that whilst women, particularly young women, are culturally defined as being more liable to demonic possession than men, a focus on culture alone ignores the processes through which people become possessed. Secondly, I have argued that there are many roads to demonic possession, and that at Kudagama people become possessed through many different processes. Thirdly, I have argued that questions of authority are frequently of central importance to demonic possession, and that through possession issues of authority are fought out, negotiated and mediated. Just as the overall structure of the demonic pantheon at Kudagama can be viewed as a commentary on the power of Catholics in Sri Lanka as a whole, so individual cases of possession are concerned with issues of power and authority within and between households. And the success of exorcisms at Kudagama, success in so far as they maintain the authority of parents over children and men over women, works to justify and validate the more ambitious claims of Kudagama to restore the position of the Catholics in Sri Lanka.

Yet not all cases of suffering lead to demonic possession. Rather than be viewed as something to be escaped from, suffering can be and often is seen in a much more positive light.

When I first met Elizabeth in the late seventies, she was about fifty years old. Her husband had died leaving her to bring up three children who by then were in their teens. One was still at school but the other two did little but loaf around the house. Elizabeth made a precarious living by taking in sewing and was always extremely hard up. She also suffered from some sort of stomach problem and complained of continual pains in the night. Yet unlike the cases I have described so far, Elizabeth did not see her suffering in terms of demonic possession. Indeed, she vigorously denied that there was any possibility of her being possessed. Instead, she revelled in her suffering. She talked of her life as being one continual process of *dukkha* (suffering): her poverty, the lack of her husband, her illness and the behaviour of her children. But rather than see this state of being as demonically inspired or as something evil from which she wanted escape, she presented it as an opportunity for sacrifice. When she could, she would go to Kudagama and there become part of a community of sufferers in which suffering was sacrifice.

For Elizabeth, her suffering was a sacrifice. Thus she claimed that everyone was a sinner: that to free oneself of sins one had to suffer. Furthermore, her suffering was not just a sacrifice for her own sins but also for the sins of others, notably her dead husband and her children. Her husband by all accounts had been a bit of a rogue: Elizabeth thought that he was now in purgatory and that through her prayers and through her suffering she could reduce his time there. Similarly, her children were a problem. They refused to go to church; they refused to look for jobs. Not only was their behaviour part of her suffering, but her suffering was a recompense for their sins. In a sense, Elizabeth's suffering became a crucial part of her sense of identity. To her, suffering was a golden opportunity, a way of ensuring her own salvation in a future life. She would talk of suffering as a means of purification, even of 'burning her sins', which ensured her a place in heaven. And she would at times pity those who were rich, whose husbands were alive and children successful, who did not have the opportunities to suffer that she was blessed with.

Clearly, Elizabeth's attitude towards suffering harks back to a form of Catholicism, encouraged by the nineteenth-century missionaries, which viewed mankind as inherently sinful and thus impure, and stressed the necessity for repentance and purification. This was a form of Catholicism which encouraged on the one hand mortification of the flesh – usually such minor things as fasting or kneeling with arms outstretched during Holy Hours, but occasionally more spectacular – and on the other the acceptance of suffering as a means of atoning for one's sins. Such a view of suffering is not totally antithetical to that which I have discussed earlier. Elizabeth's suffering is also the result of the inherent sinfulness of mankind which again has its origins in the Garden of Eden. But whereas in the cases of suffering discussed previously, suffering is a manifestation of evil, in Elizabeth's case suffering is the means by which evil can be overcome. Elizabeth made her suffering part of her persona and thus a suitable form for her sacrifice.

Elizabeth was not alone in her indulgence of suffering: like her, many other middle-aged women so represented their suffering as a sacrifice (*puja*) or a penance (*tapasa*) for their own sins or for the sins of others. What is striking about them is how they tend to come from a different age category than women who are possessed. Admittedly, there are middle-aged women who are possessed, but they are relatively few: the young tend to get possessed whilst older women do not. Here, what appears to be important is the presence or absence of control. Middle-aged women, particularly widows such as Elizabeth, are not subject to the same degree of control by others as are young women. Free of such control they are less liable to be possessed, and more able to channel their experience into religiously acceptable forms.[10] Just as women are seen as sacrificing their own interests for those of their families at the domestic level, so in the religious arena they offer their sufferings as a penance for the sins of their male relations: sons, husbands and, less often, brothers. Thus the religious division of labour between male and female amongst the laity uncannily reproduces the gender division of labour in the secular world. Whilst women offer themselves to God, men tend to avoid such an indulgence in suffering. They either offer their female relations, or make financial or physical offerings to the Church.

The model for this elaboration of suffering as sacrifice is of course Christ himself. What is striking at Kudagama is that of all the images of Christ that are available in the Catholic tradition – Christ the King, Christ the miracle-worker, Christ the teacher and so on – here one and only one image of Christ is stressed, and that is the picture of the crucified, suffering Christ. In the rituals of the shrine this is most clearly seen in the Way of the Cross. It is also apparent in the images of the crucifixion which dot the shrine: a large concrete set of statuary at the end of the Way of the Cross; a smaller statue in the grotto; pictures and images of the crucified Christ in the church. Indeed, the interior of the church is dominated by a huge painting of the crucified Christ, the blood that spurts from the wound on his chest being caught in a chalice held by a priest around whom wait the laity. Such scenes are interpreted in terms of sacrifice; of Christ's sacrifice to redeem the sins of mankind. In her own way, Elizabeth is attempting the same redeeming sacrifice and she explicitly compares her suffering with Christ's agonies on the Cross. In the process, her suffering becomes less of a penance for her sins and more of a sacrifice for the sins of others.

In terms of suffering, however, the most important human character at Kudagama is Father Jayamanne. One of the most frequent admiring comments made about him by the pilgrims at Kudagama is that his life is a life of suffering, and that this suffering is a sacrifice for the sins of mankind. Moved by pity for others he is thought to deliberately seek out suffering. His mission house is bare and spartan, and he leads, at least publicly, an exceedingly ascetic life. Each weekend he fasts from Thursday night to Sunday night and during the rest of the week eats no more than is absolutely necessary. His performance of rituals is markedly emotional, his face riven with pain. Nowhere is this more obvious than during the Way of the Cross. Here, Father Jayamanne is not content simply to lead the prayers but acts out the part of Christ. He carries a large cross on his shoulder; he walks up the hill from station to station in bare feet; he cries and stumbles at the points where Christ stumbled.

In his elaboration of suffering, Father Jayamanne is not just acting as a model for the laity, a model seized upon by pilgrims such as Elizabeth. He is also acting out a critique of other priests. One of the standard comments made by the faithful at Kudagama is that today's priests don't suffer; that they are too involved in everyday life; that they lead a life of luxury in their mission houses. In contrast, it is claimed that the missionary priests of the past suffered and through that suffering were better priests, for they acted as surrogates for their sinful parishioners. Whether this was really so – whether the missionaries actually suffered very much – is a debatable point, but this is the image which today's laity now has of them. Good priests should suffer.

At Kudagama priests are not the only surrogate sufferers: so are the sick, the unfortunate and the possessed who are brought to the shrine to be healed. Around the patients there are always crowds, on the one hand hoping to see miraculous cures, but also in a strange sense admiring those who are suffering, and the more extreme, the more grotesque, the more horrifying the form of suffering the greater the crowd. In some ways, the suffering of the possessed, the sick and the crippled is a sacrifice for others and is described as such. The patients are redeeming the sins of the healthy. Occasionally, the patients are said to be in purgatory, a purgatory on earth, but whether they are suffering to redeem their own sins or the sins of others is at times unclear. So too is the significance of the prayers said over the sick and the possessed, for whilst they are prayed for, there is also a sense in which, like the souls in purgatory, they can also be prayed to. In a way they are closer to salvation than those who have no opportunity of redeeming either their sins or the sins of others.

However, just as the successful exorcism of the possessed can be a metaphor for the hoped-for resurgence of the Catholic community in Sri Lanka, so the sacrificial interpretation of individual suffering can also be invoked to view the present-day travails of Sinhala Catholics as an almost heaven-sent opportunity. The whole community of Catholics now becomes the sacrifice, or rather their sufferings become that sacrifice. These sufferings are a means of purification; of cleansing; of reparation. They act as martyrdom writ small, not to be fought against but rather to be joyfully accepted. And here the past of Kudagama is invoked to explain the present. Thus the contemporary difficulties of the Catholic community are often seen as the result of the sins of Catholics in Sri

Lanka. Today's sufferings are a reparation for these sins, an opportunity not to be rejected. Yet such sufferings are not new: popular histories of the shrine claim that in the Portuguese period there was a Catholic community and church in Kudagama but that the church was destroyed and the Catholics butchered on the orders of the Buddhist king of Kandy. This is almost certainly historical nonsense, but the significance of the story is that it links the present day shrine with the past. Historically, Catholics had much more trouble with the Protestant Dutch than with the Buddhist Sinhalese, but today the latter are significant and the former have faded into the past.

Thus the same events, the same experiences, can be given radically opposed values. Poverty, sickness, illness or whatever can be given a significance in terms of evil and be seen, as in the cases I described earlier, as a manifestation of evil. On the other hand, exactly the same experiences can be grasped as an opportunity for sacrifice. Poverty, sickness or whatever can be given a positive value, a positive sacrifice to atone for one's own sins, for the sins of others, for the sins of Sinhalese Catholics, or even for the sins of mankind. It is not that these two visions are unrelated to one another: far from it. For the sins which mankind has to atone for are precisely those sins which cause mankind to court evil, and have their origin in the Garden of Eden. Suffering as a manifestation of evil and suffering as a penance for evil are thus two sides of the same coin.

Ways in which suffering is constructed and interpreted at Kudagama depend largely on relations of power. For many of the young women brought to the shrine, the symptoms which are defined in terms of suffering, sorcery and possession were previously seen in a rather different light. Through becoming defined as the result of demonic attack, these symptoms become defined as suffering. Their miraculous cures are then seen as evidence of the power of the divine. Through the whole possession process suffering is, for many, both created and negated, and in this process not only are relations of authority within the household re-established, but power relations within the larger world recast in terms of good and evil.

Yet at the same time and in the same arena, suffering is also given a different significance: as sacrifice. Here, suffering is a road to salvation, akin to martyrdom. And if possession and exorcism both create and negate suffering thus creating and recreating relations of domination and subordination, suffering can also be used as a means of exploring autonomy from such relations.

Caroline Bynum in her work on medieval European women has also pointed out the positive values which can be placed on suffering in the Christian tradition (Bynum 1987. See also Dahlberg 1987, 1991; Kreisler 1978: 259–64; Kselman 1983: 102–6). In the Sri Lankan Catholic context there are similarities, notably in the ways in which suffering can be seen both as a sacrifice for others and as a means of attaining autonomy. Yet there is one major difference which should be noted. In Europe the stress is on physical suffering; on the image of God made flesh and the importance of the body in Western Christian thought (see also Brown 1989). In Sri Lanka the emphasis is different. Physicalness remains important but much more stress is laid on existential problems: on poverty, on the tribulations of being a woman, on poor relations with kin, on psychic discomfort. Here we are moving into a wider vision of the nature of suffering which owes much to Buddhist notions of *dukkha*. Thus for some at Kudagama, the very nature of life itself *is* suffering; is *dukkha*. Life itself becomes one's sacrifice.

# 7

## Holy men and power

### Introduction

Despite its pre-eminence, Kudagama is only one of several shrines which have developed in Sri Lanka since the early seventies. Although many priests may have reservations about it, Kudagama is still firmly within the framework of the institutional Church. Father Jayamanne is a priest in holy orders and has done nothing which puts him beyond the pale of the Church. He still has the support of his bishop and many of his fellow priests, and little which goes on at the shrine and which has his approval could be described as heterodox. However, other shrines are much less orthodox, existing on the margins of the Church and are either ignored or attacked by the priesthood. They centre on individuals who have no place in the ecclesiastical hierarchy but who claim in one way or another to have special gifts. They provide access to divine grace independent of the Church and represent a challenge to both the Church and its priesthood.

In this chapter I shall be concerned with three of these shrines. The first has developed around a man called Lambert who claims to have been given special powers by the Virgin Mary. His shrine, which he calls Suvagama, is closely modelled on Kudagama. The second is in some ways much more radical than Suvagama. Here, a young man called Lalith Aponsu claims to have been ordained a bishop by Christ himself and attracts a regular following to his shrine of Our Lady of Katunayake. The third is rather different: here St Sebastian possesses a man called Norbert every Monday, Tuesday and Wednesday.

As at Kudagama, devotees go to these shrines for all sorts of reasons, and again the exorcism of the demonically possessed is central to their claims to fame and power. Here, however, I am not so much concerned with the devotees but rather with the central figures and the bases of their power. In the last chapter I examined two aspects of suffering at Kuda-gama: suffering as something which could be overcome with the help of the divine, and suffering as a sacrifice of self to the divine. When we turn to look at the bases of the power of such holy men as Lambert and Lalith, once more suffering is central, but this time as the road to power. On the other hand, Norbert's power depends not upon suffering or sacrifice but on the presence of the saint.

### Brother Lambert of Suvagama

Lambert founded the shrine in 1980 after a series of incidents which persuaded him he was favoured by the Virgin Mary. He called it 'Suva-gama', which can be translated as 'village of healing' or 'village of relief'. It is not so much a village as a large compound on the outskirts of Puttalam, a predominantly Muslim town about eighty miles north of Colombo. Each evening a small crowd comes to pray, whilst at weekends crowds of 200 to 400 people gather for the weekly rituals.

Lambert was born in 1957 near Puttalam. Although he claims to be Sinhala, he grew up in a mixed Sinhala, Tamil and Muslim area and is fluent and literate in Sinhala and Tamil. He claims that,

From the very start I had a great desire to be a priest, so I used to pray to Our Lady very often ... When I was studying I prayed a lot to obtain this desire.[1]

But he came from a poor family and could not even afford a rosary.

With difficulty I made a rosary from broken pieces of rosaries I had collected ... When it broke I repaired it with thread. When this make-shift rosary was beyond repair I collected *olinda* (wild liquorice) seeds and made another rosary.

Lambert describes his early childhood as a life of extreme poverty and privation until he was about ten when his family obtained some land outside Puttalam. There they began to prosper, but a fire destroyed their house and crops, his father died, his elder brother left home and failed to support the family, and his elder sister's husband also died.

That is what I call troubles. We were having enough sorrow and pain. Nothing was coming right for us. We were always shedding tears. We had no one to turn to and no one to give us consolation.

Lambert still wanted to become a priest but the family were too poor and his mother wanted him to get a job. He was apprenticed to a radio repairman in Chilaw but this was not a success. He was then sent to work for a photographer in Puttalam but again he was unhappy.

I bore all these sufferings and prayed. I prayed as much as I could. Even when I was walking to and from the studio I used to pray. I prayed to the Blessed Virgin Mary asking her when she was going to relieve me of my troubles. I prayed asking Jesus why he sent such suffering to me.

When Lambert was twenty he left the studio and began to work as an untrained teacher for a government resettlement scheme. This seems to have been a time of relative happiness but his success aroused the jealousy of others. He became the victim of sorcery and ate a charmed *kavum* (oilcake). As a result he became ill and couldn't teach.

Lambert had heard about Kudagama and decided to go and seek help for his illness, taking with him a Buddhist friend called Gamini. Whilst Lambert prayed, Gamini wandered around Kudagama and was impressed with what he saw. He bought two pictures, one of Our Lady, the other of the Sacred Heart. When he brought them back to Puttalam he wanted to put them next to his Buddhist pictures, but Lambert objected, took the pictures from Gamini, and put them on his private altar.

It is my custom to light lamps at the altar. Before I lit the lamp that day Gamini had gone for a bath. When I went to light the lamp I found the pictures damp and wet. Water was dripping from the pictures. Just then Gamini returned from his bath and I scolded him. I thought he had returned from his bath, gone before the two pictures and combed his wet hair, thereby wetting them. I told him this and scolded him. Gamini protested and said, 'No. No. I did not comb my hair near the pictures. I did not wet them.' I insisted that I did not believe him, scolded him thoroughly and told him that he was mad ... I cleaned the pictures in his presence and went to bring the oil lamp to light before the pictures. When I returned, the pictures were again wet. I was very angry and hit Gamini saying this was his doing. I told him to get out and that our friendship was over ... I closed the room where the pictures were and, taking the key with me, went to another room and laid down on the bed ... After an hour or so I woke, thought of the pictures, and decided to go and have a look at them. When I opened the door and looked, again water was pouring down the pictures. I started shivering and also to sweat ... I shouted to my mother and ... she came running with my sister. When they looked the pictures were still damp and dripping water. My elder sister ... ran out quickly and brought a white sari and made a canopy over the pictures ... This was a miracle wasn't it? People heard about it and started coming. They gathered together and holy hours were observed. When the people prayed the pictures didn't drip water. As soon as the prayers stopped the dripping resumed. Then suddenly the water that dripped looked like blood drops; like the colour of water in which beetroot has been washed. It poured red in colour. Then we became really afraid wondering what crime we had committed ...

The pictures continued to drip water for a number of weeks and local people began to pray before them. Lambert's illness got worse until one night after praying he vomited the charmed oilcake and began to recover, even going back to his old job as a teacher. One day, however, he stayed at home and had his usual afternoon nap.

Usually I do not sleep for long but that day I went to sleep about 2.00 p.m. and woke at 5.58 ... When I shook my sheet ... a necklace dropped out of the sheet onto the floor. When I saw this I started to shiver and called out, 'Aiyo. Is there no one? Come quickly.' Neighbours came running in. I told my neighbours [about the necklace]. The people said, 'Pick it up' ... but I was afraid. I said, 'Aiyo. I won't pick it up. Someone may have charmed it.'

Lambert used a bit of stick to lift the necklace onto the altar and put it next to the miraculous pictures. He began to pray, and whilst praying noticed that what he had thought was a necklace was really a rosary. So he began to treat it as a miraculous object and left it with the pictures.

A few days later, again at prayer before his altar, Lambert became aware of a force preventing him from praying.

I heard a sound, someone saying, 'Stop praying, son, there is something in this house, something in this very room, which offends me' ... I thought this was a temptation. However I continued praying and again I heard the voice ... Then, like watching a film, I saw the almyrah, all the cracks and crevices in the almyrah.

Lambert searched the almyrah and hidden in the corner he found a piece of plastic tubing with the ends sealed. He picked it up and began to pray. As he did so, he had a vision of his elder sister's second husband going to a *kattadiya* (sorcerer) who was putting a charm into the plastic tubing. Lambert could also see that his brother-in-law was doing this to test whether or not Lambert's miraculous objects were truly powerful. When his brother-in-law returned home, Lambert challenged him and found that all he had seen was true.

Lambert next went to Kudagama to show the rosary to Father Jaya-manne. The priest took the rosary and

went into his room. I was standing outside and began to cry. When he took the rosary he kissed it and said, 'It gives off a sweet smell doesn't it?' I thought this was the last time I would see it and I prayed to the *maniyo* (Virgin Mary) to have it given back ... The Father returned and gave the rosary back to me, but said I should leave it with him when I returned home. I thought he said this because he was jealous of me.

However, Father Jayamanne relented and allowed Lambert to keep his rosary.

After his traumatic interview with the priest, Lambert went into the church at Kudagama and prayed. Whilst he prayed, a possessed child entered a fit and started shouting at him, 'Take that and go elsewhere. Take your dowry (*davadda*) and go from here.' The possessed child then started rolling up the hill to Calvary shouting, 'Because of you, because you brought it here, I have to depart today.' Many people saw this miracle and started asking Lambert about his rosary.

Lambert went home and that night dreamt that the Virgin Mary appeared to him and told him to use his rosary to cure the sick.

So what did I do? I took the rosary and placed it on the foreheads of the sick that had come with the crowds to pray. Then just imagine what happened! Some of the sick started to get fits and fall on the ground ... The afflicted also shouted and scolded me saying, 'What is this you have brought? I am burning. For years I have stayed [in possession]' ... I became afraid that those who fell unconscious would not revive. I didn't know did I? I had never cured anyone yet had I? I prayed to the *maniyo* asking her, 'Please make these people conscious.' The whole place was full of noise, the possessed dancing and shouting, 'You have brought it. You have been given power. You must be destroyed, must be wiped out. Your legs will be broken.' But after some weeks some of the possessed were cured.

From then on, Lambert's confidence grew. More and more people came to the shrine, even people who had gone to Kudagama. In a dream, the *maniyo* told him to treat the rosary as a holy relic (*suddha dhatuva*) and to light a lamp before it every night. She also told him to use the rosary to bless individuals as some 'evil people' were claiming that he used charmed oil to make the patients collapse. Instead, Our Lady told him that all he had to do was bless people with his hand on their foreheads and recite the *jamma dosaya* (a prayer to Our Lady). Thereafter, no one but Lambert was allowed to touch the miraculous rosary.

In yet another dream, the Virgin told Lambert that there was a miraculous statue of her in a boutique at Kudagama and that he should buy it for his shrine. She instructed Lambert to collect money from his patients, go to Kudagama and ask the boutique keeper for the statue which had two small flaws, one in the hand and one in the foot, as well as a slight crack.

I collected some money ... and went to Kudagama. When I enquired at the boutique ... they said that all the statues had been sold ... and that I could buy one next week. I said, 'No, no. There is one available. I was told that there is one kept aside because it has two small flaws.' The boutique keeper said that the statue had been kept aside for the use of the boutique and that no statues were available for sale. I again asked whether the statue had been chipped on one leg and the boutique keeper said 'Yes' ... I told him that it would not be right for him to keep the statue as I had been told about it in a dream and so it was really mine. When I said this the boutique keeper thought for some time. Then he gave me the statue.

Almost immediately Lambert was given proof of the statue's supernatural powers: on the bus on the way home a woman went into a trance because of it. When Lambert got back to Puttalam he enshrined the statue at Suvagama, and the shrine began to grow in popularity. People who had seen the power of Lambert's rosary at Kudagama, and others who heard of its fame, began to come to the shrine of Our Lady of Lourdes at

Figure 2    Brother Lambert's shrine at Suvagama

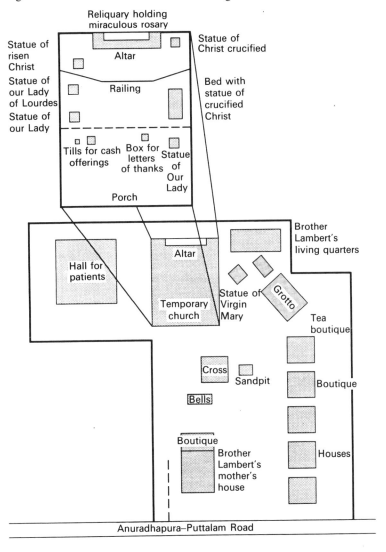

Suvagama. As the shrine grew so did its wealth. Those who received help gave thank-offerings; others gave gifts out of faith. Over the next couple of years Lambert used this money to build a small chapel, a grotto, a hall for the sick and a house for himself, as well as having a huge cross erected in the middle. Each time he was guided by the Virgin who continued to appear to him in dreams, telling him what to do with the money and how to run the shrine.

### Suvagama and Kudagama

Quite clearly, Suvagama is closely modelled on the more famous and successful shrine at Kudagama. Lambert greatly admires Father Jaya-manne, describing him as the most devout priest in the whole of Sri Lanka and as epitomising the true meaning of the Church. In all, Lambert has visited Kudagama fourteen times, the first ten when he was ill and the last four after he had started dreaming of the Virgin. The miraculous statue and pictures come from Kudagama, whilst Lambert took the rosary to Kudagama for Father Jayamanne to pronounce on its status.

The influence of Kudagama is also apparent in the rituals held at Suvagama. The 1983 'Order of service' at Suvagama is shown in table 3: of course the rituals never run to time, but the list gives an overall view of what happens. As at Kudagama, they start with the Way of the Cross on a Friday night and continue with a series of novenas and blessings. Just as Father Jayamanne prays over his miraculous statue and then immerses it in water which he then distributes to the faithful, so too does Lambert. Whilst Father Jayamanne at first blessed people with the Thorn, and then used his hand, so too Lambert blesses with his hand. Just as the possessed run and roll screaming to the cross at Kudagama, so too at Suvagama.

Admittedly, there are differences. Lambert does not say mass: rather he exhorts his followers to go to the local church on Sundays and is a regular attender himself, much to the embarrassment of the local priest. At Suvagama, the possessed are often tied to the cross, a form of exorcism which was once popular at shrines such as Talawila (Modder 1908) but is now banned at all Church-controlled churches. One of the peculiarities of Suvagama is that shoes and sandals cannot be worn within the bounds of the shrine, perhaps the only Sinhala Catholic holy-place where such a restriction exists. Finally, at Suvagama there is a special pit of sand which Lambert blesses and from which the faithful can take sand home.[2]

Lambert is quite willing to acknowledge the similarities between his shrine and that at Kudagama, but rather than explain Suvagama as modelled on Kudagama, he sees them as equivalent. Furthermore, despite

Table 3. *Order of service at Suvagama*

| Friday | 5.00 p.m. | Way of the Cross |
|---|---|---|
| | 6.30 p.m. | Recitation of the rosary |
| | 7.30 p.m. | Perpetual novena dedicated to the shrine |
| | 8.00 p.m. | Free time |
| | 9.00 p.m. | Requests |
| | 9.30 p.m. | Offering of *panduru* |
| | 9.30 p.m. | Our Lady's blessing |
| | 10.00 p.m. | Blessing with holy water |
| | 10.30 p.m. | Adoration of parents |
| | 11.00 p.m. | Hand blessing by Brother Lambert |
| Saturday | 9.00 a.m. | Novena |
| | 10.30 a.m. | Telling of troubles to the Virgin |
| | 6.00 p.m. | Novena |
| | 8.00 p.m. | Our Lady's blessing |
| | 8.30 p.m. | Hand blessing by Brother Lambert |
| Tuesday | 5.00 p.m. | Novena |
| | 6.30 p.m. | Rosary |
| | 7.00 p.m. | Requests |
| | 7.30 p.m. | Our Lady's blessing |
| | 7.45 p.m. | Kissing of the statue of the Virgin |
| | 8.00 p.m. | Hand blessing |

the fact that Father Jayamanne is a priest while he is only a layman, Lambert sees their powers as being equivalent. In both cases he believes their powers are *personal* gifts, and contrasts these with, say the power of Madhu and Talawila which inheres in the *place*. Thus he claims that if he moves or Father Jayamanne is transferred, Suvagama and Kudagama would sink into oblivion.

Yet even if Lambert copies Father Jayamanne in many ways, and even if Suvagama is a local and less famous imitation of Kudagama, there is still a certain tension between the two shrines and the two men. Lambert was afraid Father Jayamanne would appropriate his rosary. 'After all', said Lambert, 'Father Jayamanne is still a human being and might be jealous that the *maniyo* favoured me and not him.' The tension also comes out in Lambert's repeated claims that those who have not been healed at Kudagama find a cure at Suvagama.[3] Where the tension is most marked is amongst the faithful at the two shrines. Although there are people who go to both, each shrine tends to have its own clientele who are quick to criticise the other shrine. Admittedly, many of the pilgrims at Kudagama have never heard of Suvagama, but those who have are outspoken in their criticisms. They see Suvagama as the work of the devil where people are healed or gain boons not through the intervention of the Virgin but through demonic powers. Others claim that Lambert is only interested in money and that the shrine is one big fraud. Similarly, devotees of Suvagama are often critical of Kudagama, although not of Father Jayamanne. Rather they focus on the pilgrims at Kudagama who, they claim, have turned the shrine into a carnival. Father Jayamanne may be a holy man but his power is corrupted by his devotees.

Such criticisms are a crucial part of the dynamics which generate shrines such as Suvagama and Kudagama. As I indicated in chapter 4, the rise of Kudagama was in part a reaction to the loss of power of the older shrines such as Madhu and Talawila, a loss in part due to the behaviour of pilgrims. Similarly, as Kudagama grew in popularity so it attracted more and more visitors who were at best only marginally involved in religious activities. They came to buy and sell, to watch the possessed and to socialise. The holiness of shrines is thus always at risk.

### Bishop Lalith Aponsu of Katunayake

Katunayake is about sixty miles south of Suvagama in the outer suburban fringes of Colombo. Colombo International Airport and the Free Trade Zone are only a couple of miles away, and although there are a few poor fishermen, day labourers and petty traders in the area, many people commute to Colombo or work in the Free Trade Zone. But to quote the *Voice of Our Lady of Katunayake* (an occasional publication put out by supporters of the shrine),

In this sleepy village bordering the lagoon through which run the streams of modern life is a place sanctified as sacred ground. A place so ordinary that at first glance one tends to pass it. But a place to which it is claimed, power has come from the Divine. Divinity favours the simple, or ordinary, the unostentatious. That is why it selected a humble stable, and an ordinary carpenter and his wife to be the first, for its manifestations. Through the ages the Divine Power has worked through the simple and the lonely shunning the powerful, the rich and the ostentatious.

Lalith Aponsu was born on 2 February 1956, the second son of a betel seller who had become a successful baker in Katunayake.[4] Like Lambert, it is claimed that Lalith led a very pious childhood: he preferred rosaries to toys, medallions to sweets, playing at being a priest rather than a train driver. As young as ten he witnessed his first miracle seeing the eyes of a statue of Christ moving and winking.[5] Lalith attended one of the major Catholic schools in the area and when he was sixteen joined the junior seminary in Colombo. According to his elder brother the whole family was against this:

The reason is this. We are at a stage where we have very much lost faith in the activities of the Catholic Church and the Catholic priest.

Lalith insisted on going to the seminary but left after two years. According to his brother, this was because the rector of the seminary thought he would be better suited to a religious order than to the secular clergy, and so it was decided that he should transfer to the Oblate seminary in Wennapuwa. To fill in time before starting at the new seminary, Lalith helped the Katunayake parish priest as a catechist. According to his brother, Lalith was so good at this task that the priest became dependent on his help. Such was Lalith's popularity that he was selected to unveil a new statue of St Sebastian outside the village church. But Lalith was not destined to join the Oblates. Instead,

One Sunday about five or six in the evening one angel appeared to him and told him that he would be selected for some special purpose by God. After that he was frightened. He told his story to mother and me. I laughed and said he must have seen a dream.

The angel had told Lalith he would return a week later, and so the next Sunday his brother returned from Colombo to see what would happen.

On the Sunday morning we went for mass and came back and after lunch he was sitting doing his work in the office room. Then I was talking to my mother. About 3.30 in the afternoon he called my mother and we went into the room as the call was in an excited voice. Then he said that an angel had come and I asked, 'Where?' 'There. Sitting in front of me' [he said]. Then the angel spoke [through Lalith] and told everything, that he was sent by God. Then I asked, 'Who is the true God?' And he [i.e. Lalith] pointed out the crucifix. And I asked, pointing to a statue of Our Lady, 'Who is this?' 'This is the mother of you and I.' And God had selected him for this purpose since the time that he was born. I asked all sorts of questions about heaven and hell and so on, and then the angel said, 'He will be ordained, and from time to time I will come according to the instructions from God.' So then after that it was mentioned that he would be tempted by the devil for one week until he is ordained.

Lalith's brother, suspicious that the angel was really a demon, kept on questioning the angel through his brother but in the end he was satisfied. The next day the angel appeared once more to Lalith telling him to use his crucifix to bless people and drive out demons. From then on the angel appeared regularly and gave Lalith instructions about his forthcoming ordination: how the altar should be constructed, what rituals should be performed, and the vows Lalith should take.

The next stage was a series of 'temptations'. First, Lalith returned to his room to find all his belongings strewn around. Then a huge demon, 'with long hair and a tongue hanging out and all ...' tried to attack him. Sometimes demons appeared as black dogs. At other times they had, 'Five or six hands. They were black ... as we have seen in the photographs of demons.' Each time Lalith drove them off either with his crucifix or with holy water his brother had brought from Fatima church in Colombo.[6] Lalith's brother considered informing the bishop but decided not to as the bishop might think that Lalith was 'under an evil spell or something like that'. Then, the Virgin Mary began to appear to Lalith. The first apparition of the Virgin took place when Lalith was travelling from Colombo to Katunayake by car. At Ragama junction there is a large statue of the Virgin marking the turning to the famous Marian shrine of Teewatte. As they went past, Lalith demanded that the car be stopped. He got out and started praying before the statue. Our Lady appeared to him. She told him not to be afraid, that he must have faith, that the angel had been sent to help him, and that he would soon be ordained.

The Virgin appeared to Lalith on five subsequent occasions, each time giving him instructions on his forthcoming ordination. Throughout this period the demons continued to tempt him: 'If you have so much faith in Christ then jump in front of that car and he will save you.' However, with help from the Virgin and the angel Lalith kept the demons at bay.

Finally the day of the ordination arrived. By this time Lalith was experiencing 'unbearable pains', but he did all that the Virgin and the angel told him to do. He dressed in white, an altar decorated with flowers was erected in his house, and a chair put by it for the angel. A white cloth was laid in front of the altar and around it a line was drawn over which no-one but Lalith could pass. Lalith was told that Christ would come to ordain him in one minute, but he was still in excruciating pain. 'He was rolling on the bed. Everyone who was watching started crying for they could not bear his sufferings.' Suddenly the pain went and Lalith saw the Virgin again. He saw her destroy six devils who were on each side of her. Then a serpent appeared and 'she crushed its head under her feet'.

The ordination ceremony appears to have been an almost exact copy of a Catholic ordination – but without priests or bishops. Instead, Christ and the angels performed the functions usually reserved for the clerics. In Lalith's own words, as recorded in *The Voice of Our Lady of Katunayake*,

I saw Christ appearing before me. He had long hair with ringlets at the end of each lock. He wore a crown the majesty of which no human being had ever seen. It was so brilliant as if seeing the sun at close range. Yet I did not feel any discomfort whatsoever. He was carrying a staff in his right hand. Dressed in a snow-white robe he had a brilliant red shawl over the robe.

Christ blessed Lalith and invited him 'to put my finger into the stigmatic wounds in his hands'. After Christ disappeared he left his footprints in blood on the white cloth which was subsequently treated as a miraculous relic. Lalith now pronounced himself 'The Primate Bishop of the Immaculate Heart Church' and began to carry out all the functions normally reserved for a bishop: saying mass, solemnising weddings, carrying out christenings, confirmations and funerals.

The Virgin continued to appear to Lalith, and by 1979 he had experienced eighteen apparitions. Each time the Virgin appeared standing on a bed of roses, and she usually gave Lalith messages. Typical of these is the following:

I come from heaven. I am now in your midst. I am the mother of God given to you by [the] heavenly saviour. You all know that my son suffered for your sins. I too have shared all his suffering. Accept me as your mother. Give a consolation for my heart . . . To soothe away sorrows recite the rosaries always and bind [?] my heart with the cooling stream of the rosary. Turn each and every inch of my land into a place where I can appear. Then I shall come to you again.

Other messages were more specific, such things as thanking Lalith for building a chapel in her honour. Still others expressed criticism of the hierarchy:

Go to them and preach the message of Christ and spread devotions to my Immaculate Heart. That is not done even by the present day bishops.

Besides the Virgin, Lalith also saw apparitions of Father Pio, Pope John XXIII and various saints.

There were also a number of more spectacular and public miracles. Lalith began to experience stigmata, bleeding for forty-eight hours on the first occasion. By 1979 his hands had bled seven times. Most spectacular of all were the two or three occasions when the wine and the host turned to blood and flesh during the mass. Each time the air was filled with the smell of jasmine. As with Kudagama and Suvagama, the major attraction of Katunayake and the visible proof of Lalith's powers was his ability to exorcise demons. The exorcisms followed much the same pattern as at the other shrines. And again, people also came for other boons: jobs, health, money and so on.

By the late 1970s, a congregation of between two and three hundred people were gathering each weekend at Lalith's chapel. He set up a *dayaka mandalaya*, a parish council, to administer his parish and was considering building a larger church, setting up his own seminary and ordaining his own priests. Lalith claims the right to administer the sacraments not only in his chapel but in all Catholic churches, and on one occasion he tried to officiate at a marriage in Negombo's most famous church, St Mary's. On a national level he has demanded equal rights with the Catholic bishops to meet the President, and on one celebrated occasion even managed to have his photograph taken with the Papal Nuncio! In his sermons, Lalith is an outspoken critic of priests, expressing sentiments which are shared by his followers. Here, once more, is his brother's comment:

The Catholic Church is just a money-making thing. This is what has happened at Fatima and Lourdes today. There is no spirit at these places, not even at Madhu and Talawila. Our present day priests are like devils. They are devils. They don't fast, they don't pray. But Bishop Lalith does all these things and he has all the power a priest should have. Other priests cannot do these things because they are not leading that life.

Of course, the reaction of the hierarchy has been to dismiss Lalith's claims as nonsense. According to priests who say they knew Lalith as a youth, he was 'sacked' from the seminary because he was considered unsuitable to be a priest. He had been weak intellectually, had got on very badly with other students, and had refused to eat at the seminary, his brother bringing him food each day. His transfer to the Oblate seminary was a way of getting rid of him, and the Oblates were not too keen on having him. The priests interpret his subsequent behaviour as indicative of his madness, although one priest I talked to claimed that Lalith was possessed by the spirit of his father.

The parish priest in Katunayake had a particularly difficult time with Lalith. He claimed that Lalith had been wished on him by the bishop and that he had given him catechetical work to keep him quiet. This had been a disaster and so was stopped. Then Lalith started his own church and the parish priest was instructed to stop him. Receiving no advice and little support from his superiors and already unhappy in his parish, the priest requested a transfer. When this was refused, he resigned, married and became a teacher.

### Priests and holy men

In terms of the long-term history of the Catholic Church there has always been a tension between the institutional Church and individual 'holy men', a tension which centres around the workings of grace. The institutional Church claims to be the mediator between man and God on the grounds of the apostolic succession, the Church of Rome being the direct successor to Christ and his apostles. Through the rituals of ordination special powers are given to bishops and priests, powers which have come down through the centuries from Christ himself. Furthermore, through what Weber called the 'depersonalisation of charisma', these powers adhere to the office of the priest, not his person. Thus the personal character of a priest is irrelevant to his competence as a priest (Bendix 1966 [1959]: 311). But there is a sense in which Weber overstated the distinction between office and incumbent, at least in the clerical context. In theory, once a man has been ordained he always has the powers of a priest. Admittedly he may not be allowed to exercise them, but this is a matter of ecclesiastical authority not a loss of sacerdotal powers. The rituals of ordination are magical acts which change the very *persona* of the priest thus making the distinction between office and incumbent somewhat fuzzy. After all, a priest is always a priest in a way that being an incumbent of a bureaucratic position does not change an individual's *persona*. It is this confusion, this blurring, which opens the way for criticisms of the character or activities of individual priests to develop into doubts over their competence to carry out their priestly functions. More generally, this confusion implies that as a gap develops between the ideal of the priest and the activities of the clergy, so questions will be asked about the competence of the priesthood as a whole. Finally it allows particular priests, such as Father Jayamanne, to be seen as particularly effective because their lives more closely coincide with commonly held ideas about what a priest should be.

Yet whilst on the one hand the Church has attempted to monopolise mediation between man and God, at the same time it has always recognised that the workings of God's will are unknowable, and that grace can make its presence felt in the most unlikely places. Most importantly, particular people can be imbued with, or have a special relationship with, the divine. Such personal gifts are, in Weber's terms, pure charisma. Such personalisation of grace constitutes a challenge to the authority of the Church in that it challenges the Church's control over mediation.

Historically, there has been a continual tension between these two channels of mediation, between the Church and the holy person, the priest and the prophet. Institutionalised grace and personalised grace form two poles in a fluctuating and dialectical process. Those whom the Church accepts as making valid claims to such personalised grace become saints; those whose claims it rejects are heretics. And frequently there is a great deal of uncertainty as to whether a particular individual is a saint or a heretic, particularly, as Bell (1985) points out, because such individuals are often religious innovators who develop new forms of religious expression and ritual which the Church may or may not take up.

Again, Weber's characterisation of charisma does not quite fit these Sinhala holy men. It is not just a matter of charisma being parachuted down from on high to individuals who simply accept with surprise that they have been chosen. Rather the material on Sinhala holy men shows us that a lot of hard work goes into receiving the gift of grace. These men's lives, at least with hindsight, have been preparations for their divine missions. Furthermore, the model to which each holy man aspires is not created in opposition to that of the priest but as exemplifying those qualities of the perfect priest which today's clergy are thought to lack. Both Lalith and Lambert appear to have had childhood ambitions to become priests, and they model themselves on various clerical prototypes. Thus Lalith claims to be a bishop whilst Lambert calls himself 'Brother'. What both are attempting is the unification of two modes of communicating with the divine, to be both priests and holy men. Not surprisingly, Father Jayamanne's shrine at Kudagama is pre-eminent because he is both priest and holy man. Doubly legitimated, his shrine is both the most popular and the most stable.

### The model of Christ and the construction of the holy man
One of the problems in understanding these personal histories and their significance, in common with the stories of the demonically possessed, is that they are *post hoc* stories. Lambert and Lalith already claim the status of holy men and their personal histories are motivated histories in which the incidents reported are not so much significant in themselves, but in terms of what holy men's lives should be. Like stories of medieval European saints or the Buddhist forest-dwelling monks described by Keyes and Tambiah, they are primarily hagiographic.[7] To use them to reconstruct the past is extremely dangerous. Rather, what they tell us is something about the way in which one sort of holiness is constructed in contemporary Catholic Sri Lanka.

As I indicated in chapter 4, Father Jayamanne was not the greatest of informants and was generally unwilling to talk about his own life. What information I gave there was based largely on what other priests, not necessarily his supporters, chose to say. Yet amongst his followers, a different story, or rather set of stories, is told.

At Kudagama, it is claimed that Camillus Jayamanne was brought up in a poor home. He led a life of childhood piety and managed with a great deal of difficulty to be accepted into the seminary. There, so it is claimed, he was an extremely pious student and also very successful at his studies, so much so that he was envied and shunned by the other seminarians. After becoming a priest, he served as an assistant to a number of priests, once more being the object of jealousy owing to his piety, his knowledge and his ability to heal people by praying over them. But priests opposed to him prevented Father Jayamanne from being given a parish of his own, and so he became very depressed, wandering off into the jungle and considering leaving the priesthood. Some people say that he was tempted by the thought of marriage. Others claim that when he was in the jungle he was tempted by Satan who promised him worldly power if he left the Church. In the jungle he began to have dreams of the Virgin Mary. She told him that she had a special function for him, and that she would support him because of all the trials he had undergone and because of his devotion to her. So he returned to his Bishop and soon was given charge of Kudagama. The Virgin Mary continued, and still continues to appear to him. She told him what to do when he found the Thorn; she tells him what to say in his sermons and the prayers to repeat at the shrine. And she gave him the miraculous statue which he keeps in his mission house and uses during the rituals at the shrine.

Clearly, popular versions of Father Jayamanne's life parallel those of both Lambert and Lalith.[8] In all three versions, summarised in table 4, most of the incidents are repeated in each story.

A number of features stand out in these personal histories. One of the most striking is the importance of the Virgin Mary. All three shrines are dedicated to one or other advocation of the Virgin, and all three men have strong devotions to her. To each she has appeared either in dreams or in apparitions, and it was with her help that they overcame their trials. Each receives directions from the Virgin, and Father Jayamanne and Lambert have received miraculous objects from her, Father Jayamanne receiving a miraculous statue, Lambert a rosary and a miraculous statue. In these cases there are two rather bizarre features which should be mentioned. The first is the claim by a demon that the rosary Lambert received from the Virgin was his 'dowry'. What precisely this means is unclear. The second is that Father Jayamanne is said to sleep with his miraculous statue of the Virgin. Again, the precise significance of this claim is unclear, but what both point to is the close relationship with the Virgin which is claimed by and for these two men.

In all three cases, it is the Virgin who appears to be the dynamic component of the divine, appearing in this world to influence events.

Table 4. *Mythic construction of holy men*

|  | Father Jayamanne | Lambert | Lalith |
|---|---|---|---|
| Childhood poverty | × | × | ○ |
| Childhood piety | × | × | × |
| Ambitions to priesthood | × | × | × |
| Doubters | × | × | × |
| Suffering | × | × | × |
| Intercession of BVM | × | × | × |
| Temptations | × | ○ | × |
| Gift of miraculous objects | × | × | ○ |
| Miraculous powers | × | × | × |

Christ is a somewhat otiose figure, ever-present as we shall see, but not actively intervening in the mundane. It is through the Virgin that these small shrines in a relatively insignificant corner of the Catholic world are brought into conjunction with the great shrines of the Catholic Church. But whereas in Portugal, Spain or Yugoslavia the Virgin chooses in general to appear to young children, or rather, their visions of the Virgin tend to find greater acceptance (Christian 1972, 1987) here she appears to adult men.[9] This appears to be linked to the different manner in which holiness is constructed in Europe and Sri Lanka respectively. Whilst in Europe the stress appears to be on innocence, particularly the innocence of children, in Sri Lanka the stress is on the ideal of the perfect priest.[10]

Yet if the Virgin is the being who intervenes in this world, Christ is equally important not so much as an interventionist figure but as a model for emulation. This is particularly true of Father Jayamanne and Bishop Aponsu, and given the stress on the priest as imitator of Christ in the pre-Vatican II Church, it would be surprising if it were not. Thus in the stories of Father Jayamanne and Bishop Aponsu, stress is laid on incidents which parallel Christ's life. Each is presented as a pious child; each goes through periods of trials and tribulations. Each is tempted by worldly power before finally achieving grace. In Father Jayamanne's case, he acts out the Passion of Christ each Friday night. He walks barefoot up the hill from station to station, dressed in his oldest cassock and carrying a huge cross. When people are asked why he is doing this, they describe it as his penance for the sins of others, sometimes likening this penance to Christ's penance on the Cross. The identification with Christ is even more clear in the case of Bishop Aponsu. Not only was he ordained by Christ himself but he now even bears the stigmata of Christ's sufferings on the Cross.

However, even if the image of Christ which dominates these shrines is of Christ as the sacrificial victim dying on the Cross to redeem the sins of mankind, there is also an alternative. This is the model of Christ as the miracle worker, the Christ who drove out devils, who turned the water into wine and raised the dead. The image resonates more with medieval ideas of the miracle-working saint than with images of the martyrs of the post-Reformation Church. But more importantly, it is an image which views power as something which can only be attained through suffering. It is precisely because Father Jayamanne suffered and still suffers that he has the power to overcome evil and relieve others of their suffering. Each Friday by experiencing the suffering (*duk vindinava*) involved in the Way of the Cross, he is thought of as recharging his spiritual batteries. As some at the shrine put it, if he did not suffer then he would cease to have power over the demons. Similarly, Bishop Lalith's stigmata give him intense pain, but this pain is thought of as a necessary part of his holiness and his power. Suffering is not simply something to be avoided; nor is it just a penance for one's own sins or the sins of others. It can also be a source of power.

**The dilemmas of asceticism**

Put in a slightly different context, the suffering experienced by all three holy men can also be seen as a form of asceticism. Indeed, experiences which are at one moment described as *dukkha*, 'suffering', can also be described as *tapasa*, 'asceticism'. Thus Father Jayamanne fasts each weekend. This is referred to both as *dukkha* and as *tapasa*. When Lambert talked of his trials before he received his miraculous rosary, the words were used interchangeably. All three men are seen as ascetics, as world renouncers. Thus all avoid women, they fast and they lead lives of ostentatious simplicity – at least in public. Lambert lives in a shack by comparison with the splendours of the buildings holding his shrine. According to his brother, Bishop Aponsu lives in a 'cell' and eats very little. All three disdain money. Father Jayamanne refuses to have anything to do with the offerings made at Kudagama, his bishop having to appoint an administrator to deal with the funds. At Katunayake, Lalith's brother looks after the books, and at Suvagama Lambert makes a great play of knowing nothing about the finances of the shrine. The criticisms which are most offensive and most vigorously contested are those which accuse holy men of being interested in sex and money.

Yet if these holy men are ascetics, world-renouncers in the great tradition of Catholic religiosity, the majority of people who go to their shrines are by no means ascetically orientated. As in medieval Europe, 'the cult of the saint ... [is] everything that the saint [is] not' (Weinstein and Bell 1982: 239). As we have seen in earlier chapters, people go to these shrines and cluster around holy men for practical purposes. 'Venerated for their holiness but invoked for their power, saints stood as a reproach to the wonder-seeking crowd even as they served its humble ends' (Weinstein and Bell 1982: 5). For the few hours or days that they are at the shrines the pilgrims may become temporary ascetics, constantly praying, eating little and avoiding the pleasures of normal life, but this is a transient state: 'humble ends' are what have drawn them there. Precisely because these holy men have renounced the world, and as a result sought and found divine grace, they become channels for such divine power, conduits which mediate between the material and corporeal interests of the mundane world and the immaterial and spiritual, but also infinitely superior and more powerful, world of the divine.

Running through the construction of holiness at these shrines is a dialectic between this world and the other world, between non-involvement and involvement, between succour and suffering. The more one renounces the world and the more one suffers, the greater one's power over the world and the greater one's power to relieve suffering. On the one hand this dialectic is central to the Christian tradition: Christ is both the suffering world-renouncer who turned his back on earthly powers, but also the world-ruler, Christ the King, whose earthly kingdom may not be here today but will surely come tomorrow. The same sort of tension is apparent in Buddhism: Buddha was both the great world-renouncer and the world-conqueror, a theme which is played out constantly in concepts of Buddhist kingship and in the relationship between the king and the *sangha*. Similarly, in the Buddhist ascetic tradition, meditation and renunciation can give supernatural power, the power to perform miracles. To gain power over the world one must first renounce it.

The result is in one sense unedifying. The holy men, be they Buddhist or Catholic, attempt to achieve their own salvation through rejecting the mundane. As a result they become channels for supernatural powers and are therefore pursued by the masses intent on tapping this power. At the shrines discussed in this chapter, there is a certain ambivalence on the part of the holy men towards the miracles they perform. On the one hand these are proof of their status. Yet too strong a focus on worldly benefits turns a holy man into a mere magician. Thus it is not Father Jayamanne who boasts of his miracles: he would prefer his followers to emulate his behaviour rather than see him as a wonder-worker. Similarly, Brother Lambert often criticises people at Suvagama for searching for miracles rather than seeking God.

### Personal powers and the power of words
The peculiarly personal powers of these holy men come into sharper relief when they are seen in contrast to the sorts of power exercised by other practitioners of the sacred in Catholic Sri Lanka, for besides the priests there were and still are a number of other people who claim divine powers.

As was mentioned in chapter 2, during the Dutch occupation of the Maritime Provinces, priests were few and far between in Sri Lanka, and as a result they were forced to experiment with means of maintaining Catholic practice in isolated Catholic communities. In part this consisted of translating texts into the indigenous languages. These included the creed, various litanies and most famously, the 'passion books' (*pasan pot*) which told the story of Christ's passion and were used at Easter.[11] Besides these liturgical texts there was also a second series of writings, sometimes called 'books of protection' (*araksha pot*). These consisted of collections of prayers for specific purposes: illness (both human and animal), crop failures, plagues of pests, toothache and exorcism. Like the liturgical works, the *araksha pot* were closely modelled on indigenous Sinhala and Tamil literary forms. They were copied and passed down from one generation to the next, and were used by the *muppus* and *annavis* as well as men known as *prarthanakarayas*, 'litany readers'.[12]

When the Church hierarchy reasserted itself in the nineteenth century, the missionaries found these texts in widespread use. Their existence posed a problem for the priests: their form was viewed as dangerously non-Catholic because they followed indigenous models so closely, included prayers which were normally reserved for priests, and provided channels of communication with the divine outside priestly control. Individual priests differed over how they should deal with these texts. Some refused any compromise with such 'folk-Catholicism', attacking the *muppus* and *annavis* who used them and the laity who had recourse to them. Other priests were less rigorous and allowed their use to continue. At times the *muppus* were even allowed to borrow statues and take holy water from the church to use in their rituals for the sick and the possessed.[13]

In the 1970s the *araksha pot* were still in use in Catholic Sri Lanka particularly for exorcisms. However, their use and the number of laymen

F

active in exorcisms appear to have steadily declined since the nineteenth century. The few exorcisms I witnessed which involved the use of these traditional prayers were all held in private houses and involved rituals clearly modelled on Sinhala Buddhist prototypes. In all, the words of the exorcism were seen as being of central importance.

The most important point about the *araksha pot* was that they can be used by ordinary men. 'Prayer men' are not considered to have any special innate powers: they simply have a skill which anyone can learn. All they need is access to an *araksha potak* and a teacher. In the past access to such books may have given the owner a certain status, but by the 1970s this was not the case. Admittedly they have to be 'strong men' and not easily frightened, for if the rituals go wrong there is a danger that the demons might attack them. Before they begin the rituals, they say prayers in their own houses to prevent demonic attack. Also, they have to be pure (*suddha*), but this is short-lived, a matter of avoiding sex, alcohol and meat for a few days before the ritual.

What gives these men the power to cure and to exorcise demons is their knowledge of the particular words which make up the prayers and of the way in which these prayers have to be used. As with the ritual forms, the *araksha pot* show strong Sinhala Buddhist influence. They are written in the style of *kavi* and *pirit pot*, traditional Buddhist forms, and this similarity is acknowledged by those who use them. Indeed, much of the power of these prayers is thought to reside in the verbal forms which they employ, a power which they share with older Catholic prayers and which new forms of prayer are thought to lack.

The users of the *araksha pot* contrast the power they exercise with the power exercised by the priests. The power of the priests, they claim, is something that comes from ordination. Priests can bless and curse at will. On the other hand, the prayer men see their power as residing in the power of words used in the correct ritual context. To a certain extent this contrast is correct, but it oversimplifies matters. First, the *araksha pot* themselves are priestly products and part of their power is a matter of their priestly origin. Secondly, priests themselves have to use words in particular ways, and the correctness of these words is extremely important. The mass is never said without the priest referring to the written word, and the actual language of the mass is as important an element in the transformation of the bread and the wine into flesh and blood as is the presence of the priest. Thus priest and prayer men are related not just in contrast to one another; they also share certain elements in common.

The importance of words and verbal form is also evident in other contexts. Items such as holy water and oil are powerful because of the words the priests chant over them. Amongst the laity, rosaries are known as *japamalaya*, 'muttering prayer beads', and are thought to become more powerful the more they are prayed over. The alternative name for them is *kontaya*, 'javelin', and I was told that a well-used rosary, frequently prayed over, would protect its owner not just against demonic attack but also against physical attack. Similarly, *boralikkamas*, 'medallions', are considered to gain power through being prayed over, whilst miraculous statues are also often thought to owe their power to the prayers of the faithful.

In sum, power accretes in objects through prayer. Formalised, formulatory and stylised language has a power which can be transferred into objects and people. Thus objects such as rosaries, medallions and statues gain power through prayer, and people are made priests through being ordained by other priests using the particular language of ordination. The use of language in formalised ritual contexts can give power. In contrast, the power of the holy men described in this chapter does not depend on knowledge of words or rituals. It depends upon the grace they have been granted from on high. In part this is made concrete in the miraculous objects they have been granted. Brother Lambert's pictures, statue and rosary owe their power not to having been prayed over but because of their origin. Similarly, Father Jayamanne's Thorn and his miraculous statue of the Virgin also have power in their own right and not as objectified words. But even more important is the power these men have in themselves. Theirs is not a power generated by words in ritual contexts but is a power granted to them by the divine.

However, all three men use words and perform rituals. Father Jayamanne and Bishop Lalith simply perform their sacerdotal duties. Along with Brother Lambert they see their primary role as the restoration of faith, and prayer, rituals and curing are all means to that end. For most devotees what is important is the miraculous power that adheres to these men. Father Jayamanne's touch heals: he blesses with his hand. Brother Lambert and Bishop Lalith have similar powers which can be transferred to the objects they touch. Thus at Kudagama when Father Jayamanne blesses the salt, candles, rosaries and so on, the important thing for the devotees is that some of the water he uses to aspirate the crowd, water which he has touched, should in turn touch their objects. They open their bags of salt and bottles of water to allow the blessings in. At all the shrines rosaries, scapulars, prayer books and all manner of objects are presented to the holy man to touch. And this touch can even work on images of the object or person to be blessed. Photographs of loved ones and plans of houses yet to be built can all benefit from a blessing from one or more of these holy men. Furthermore, the holy men's possessions are also imbued with their holiness. To touch Father Jayamanne's robes is to partake of his power. As one man at Kudagama put it, Father Jayamanne is already 'like a relic'.

### Saintly possession

Brother Lambert and Bishop Lalith both owe their power to being chosen by the divine. Both have had, and still have, apparitions, and so too, it is claimed, does Father Jayamanne, but all three remain unambiguously human. In all three cases their power is closely associated with their asceticism, and this in turn can be viewed in terms of both the Catholic tradition of saintly power and the Buddhist tradition of world-renunciation and the power over the world which this gives. Yet at the same time, another sort of holy man is also at work amongst Sinhala Catholics. In these cases their power derives not from asceticism but from possession by the saints. And whilst the holy men so far discussed in this chapter are self-conscious ascetics, the men possessed by the saints are very much part of the world and build upon a different model which ultimately derives from the traditional Sinhala priests of the gods, the *kapuralas*.

Probably the most successful of these men who become possessed by saints is a man called Norbert who lives in a small town known as Mirisgama about fifteen miles north of Negombo.[14] Norbert comes from a fairly prosperous middle-class background and was educated at one of the foremost Catholic schools in the area. When he was at school he lived, by all accounts, a very pious life and spent his time praying and helping the teaching Brothers at the school. Whether or not he wanted to be a priest is unclear, but being an only child his parents were opposed to it.

The major crisis in Norbert's life came when he left school and started looking for a job. Norbert appears to have been a rather shy young man, afraid to leave home, and relations with his father began to deteriorate although he remained on very close terms with his mother. Then, to quote Norbert's words during interviews with me,

I applied to join the army. So I went to a church dedicated to St Sebastian for he was a soldier and I made a vow to him. That night I fell into a trance in front of my mother. St Michael spoke through me and said that I had to prepare for a special task. My mother wrote down what was said. It was like a timetable. I had to fast every day from noon. I had to pray every day and anoint my head with oil. These prayers included the rosary, Holy Hours, Ways of the Cross and various litanies. Every three months for nearly eighteen months St Michael would appear and change the routine. I also had to visit various churches.

My mother helped me but not my father. He tried to stop me and didn't believe me. But I persevered. Then St Michael told me that on 16 February [1972] the purpose would be revealed. I had a trance that night and I gave a sermon to my family. This was St Sebastian. Then my father began to have faith. I was given a choice as to whether I would be a priest or a layman. I chose to be a layman as I didn't want to be cut off from my family and I wanted to marry and have children.

At first Norbert fell into a trance in his parents' house. Each time St Sebastian announced his presence and delivered a sermon. Then more distant relations began to come and Norbert's fame began to spread. The first outsider to come was Jayakody, a friend of Norbert's mother's brother, who had a cancer in his leg. The doctors wanted to amputate it but the saint, speaking through Norbert, said that the problem was really sorcery. Saint Sebastian named the sorcerer who later died of a heart attack.

The saint [speaking through me] told Jayakody to go with his family to St Anthony's church at Daluvo (a village on the Kalpitiya peninsula west of Putta-lam). There they met an old beggar dressed in rags. The beggar insisted on putting some oil on Jayakody's leg. Eventually Jayakody agreed. When the oil was applied he fell senseless to the ground but recovered after a few minutes and found that he had recovered the use of his leg. So Jayakody and his family went to [Daluvo] village to buy the beggar a present, but when they returned the beggar had gone. So they came back here to Mirisgama. I was in a trance. I asked if they had seen a beggar at Daluvo. They were surprised and said yes. Then I told them that the beggar was really St Anthony whom I [St Sebastian] had asked to be there to help.

After this, Norbert's fame began to spread and people came seeking the aid of St Sebastian. At first Norbert held public services at his parents' house every day except Sundays but St Sebastian said that Norbert was becoming overtired and limited the services to Mondays, Tuesdays and Wednesdays. By 1975 the crowds were so large that a special chapel was built by some of the wealthy devotees whilst another devotee paid for the construction of a Lourdes grotto.

By the mid-seventies, a regular set of rituals had developed at the shrine (see figure 3). Each morning at around 7.00 a.m. Norbert started praying to the Holy Spirit, to God and to the saints for help whilst some of his helpers would be outside leading the congregation in prayers to St Michael, the Virgin Mary and the Holy Ghost.[15] Around 8.00 a.m.

Norbert entered the enclosed area of his chapel and prayed to the Trinity. Then he entered a trance. Each time St Sebastian possessed him, but the saint also invited other saints to enter Norbert. If it was only St Sebastian, then Norbert would don a short red cloak, but other saints would be accorded other coloured cloaks. Then, properly attired and possessed by the saint, Norbert moved out onto the verandah of his chapel.

The saint then blessed the congregation and delivered a sermon which could last up to an hour. The subject varied: it could be concerned with God's power, with exhorting the congregation to attend church regularly, with a discussion of family life or with the nature of evil. Usually the sermons were remarkably similar to those delivered by more traditionally-orientated priests, and always they were on the general theme of the 'good' Catholic life. Although St Sebastian spoke through Norbert in Sinhala, there could be problems when other saints were present. Thus St Joseph could only speak Hebrew whilst other saints could only speak

Figure 3    Norbert's shrine at Mirisgama

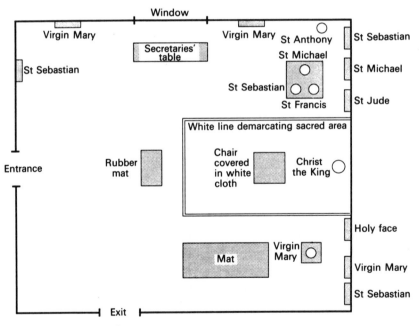

Latin. Thus after they had finished speaking St Sebastian had to translate. After the sermon there were sometimes hymns and always prayers. St Sebastian called on God to purify the world, to drive out evil and to prevent illness and suffering. There was a final general blessing from the saint who then would retire into the interior of the chapel.

After this the congregation would divide. Some would go home whilst others would pray at the grotto. The rest would form a queue outside the chapel and await individual audiences with the saint.

Inside the chapel, the saint sat on a chair covered with a white cloth. On the floor around the chair was a white line across which only the saint could pass. Around the walls were numerous pictures and statues of the saints, mostly presented by grateful devotees, whilst above the saint was a representation of Christ the King. Individuals would then be brought in one by one and explain their problems to the saint: jobs, illness, education, family problems and so on. In each case the saint would tell them what should be done: what prayers to say and when, how many candles to light, what churches to visit. His words would be written down by the *lekama* or secretary, usually Norbert's mother, whilst other assistants would supply items such as blessed water and oil.

After the last interview, St Sebastian would lead his assistants in a short prayer of thanks to God. Then they would all commit themselves to God, the saint would bless his assistants, remove his cloak, shudder and leave Norbert. Norbert would then go off to eat and rest.

Norbert's shrine has never gained the same degree of popularity as have the other shrines discussed in this chapter, and nothing like the fame of Kudagama. Each day when the shrine was open only around 100 to 150 people turned up, and some days there were as few as 50. Yet what is interesting about this shrine is that it displays a different working out of strains inherent in the Sinhala Catholic tradition from those at the other shrines. In particular it has made possession its central legitimating feature.

Returning for a moment to Bishop Aponsu, he like Norbert was possessed by the saints. However, this was only the first stage on the road to ordination, and after being ordained he ceased to be possessed although he did continue to have visions. In the case of Brother Lambert, there appears to have been no possession. For both individuals, their power resides in having been chosen by the divine to have special powers, and this in turn is related to their ascetic practices. Devotees at both Katunayake and Suvagama claim that if Bishop Aponsu or Brother Lambert gave up their ascetic lifestyles then they would lose their special relationship with the divine.

Norbert claimed that he too had the choice of being ordained, but that he deliberately turned it down. Instead of becoming a priest or a brother, he became a vehicle for the saint. Furthermore, he has no idea why he was chosen, and after he had been 'trained' he simply started being possessed by St Sebastian.

One of the features which is striking about Norbert's shrine is that whilst there was as much criticism of modern priests as could be found at the other shrines, there was not the same degree of public hostility to the Church. Thus St Sebastian went out of his way to encourage regular Sunday attendance at the mass and was careful to cancel services at the shrine when they clashed with Church feasts. Similarly, Norbert went out of his way to maintain relationships with local priests and was extremely proud of being able to lend crosses and statues to poor churches. As far as Norbert is concerned, what happens at his shrine is complementary too, not antagonistic towards, the institutional Church. He is not ordained, and even St Sebastian cannot hear confession or administer the sacraments.

From one point of view, all that is happening at Mirisgama is an intensification of an age-old tension between God-centred and saint-centred practice in the Catholic tradition. Yet at the same time, the form it takes at Mirisgama owes much to the Sinhala Buddhist context in which the shrine has arisen.[16] As I mentioned in chapter 2, there is a remarkable congruence between the God/saint distinction in the Catholic tradition and the Buddha/gods distinction in the Sinhala Buddhist tradition. Like the *kapuralas* of the Sinhala Buddhists, Norbert becomes possessed by his saint. Like them he is no ascetic: he makes no attempt to deny that he leads a normal life, and enjoys the pleasures of life. In 1979 he got married, and this seemed to have no effect on the number of devotees at the shrine. Indeed, in some respects he is even less ascetic than the *kapuralas* or the 'prayer men' mentioned earlier in this chapter in that he does not even practice temporary asceticism on the days he becomes possessed. And whereas the period leading up to Bishop Aponsu's ordination is described in terms of 'suffering' and 'asceticism', Norbert talks of the period before he became possessed by St Sebastian as a period of 'training', just as the *kapuralas* are trained.

### Conclusion

Whilst the rise of Kudagama, Suvagama and Katunayake is in some ways reminiscent of recent developments in Sinhala Buddhist contexts (Gombrich and Obeyesekere 1988), an aspect I shall discuss in the next chapter, they also display the widespread unease amongst the laity over the direction the Sri Lankan Church was taking in the 1960s and 1970s. Anti-clerical and anti-hierarchical statements are frequent and explicit at these shrines: 'I tell you straight. All the Church is interested in is money.' Continually, contrasts are made with the past, a glorified past in which priests were paragons of virtue and Catholics a privileged minority. The growth of these shrines is also a manifestation of the failure of the Church to control its members. Thirty years ago Suvagama or Katunayake would have quickly been squashed, but today the Church lacks the power and the authority to control its members. These shrines are part of an entropic process within the Sri Lankan Church, the result being greater and greater diversity of thought and practice amongst Sinhala Catholics.

# 8

# Patronage and religion

## Introduction

So far, I have tended to concentrate on what separates Sinhala Catholics from Sinhala Buddhists. Yet it must have become clear in the course of previous chapters that to treat Sinhala Catholics as an isolated autonomous community is to oversimplify the situation. Ideas about demons and possession at Kudagama, for example, depend upon a fairly detailed knowledge and reworking of Sinhala Buddhist ideas about gods and demons. The forms of prayers used by lay exorcists are based on Sinhala Buddhist prototypes, a fact well known to and appreciated by those who use them. Ideas about asceticism and holy men discussed in the last chapter owe at least part of their power to the Sinhala Buddhist tradition, and even the most ardent Catholics express at times their admiration for the ascetic feats of forest-dwelling monks. Furthermore, Catholics attend Buddhist shrines, and despite their vigorous anti-Buddhist aspects, shrines such as Kudagama do attract some Buddhists.[1] Thus whilst at one level such shrines are concerned with parochial Catholic interests – a hankering after a vision of an older style of Catholicism and a world in which Catholics regained their lost privileges – at the same time all who attend these shrines are Sri Lankans and, no matter what their religious identity, all share certain common experiences and common problems.

Turning for a moment to Sinhala Buddhists, here too we find a series of changes in religious practice over the last few decades which parallel those found amongst Sinhala Catholics (see Gombrich and Obeyesekere 1988; Obeyesekere 1970a, 1975a, 1977, 1978a). One aspect of this is the rise of so-called 'Protestant Buddhism', a group of fundamentalist renditions of the Buddhist tradition in which there is little room for the gods of the traditional Sinhala Buddhist pantheon, but of more relevance here are changes in the pantheon of the gods and in relations between people and the gods amongst Sinhala Buddhists.

As I described in chapter 2, the traditional pantheon of the gods formed an ordered hierarchy of greater and lesser deities. However, in recent years, this pantheon has been subject to a number of changes. Probably the best known and most important of these changes is the rise to prominence of the god Skanda, often referred to as Kataragama after his main shrine in southern Sri Lanka (Obeyesekere 1977, 1978a). In the past, Skanda was only one of the four main 'guardian deities' of Sri Lanka. He was particularly associated with war and with the southern part of the island. During the nineteenth century Skanda declined in popularity, but during the twentieth century this trend was reversed. By the 1960s he outranked all other gods, including the other guardian deities, in popularity. Today over 500,000 people a year visit his main shrine. What characterises devotees' relations with Skanda is, according to Obeyesekere, an extreme form of devotionalism which he terms, '*bhakti* religiosity' (Obeyesekere 1978a). At his main shrine, people walk on fire, hang from hooks and otherwise engage in extreme forms of devotional behaviour.

The rise of Kataragama is only part of a wider set of changes affecting the gods. In urban areas Kali and a god known as Huniyam have become increasingly important (Gombrich and Obeyesekere 1988). Huniyam is particularly interesting in that he was once a demon and still retains demonic attributes. Kali on the other hand appears to have gained precedence at the expense of the less frightening and vindictive traditional goddess known as Pattini. Once again relations between these divine beings and their followers are based on devotion.

Associated with the rise of Kataragama, Kali and Huniyam there has also been an increase in the incidence of possession. On the one hand demonic possession has increased, but at the same time, other benevolent forms of possession are becoming more common marking a break with traditional attitudes towards possession. Increasingly, women are claiming to be possessed by gods and are acting as priestesses of their divinities. And finally, both the practice of sorcery and accusations of sorcery are increasingly common.

According to Obeyesekere, these developments in Sinhala Buddhist religiosity have to be seen in broad psychological terms. At the most general level, the growth of the cult of Kataragama and the other changes outlined above have to be seen as the result of a 'collapse of "traditional" order' and the resultant lack of a 'coherent system to social life' (Nissan 1988: 267), what Obeyesekere describes as a 'disordered modern society [containing] many ... bafflements and frustrations' (Gombrich and Obeyesekere 1988: 100). Changes in modern society have, according to Obeyesekere, destroyed the village communities of the past. With the failure of the economy to meet the aspirations of the people, and a political system which encourages unrealistic ambitions, psychic tensions are built up, and one way in which such tensions can be resolved is through recourse to new forms of religious expression.

Yet as Nissan (1988) and McGilvray (1988) have pointed out, there is a certain looseness in Obeyesekere's writings concerning changes in Sinhala Buddhist religious practice. It is often difficult to identify the precise line of reasoning which links particular forms of behaviour to particular psychological states, and frequently the states of mind of the actors are imputed from their behaviour. As was remarked in chapter 6 when discussing possession, Obeyesekere tends to focus on a handful of informants, beyond doubt the crucial innovators in modern Sinhala Buddhism, and from a close analysis of these individuals moves on to make generalisations about all devotees of Skanda (Nissan 1988: 267).

Although the developments amongst Sinhala Catholics which I have been discussing in previous chapters are by no means identical with those described by Obeyesekere in Sinhala Buddhist contexts, there are similarities, most notably the stress on devotional forms of religiosity and a strong interest in possession and sorcery. In this chapter, the focus is upon the social contexts from which shrines such as Suvagama and Kudagama attract their followers. Whilst the ethnographic context remains that of Sinhala Catholics, the questions addressed are of more wider relevance and concern processes in Sinhala society as a whole which give rise to new forms of religiosity amongst both Catholics and Buddhists. For in a sense, Kudagama and the other new Catholic shrines are 'overdetermined'. Whilst being manifestations of peculiarly Catholic preoccupations – the place of the Catholic community in post-colonial Sri Lanka and the nature of Catholic teaching after Vatican II – they are also manifestations of vicissitudes affecting all Sinhalese no matter what their religious identity.

### The social composition of the pilgrims

In 1975 I carried out a survey over four weekends of the pilgrims at Kudagama. This was not a random survey but rather a sample of those who were willing to talk to me and had the time to do so. Collecting numerical data at a shrine such as Kudagama is not as easy as it might appear. People come and go, and it is difficult to ensure that the same

Table 5. *Religion of pilgrims at Kudagama*

| | |
|---|---:|
| Roman Catholic | 212 |
| Other Christian | 4 |
| Buddhist | 33 |
| Hindu | 7 |

people are not interviewed over and over again. The pilgrims arrive in family groups and again it is difficult to ensure that members of the same group are not interviewed at different times. Given that the interviews took place publicly, it is difficult to judge how far the information obtained was reliable. Nevertheless, for what they are worth the figures are presented in tables 5–9. In all, I interviewed around 260 family groups to which the tables refer.

Not surprisingly, the majority of those who came to Kudagama claimed to be Catholic (see table 5). Less than 2 per cent were non-Catholic Christians, around 3 per cent were Hindus and 13 per cent Buddhist. In my sample there were no Muslims although a few do turn up from time to time at Kudagama. Given the level of Catholic chauvinism at Kudagama it is perhaps surprising that 17 per cent of the pilgrims should turn out to be non-Catholic. In part they were there out of curiosity, whilst others came for trade. Some Buddhists at Kudagama were in the process of conversion, but most were there in a desperate search for healing. Thus the paralysed, the senile, those with cancer and those with congenital deformities are brought to Kudagama after having been the rounds of all the other shrines of Sri Lanka. Even so, what is striking at Kudagama is how few non-Catholics are present compared with shrines such as Madhu and Talawila where quite sizeable numbers of Buddhists and Hindus are to be found, or non-Catholic shrines where Catholics are common.

Only 18 per cent of those I interviewed said that this was their first visit to Kudagama (see table 6). Around 20 per cent had been more than 10 times and some of these had come on anything up to 200 previous occasions, one man claiming precisely 187 visits. Given that few non-Catholics come more than once, these figures appear to imply that almost all the Catholics at the shrine had been before. On impressionistic grounds I find this rather surprising: my guess would be that each week nearly a quarter of the Catholics were on their first visit to the shrine. Even so, these figures reinforce my impression that a steady and regular clientele turned up week after week at Kudagama.

Table 6. *Number of visits by pilgrims to Kudagama*

| | |
|---|---|
| 1– 5 | 159 |
| 6–10 | 39 |
| 11–15 | 9 |
| 16–20 | 4 |
| 21–25 | 7 |
| 26–30 | 7 |
| over 31 | 24 |

Table 7. *Reasons for coming to Kudagama*

| | |
|---|---|
| Victim of sorcery | 109 |
| Possession not linked to sorcery | 58 |
| Physical illness | 84 |
| Mental illness | 11 |
| Financial or economic problems | 44 |
| Out of faith/just to see | 47 |

Table 7 gives an impression of the reasons people gave for visiting Kudagama. It also shows the number of people who thought themselves demonically possessed, whether or not as a result of sorcery. Out of the 247 people interviewed, a minority came simply out of faith or interest or curiosity, but the vast majority came for specific reasons, individuals often giving more than one reason for their presence at the shrine. Around half of these reasons involved physical or mental illness, and a further quarter focused on financial or economic problems. In the vast majority of these cases of misfortune demonic possession was thought to be the cause of the trouble, and in 109 of the 167 instances where demonic possession was mentioned sorcery was seen in turn as the cause of this demonic attack.

Finally, there is the social composition of the pilgrims. Over 80 per cent came from the Western and North-western Provinces, the two provinces where most Sinhala Catholics are to be found. Most claimed to come from 'villages' rather than towns, but this should not be taken at face value for when one looks at occupation, the pilgrims were in general not farmers or fishermen, the archetypal 'villagy' occupations. Rather the majority were involved in white collar jobs such as professionals including teachers and lawyers, and skilled non-agricultural occupations such as bus drivers, railway workers, mechanics and printers, or in unskilled non-agricultural labour. In other words, 'traditional' occupations are under-represented at Kudagama whilst 'modern' occupations are over-represented.

Table 8. *Origin of pilgrims at Kudagama by province*

| | |
|---|---|
| Western Province | 151 |
| North-western Province | 64 |
| Central Province | 22 |
| Sabaragamuva Province | 9 |
| Pollonaruwa Province | 3 |
| Southern Province | 1 |
| Eastern Province | 1 |

Table 9. *Occupations of pilgrims at Kudagama*

| | |
|---|---|
| Fishers | 11 |
| Cultivators | 27 |
| Rural wage labourers | 4 |
| Urban wage labourers | 27 |
| Skilled working class | 49 |
| Professionals | 40 |
| Traders | 43 |
| Police and army | 1 |
| Civil service | 5 |
| Domestic servants | 5 |
| Clerical workers | 22 |
| Estate owners and managers | 5 |
| Beggar | 1 |

I must again stress that there are major problems with these figures, not just with their collection but also with how they are to be interpreted. We don't know what the occupational structure of the Catholic population in Sri Lanka is, and thus the particular mix found at Kudagama may or may not be representative of the Catholic population as a whole. After all, Catholics are concentrated along the west coast of the country and thus most exposed to the 'modern' sector. Furthermore, through the Catholic educational system, Catholics have had advantages that other groups have not, and the picture at Kudagama may not be very different from that for the Catholic population as a whole. Thirdly, this survey was taken at one place at one time. When Kudagama is compared with, say, Suvagama, the impression is that the latter attracts a lower-class clientele whilst Katunayake tends to attract a somewhat more middle-class category of pilgrims. Also, over time there has been a tendency for Kudagama to become more attractive to lower-class (and estate Tamil) pilgrims.

Even so, no matter what the specific statistical details are, the picture that emerges is that most of the pilgrims, not just at Kudagama but at all these new shrines, are wage and salary earners, and that even if they do not live in towns, they are not 'traditional peasants'. And this is not just a feature of these Catholic shrines but also of the new forms of religious expression which have developed amongst Buddhists in Sri Lanka. Obeyesekere variously describes the devotees at Kataragama as the unemployed educated sons of peasants, the slum dwellers of Colombo, politicians, businessmen and crooks (Obeyesekere 1977). Adherents to new forms of religiosity whether Buddhist or Catholic are firmly located outside the 'traditional' villages of rural Sri Lanka but rather in what could be termed the 'modern' sector. What interests me in this chapter is trying to show the linkages between social location and forms of religiosity.

At this point it is tempting to develop an argument in terms of the 'stresses and strains of modern society' or 'social disintegration' as Obeyesekere has in his articles concerned with the rise of Kataragama and what he calls '*bhakti* religiosity'. Of course there are situations in which 'relative deprivation' or 'sexual frustration' or 'the breakdown of traditional norms' does lead individuals to Kudagama and does predispose them to certain forms of religiosity. Yet just as there are many paths to being possessed so too there are many paths to faith in Kudagama. Thus what is important is to show how these new forms of religiosity are generated within a social context; how they gain legitimacy as forms which can be used as means of expression. And this, I shall argue, involves looking at the ways in which particular categories of persons are located in the political economy of Sri Lanka and, more importantly, how they conceptualise the workings of the political economy. Even in its most devotional forms, religiosity is still largely concerned with power. But to investigate this relationship we have to move out of the shrines into the homes of the Catholics who either accept or reject these new forms of religiosity. In what follows I shall concentrate on contrasting forms of religiosity in Ambakandawila and Pallansena.

### Religious practice in Ambakandawila
When I first heard of Kudagama I was working and living in a fishing village called Ambakandawila, about fifty miles north of Colombo near a small market town called Chilaw.[2] No one in Ambakandawila told me about Kudagama, but once I started asking about it I found that a few had heard of the shrine although at that time no one had been there. Since then a few villagers have gone to Kudagama. In the late seventies a couple

of families went in the hope of cures for two children, one mentally and the other physically handicapped, but for both it was a last resort. Otherwise visits to Kudagama have been taken out of curiosity and in general people view the shrine as an interesting oddity. Father Jayamanne was and is generally admired as a good and pious priest but people in Ambakandawila were and still are generally sceptical about the miracles which are claimed for the shrine. As for the other shrines such as Katunayake or Suvagama, their attitude was one of complete disdain. Individuals such as Lambert and Lalith were dismissed as con-men, at best only in it for the money and at worst possibly demonically inspired. Those who went to such shrines were seen as gullible fools. When people from Ambakandawila did go to shrines it was to the older centres such as Madhu and Talawila or to churches traditionally associated with particular saints: St Anthony's church at Kottapitiya, a village to the north of Chilaw, St Sebastian's at Katuwapitiya, a few miles inland from Negombo, and so on.

This rejection of Kudagama and the other new shrines was only part of a specific 'religious configuration' in Ambakandawila, a configuration which stands in stark contrast to that found in Kudagama or in Pallansena. Of course there were individual variations in religiosity within Ambakandawila as there are in any village, but in general Ambakandawila people have rejected the sorts of religiosity which one finds at places such as Kudagama.

First, both possession and sorcery were of only marginal importance in Ambakandawila. In all the years I have known the village there has only been a handful of cases involving claims of demonic possession and these claims have been generally treated with scepticism. In one of these cases a girl claimed to be possessed by Kalu Kumara. But as far as everyone outside her household was concerned the problem was nothing to do with a demon but rather with her need to get married. The claim was interpreted as an attempt by the girl to gain attention for herself. Such a down-to-earth attitude was general in the village. It is not that everyone in Ambakandawila denied that demons exist, although a few certainly do. Some thought that demons only exist 'in our minds' and because we imagine they exist therefore they do exist and can harm us. But for most, the point about demons was not whether or not they existed but that they had no relevance to their lives. Admittedly before weddings firecrackers would be let off when oilcakes (*kavum*) were being prepared, and some people would say that this was to frighten off the demons. Most people however would say that this was nonsense: why should demons be scared by a few fireworks? And they would point out that the noise was really an advertisement for the forthcoming wedding. Similarly, I was told on a few occasions that if a fisherman took meat to sea with him he would be attacked by demons. Again most people thought this was nonsense: that demons didn't live on the sea but on land where there were people to feed them and be attacked by them, and that in any case meat was only eaten in the village on Sundays and feastdays when no-one went fishing anyway. The point about demons was that if one led a good Catholic life then one was safe from demonic attack. When people sinned there were demons ready to attack them. Thus the general opinion was that as one moved away from the Catholic areas along the coast there were more and more demons.

Just as demons were relatively unimportant, so too was sorcery. Again it was not that everyone in Ambakandawila denied that sorcery and sorcerers existed. Rather, people doubted that sorcerers had the powers that were claimed for them, and in general denied that sorcery had any part to play in the village. Thus in the cases of demonic possession that I know about, there were no associated claims of sorcery. In all these cases, the reasons for demonic attack were couched in terms of the whims and caprice of demons or the victim breaking some sort of taboo. The only time that sorcery was mentioned within the village was during a row over a marriage in which the parents of the bride muttered darkly that the groom's family had ensorcelled her. But even in this case the accusation was never made public and the accusers were in no way certain of sorcery.

Thus although it was accepted that sorcery could be used in interpersonal attacks, this was a most unusual occurrence and in general thought to exist only in the Buddhist interior of the island. There were, however, other contexts in which sorcery was more frequently mentioned and thought to exist nearer to home. These involved not relations between people but relations between people and things. Thus many people in Ambakandawila claimed that fishermen in other villages, even Catholic villages, employed sorcerers to increase their catches. It was said that these sorcerers used a form of sorcery known as *pilli* which involved 'breathing life' into a dead fish which then became a sort of 'zombie' fish and would lead other fish into the fisherman's nets.[3] Of course, no one in Ambakandawila would admit to ever having used such methods and anyone who did was expected to die a very bad death. There were suspicions that wealthy and successful traders and businessmen in Chilaw and elsewhere used sorcery, but again, this involved mastery over the physical world rather than over people.

In sum then, the demonic was relatively unimportant in Ambakanda-wila. Demons had none of the immediacy and malevolent reality that they enjoyed in, for instance, Kudagama. Similarly, sorcerers had a shadowy existence. They existed elsewhere, and if they had power it was power over things rather than over people. But in general, demons and sorcerers were not a focus of interest to the people of Ambakandawila and for many they had no 'real' existence.

Turning to the saints, they also had a rather different significance in Ambakandawila from the significance they held for the devotees at the new shrines. Again views differed as to their importance and their efficacy to intervene in the world.

First of all, saints were invoked in a number of specific pragmatic situations. Particular saints were resorted to in particular situations. St Anthony, for instance, was invoked in cases of theft; St Sebastian, for various illnesses. Some people in Ambakandawila could produce a long list of saints and the particular problems they were associated with, ranging from toothache to childbirth to lost causes.[4] Almost every house in Ambakandawila had medallions of St Benedict buried in the foundations and under the eaves, and these were held by some to keep not just demons but all malevolent beings at bay.

Secondly, St Rogus (the local name for St Roche) had, besides his specific function of dealing with wounds, a more general role to play as the guardian (*arakshakaraya*) of the village. Each year at the annual feast his statue would be paraded through the village and his protection for the coming year requested. On an individual level, people would light candles to him or pray to him for all sorts of purposes, such as health, good fishing, good weather for a wedding, a safe journey. Women would shout out vows to him in an effort to delay the bus so that they could load their fish for transport to market. And each Sunday around 30 per cent of the fishermen would 'incense' (*dum allanava*) their nets. They lit candles in front of the statue of the saint in the church, then brought the candles to the beach and used them to burn the incense. The incensing of the nets was only part of the more general use of *sacra* in relation to fishing gear. Thus many fishermen tied medallions of St Anthony of Padua (the 'miracle worker' in this context) to their engines, and most fishermen insisted that the parish priest blessed and lustrated new engines or boats when they were brought to the village for the first time.

To an outsider, it did appear that most people in Ambakandawila were 'worshipping' saints. Their statues were honoured; prayers were said to the saints; their pictures and images were touched and kissed. And as far

as the priests were concerned, the religiosity of the villagers was dangerously 'saintocentric'. Yet I think that such appearances bely the reality of
the relationship between people and saints in Ambakandawila. People
'believed' in the saints in so far as they considered the saints to have a real
existence in heaven. Furthermore, there were people who held that the
saints actively intervened in the world and that the relationship between a
person and a saint was one of reciprocity. Thus if an individual reneged
on his promised gift to St Sebastian, it was held by some that he would
actually be struck down by the saint's wrath. But such people were in a
small minority. The reality was more complex.

Whenever I asked fishermen whether or not incensing the nets on a
Sunday afternoon or getting the priest to bless a boat led to better catches,
or protection from storms and loss of gear, I was treated with incredulity.
No-one, or at least no-one I ever talked to, saw such actions as having
such a direct effect. Rather such actions were seen as *lakunu*, 'signs' or
'symbols', the efficacy of which was in the minds of the actors, not in the
action itself or in some simplistic accounting procedure which viewed the
saint as giving back help in equivalence to the action performed. Rather,
what these actions did was to give 'confidence'. They made people 'feel
better'. Their efficacy lay not in the external material world but in the
inner world of mind and the heart. And they were part of 'tradition', 'our
custom' (*ape sirita*). So at a pragmatic level, it didn't matter whether or
not the priest blessed the boats or St Benedict medallions were buried in
the foundations of a house. It only mattered at the level of internal feeling.
These actions were outward manifestations of inner states – and were
recognised as such.[5] Thus when the priest (or the anthropologist) accused
people in Ambakandawila of idolatry when kissing statues or of the
worship of saints when praying to them, such calumnies would be vigorously denied. People in Ambakandawila were, in this context at least, very
well aware of what they were doing in a way that simplistic distinctions
between 'affective' and 'cognitive' fail to recognise.

Indeed, the role the saints played in the religious configuration of
Ambakandawila was to link together the pragmatic domains of everyday
life with the supramundane nature of the divine. Saints, (or perhaps
better, the *idea* of the saints), were involved in dealing with pragmatic
matters. Saints were also models of the religious life, individuals who
through their lives had overcome the pragmatic problems the villagers
themselves were faced with, and who formed ideal models of what the
truly religious life should be. But for most, even if saints had been people,
and even if saints could be called upon, they were not active interven-

tionist agents. Thus in Ambakandawila there was very little elaboration of devotion to particular saints and no idea that a particular relationship could be built up between an individual and a chosen saint because the saint existed as model and as ideal rather than as superhuman person.

Saints or demons, sorcery or possession or devotion were not central to religious life in Ambakandawila. Rather a preoccupation with personal conduct and a Catholic moral code which should order conduct was what was important. This was expressed in a number of areas. First it involved regular attendance at church. Every Sunday over 70 per cent of people in the village went to church and working for financial gain on a Sunday or a Feast of Obligation was a heinous sin. Part of being a good Catholic was to attend church. Second, it involved regularly receiving the sacraments of the Church, both the life-cycle sacraments and those of confession, penance and communion. Finally it involved obeying the moral teaching of the Church. And it was no good doing one without the other; no good behaving in a moral fashion if one didn't attend church. Religiosity in Ambakandawila was a matter of obeying rules. If one did so then one would attain salvation. Furthermore, one would also reap the benefits of being a good Catholic in this world through the workings of God's grace. But again there was no neat 'fit' between being a good Catholic and being successful on earth, for ultimately God's will was unknowable.

### Religious practice in Pallansena

A few years after my original work in Ambakandawila I spent some months in Pallansena. Although only twenty miles to the south, Pallansena was very different from Ambakandawila not only in its social composition but also in its religiosity. Indeed, my main reason for working in Pallansena was that people from here were continually turning up at Kudagama. Of the cases of possession discussed in chapter 6, four are from Pallansena.

Calling Pallansena a 'village' is slightly misleading. Once upon a time it was a much more discrete unit, a community of toddy tappers, paddy cultivators and potters, but in the years since the Second World War the character of the place has been transformed. Being beside the main road and the railway line to Colombo and Negombo, Pallansena developed into a dormitory suburb for these two towns, and today it is on the northern edge of the peri-urban sprawl which stretches north from Colombo along the coast. By the mid-seventies most people in Pallansena were dependent on wages and salaries rather than being independent producers like the fishermen of Ambakandawila. Men and women worked in schools, in government offices and for private concerns in Negombo and Colombo. Others were labourers in coconut mills or in the brickyards which grew up in the seventies to service the building boom all along the west coast. The development of the tourist industry in the Negombo area provided further sources of employment, whilst the opening of the Free Trade Zone around the international airport at Katunayake created new jobs, particularly for young women, in the textile and electronics factories. Compared with Ambakandawila, Pallansena was a highly complex, highly sophisticated village, and the people of Pallansena viewed the fishermen of Ambakandawila as rough and uncouth, as ignorant country bumpkins.

Unlike Ambakandawila, there has been a resident parish priest in Pallansena since the turn of the century, if not earlier. When I was in Pallansena the priest, Father Martin, was not too enamoured with his congregation which he considered to be 'irreligious'. In part this was because of the relatively low degree of church attendance in Pallansena: rarely more than 20 per cent went to church each Sunday, although at Christmas, Easter and at the feast of Our Lady of Sorrows (*Viksopa Maniyo*) much larger crowds turned up.[6] In part this was because the parishioners did not find Father Martin's style of religious activities to their taste (see above, chapter 3).

Whilst the church was the physical centre of religious life in Ambakandawila, it did not perform the same role in Pallansena. Admittedly, the church did act as a focus for the collective religious rituals of the congregation, especially during the village feast, but what had happened in Pallansena was that much more personalised and privatised forms of religiosity had developed. For some people, church attendance was important, but they were only a minority. For most, regular church attendance was not seen as an integral part of being a good Catholic, and this was part of a general tendency towards anti-clericalism in Pallansena. It was not just Martin who was the object of criticism but the priesthood in general, with a few exceptions such as Father Bernard and Father Jayamanne. The church was frequently regarded as a money-making venture, the interests of the priests being seen as taking precedence over the interests of the laity.

Rather than being defined in terms of attendance at church, the role of the priest and the formal rules of the Church, Catholic practice in Pallansena was much more personalised and privatised, the institutional Church being somewhat marginal to people's religious lives. So whilst *in principle* attendance at church and receiving the sacraments might generally be seen as good things, most people saw alternatives as being at least as efficacious as channels of grace and sources of divine help.

The cult of the saints was central to most people's religious lives in Pallansena. Most households in Pallansena had small altars bearing not images of the holy family as in Ambakandawila but pictures or statues of a collection of saints. The Virgin Mary, St Anthony, St Sebastian and St Jude were all very popular. Before these altars daily prayers to the saints were much more common than in Ambakandawila, the saints being asked to help and protect the household. In some cases weekly or monthly cycles of prayers had developed, often modelled on missionary teachings.[7] In some respects the cult of the saints in Pallansena overlapped with the cult of the saints in Ambakandawila. Just as in Ambakandawila particular saints were often considered to have particular specialisms, and saints were very important in pragmatic matters: getting jobs, dealing with illness and so on. But in a number of crucial regards the picture in Pallansena was somewhat different.

First, in Pallansena saints were believed to have a real efficacy in the mundane world. Thus whilst in Ambakandawila making a vow to a saint was a symbolic action, the efficacy depending on the mind of the individual making the vow, in Pallansena it was much more common for people to talk in terms of a real interaction between the saint and the person. In return for prayer or offerings the saint would give actual help to the devotee. As in Ambakandawila medallions of St Benedict were buried in house foundations and around the boundaries of the garden. But whereas in Ambakandawila it was rarely considered to be very important whether or not there actually were medallions in the foundations, in Pallansena it was considered of vital importance. Houses were spiritual citadels protected against evil through a series of substances and a series of blessings. Even the person could be protected against evil by medallions of St Benedict worn around the neck, and such protection was thought to have a material reality which it lacked in Ambakandawila.

Second, whilst people in Pallansena went to particular saints for particular purposes, there was a general tendency for individuals to turn to the same saint over and over again. Devotions to one saint for all sorts of purposes was the rule. Thus different families and different individuals within the family had their own favourite saints, and in many cases stories could be told as to why X had become a devotee of St Anthony or Y of Our Lady of Mount Carmel. On the one hand this devotion was devotion to an ideal: the true Catholic life as lived by the saint. But this ideal became a supernatural person. The relationship which was built up between the individual devotee and his or her patron saint could be extremely intense, almost personal in its nature. Before making a journey, before taking a decision the saint would be turned to for guidance and help.

Third, in Pallansena the saints took over attributes which in Ambakandawila were firmly under the control of the priest and the Church. Religious activity was focused on the saints and their cults whilst God and even Christ became rather dim, otiose and irrelevant figures. Instead the saint became the figure not just to be emulated, not just an aid in the mundane world, but also a channel of grace. Devotion to a saint became the road to salvation in the hereafter. Thus attendance at church, even receiving the sacraments, was downplayed whilst private devotion to the saints at home or in their particular shrines was stressed.

Finally, the saints were considered to make themselves manifest in particular persons. Whereas in Ambakandawila claims by people such as Brother Lambert to have a particular relationship with the Virgin Mary were dismissed out of court, in Pallansena there was continual lively interest in the claims of such people. When new shrines appeared, people from Pallansena would be among the first to visit them and assess the power of the shrine and the claims of the central characters. Places like Kudagama and men like Father Jayamanne were thought to have a very real efficacy and were not the subject of the same degree of cynicism as displayed by people in Ambakandawila. Indeed, holy people whether they be dead saints or live holy men played the role in Pallansena which the rules of the Church played in Ambakandawila.

Turning to the other side of the coin, just as the saints had a reality in Pallansena that they lacked in Ambakandawila, so did the demonic. Very few people in Pallansena denied or even questioned the existence of demons and sorcery. Indeed, ideas about demons and sorcery dominated much of social discourse in Pallansena. Illness, economic problems, educational failures, family quarrels, were all seen in terms of demons and sorcery. Claims to be the subject of demonic attack or the victim of sorcery were accepted without question. There *were* demons; there *were* sorcerers, and people in Pallansena considered each other to have frequent recourse to them. Furthermore, such was the intensity of ideas about demons and sorcery that those who considered themselves successful expected their success to be envied by others and therefore to become the victims of sorcery. My own landlord, a man called Gabriel, considered himself to be in a quiet way quite successful. He was fairly well off, had a nice house and an extremely well kept garden in which he grew orchids for sale. But he lived in perpetual fear of demonic attack. Thus he prayed each night to a series of saints as well as to his particular patron, St Anthony. He buried medallions around his garden and even sprayed his orchids with water in which he had bathed his statue of St Anthony. When his orchids began to show signs of disease he began to suspect sorcery. Then when his son fell in love with a girl who was not just Buddhist but also a member of the Dhobi caste Gabriel became positive that sorcery was involved.

If the successful feared attack from sorcery, other people tended to interpret success as the result of sorcery. Gabriel was not as successful as he thought he was and I heard no one express any jealousy of him or his household – but then, I was his tenant. But one man who had started life as a labourer in the clay fields and ended up as a major contractor employing large numbers of men and women, besides owning two lorries, was the focus of much comment. It was generally held that his success was the result of using sorcery to destroy his competitors and influence those who bought his products. When he died there was a very elaborate funeral, but this did little to reduce suspicions about him. It was held that he was doomed to become a *peretaya*, a wandering spirit too attached to the world to ever attain salvation. Although I never met this *mudalali* I did know his son who was only too well aware of the accusations made against his father. The son claimed that his father's success had been the result of hard work and business acumen plus a life-long devotion to St Anthony, and he listed the gifts his father had made to the famous church of St Anthony in Kochchikade in north Colombo. This indeed is the general picture. Whilst each individual explains his or her success as a reward to the righteous, others see it as the result of sorcery.

So whilst in Ambakandawila demonic attack and possession were relatively rare and often denied, in Pallansena they were common and not dismissed out of hand. Furthermore, whilst in Ambakandawila demonic attack was seen as the result of the vagaries of demons or of breaking taboos, in Pallansena it was usually associated with accusations of sorcery. In Pallansena sorcery was almost always thought of in terms of inter-personal relations, not of relations between people and things. And besides sorcery, Pallansena was also replete with accusations about the evil eye (*as vaha*) and the evil mouth (*kata vaha*). Success bred jealousy, and this jealousy could lead to conscious attacks using sorcerers or unconscious attacks through the evil eye or the evil mouth. Children would become ill; money would disappear; the household would experience a plague of minor ailments. Nothing as serious as demonic attack but all very vexing. The result was that houses tended to be surrounded by high walls, fences or hedges. Displays of success were to be avoided unless in the safety of one's own house and under the protection of the saints. Otherwise one risked arousing jealousy in others and the danger of being the object of a sorcerer's magic.

### Religiosity as practice

Both Pallansena and Ambakandawila are Catholic villages and the people of each recognise the others as Catholic. Here there are not two different 'cultures' or 'belief systems' or 'world views'. Rather, different aspects of a more general Catholic tradition are stressed in each village to produce markedly different religious configurations, configurations which are summarised in table 10. The problem is how to understand these two different religious configurations: the very different ways in which religiosity is expressed and the supernatural constructed. What seems to me to be of prime importance is the associated contrast between the ways in which the inhabitants of these two villages make a living and the ways in which they understand the generation of success and failure. More generally, what are at stake are the ways in which people in these two villages are related to the wider political economy of Sri Lanka.

In Ambakandawila, people understood their livelihoods as being gained through two basic factors: the sea and the market. Admittedly fishing gear was also important, but obtaining gear was in itself dependent on catching fish from the sea and selling it in the market.

The sea is an open access resource. No one owns it; no one controls it. Anyone can fish in the sea if they so wish. Furthermore, as far as the people of Ambakandawila were concerned, there was an infinity of fish in the sea. At times people would admit that there might be over-fishing in the close in-shore waters, but the fish were still there further out. There was no sense in which one man's catch was at the expense of another man. Of course, catches did vary, and these variations were seen as a result of variations in skill, industry and luck. A rich fisherman was rich because he worked hard, had a good knowledge of fishing and the sea, and was lucky. Poor fishermen were poor because they were lazy and ignorant. Or so the story went.

Catching the fish was only one aspect of earning a living. The other side was selling the fish, the means by which effort and labour were transformed into money. In Ambakandawila all the fish caught by the men of the village were sold by village women in Chilaw market. Here, hundreds of women faced an equivalent number of small traders, prices being fixed

Table 10. *Contrasting religiosities*

|   | Ambakandawila | Pallansena |
|---|---|---|
| 1 | High church attendance<br>Sundays 'special'<br>Low-level anti-clericalism | Low church attendance<br>Sundays unstressed<br>High-level anti-clericalism |
| 2 | Saints unimportant<br>Pragmatic use of saints<br>Symbolic interpretations | Saints important<br>Pragmatic and devotionalist use of saints<br>Real efficacy |
| 3 | Demonic unstressed<br>High level of cynicism<br>Possession rare | Demonic stressed<br>Low level of cynicism<br>Possession frequent |
| 4 | Sorcery unstressed<br>Directed towards objects | Sorcery stressed<br>Directed towards people |
| 5 | Rejection of new shrines<br>Rejection of charisma<br>Stress on roles | Acceptance of new shrines<br>Acceptance of charisma<br>Stress on devotion |

by bargaining between the fish women and the fish traders. Relations between buyers and sellers were impersonal and atomistic. Each transaction was immediately settled for cash and there were no long-term relations set up between buyers and sellers. Some women were slightly better at bargaining than others, but the prices they obtained were only marginally better. If the supply was low, prices were high. If supply was high, prices were low. To the people of Ambakandawila the market was an impersonal force, the working-out of the abstract principles of supply and demand.

In the present context, only a few of the implications of this situation are worth stressing. The first is the atomistic nature of life in Ambakandawila. The largest unit of co-operation in the production process was man and wife: the man catching the fish and the wife selling it. Second, success and failure of the household depended upon its relationship with two impersonal factors: the sea and the market. Third, variations in income between people depended upon variations in the catch rather than on variations in price.

If we now turn to Pallansena, the situation is very different. Again there is a stress on atomism and competition, but success and failure were not thought to depend upon people's relations with abstract and impersonal forces but on their relationships with other people.

In Pallansena, very few people were 'petty commodity producers' selling their products on the market. Rather they either sold their labour in one way or another – as labourers, office workers, hotel staff or whatever – or they were traders. In both cases what were thought to be important were personal relations. Getting a job in Pallansena in the 1970s was a matter of personal contact: you had to know someone to get one. This was particularly true of the most valued jobs: white-collar jobs either in government service or in the private sector where patrons, most often MPs, were crucial. Even in the factories of the Free Trade Zone which started up in the late seventies, such patrons were essential. Similarly, trading depended upon personal contacts: knowing the right sorts of partners through whom or with whom deals could be made. This was not the world of the impersonal market as in Ambakandawila, but rather a world which consisted of a mesh, a network of personal contacts, ties and relationships, and success and failure depended upon manipulating this network of contacts. Furthermore, this was a world of the 'zero-sum game' where one person's success was another person's failure. If X got a job or made a successful deal this meant that Y didn't get the job or didn't close the deal.

This contrast between Ambakandawila and Pallansena seems to me to be crucial to the religious differences between these two villages. This is perhaps most clearly seen in Pallansena. Here, because success and failure depended upon personal relations, sorcery – attempts by one person to influence another person through supernatural means – became an ever-present possibility. In Ambakandawila, because success and failure depended upon impersonal factors, sorcery of this variety became irrelevant. Other people did not have the same significance. Furthermore, as all shared the same situation *vis-à-vis* the market, and all received the same prices, there was no interest in trying to influence the market through sorcery. Instead, what little interest there was in the supernatural focused on the sea: incensing nets to gain a better catch or alternatively accusing others of using sorcery to make a good catch.

The contrast also comes out in the context of possession. In Pallansena, possession was frequent and almost always associated with sorcery accusations. Indeed, as I argued in the last chapter, demonic possession followed on logically from accusations of sorcery, and most cases of possession in Pallansena were of the sort where the victim was forced to be possessed. In Ambakandawila, possession was rare and was not associated with sorcery. Rather it took the form of individuals 'choosing' to be possessed rather than have possession chosen for them. Because people's destinies did not depend upon other people, sorcery was rarely suspected and thus possession rarely imposed upon the weak.

Similar aspects underlie the different ways in which the saints were conceptualised and related to in the two villages. In Pallansena, just as getting a job depended upon a personal relation to a patron, so saints were also personalised. They became active agents who could be invoked for help in specific mundane situations. And just as each individual had his or her own particular set of human patrons, so each individual had his or her own set of patron saints. In Ambakandawila where human patrons did not perform such an important role, the saints were much less important as personal patrons. Rather they were patrons shared by all: St Rogus for all who suffered from wounds, St Anthony for all who needed a miracle, and so on. In Ambakandawila saints tended to have functional specialities and people would invoke a particular saint for a particular need. In Pallansena the functional specialisms were less stressed. A person would invoke the same patron(s) no matter what the specific need. And even the household altars manifested the difference between Ambakandawila and Pallansena. In the former where the husband-wife relationship was one of crucial interdependence, altars displayed the holy family. In Pallansena where each individual tended towards a greater autonomy and where husband and wife were less interdependent, altars tended to display collections of individual saints in addition to, or as a replacement for, the holy family.

At a more general and inclusive level, whilst Pallansena stressed a devotional, personalised form of religious practice, Ambakandawila stressed a less devotional, more impersonal and more role-focused form of religiosity. In Ambakandawila, just as making a living depended on impersonal factors, so religiosity became a matter of 'moral rules'; of church attendance, of leading a moral life and avoiding sin. In a sense it involved separation of the mundane from the religious because there was no room for the supernatural in the mundane. And thus shrines such as Kudagama were of little interest to the fisherfolk of Ambakandawila. In contrast in Pallansena, where making a living depended upon contact with powerful people, saints became the object of devotion and particular people became imbued with the ultimate divine power. Father Jayamanne or Brother Lambert for instance became foci through which the power of the divine could be tapped.

Thus in the two villages sacred representations were, in a Durkheimian sense, images of the profane. At the same time they were generated out of lived experience and were not simply analogues of 'social structure' but rather, in a Weberian sense, were attempts at making meaning out of life itself. In this process what has happened in Ambakandawila is that religious life and the supernatural become divorced from the mundane, and even though there were some people who saw such acts as incensing nets as having pragmatic significance, the more general tendency was to view such actions as symbolic: non-pragmatic. But in Pallansena the construction of the religious and the supernatural went in a different direction. This involved the interpretation of the mundane with the supernatural, a humanisation of the divine – and at times a divinisation of the human.

Now, I am only too aware of the dangers of generalising from these two small villages to the entirety of the Sinhala Catholic population of Sri Lanka. Of course what I have been describing here are tendencies, slants and biases, not an absolute distinction. And of course in Pallansena there are people who in the terms I have been using should be in Ambakanda-wila and *vice versa*. Secondly, the distinction I have drawn is not clear-cut. In Vahacotte for instance there are some people who are great believers in Kudagama and others who are total disbelievers. Furthermore, there is no clear-cut social distinction between the believers and the non-believers. In the village as a whole one finds both the personalised world of Pallansena and the impersonal world of Ambakandawila. But, *as a general rule*, it seems to me that the dominant configuration of religious expression in a village, a community, an area or whatever, will be determined by the lived experience of the people, and that this dominant religiosity will in turn become part of that experience. And it is in these terms that the figures I presented at the beginning of this chapter have to be seen. What I would hold to is that most devotees at Kudagama, Katunayake or Suvagama come from social contexts exemplified by Pallansena rather than Ambakandawila. They come from situations in which the world is ruled by personal rather than impersonal forces. One crucial aspect of the rise not just of these Catholic shrines but of new forms of religiosity amongst Buddhists, Hindus and Muslims in Sri Lanka is the fashion in which a person's destiny increasingly depends upon the personal power of others. The most obvious manifestation of this dependency is the way in which patronage has come to dominate the present-day political economy of Sri Lanka.

### Transformations of power

One of the most pronounced features of the Sri Lankan polity since Independence has been the development of various systems of patronage. Before leaving Sri Lanka, the British attempted to create a political system based on the Westminster model in which one of the crucial features is a strong distinction between policy making, the job of the MPs, and policy implementation, the task of a politically neutral administration. Whether it ever worked like that in Britain is open to question, but in Sri Lanka the gap between ideal and practice rapidly broke down.

The first major impetus in the dissolution of this separation of function came with the victory of the SLFP in the 1956 election. Riding a populist wave, the SLFP attacked the administration as elitist, out of touch with the masses, and incapable of reacting to the needs of the people. This government began a process of politicising the bureaucracy and administration. Administrators lost autonomy and MPs became increasingly important figures in their constituencies – at least if they were members of the ruling party. Administrators found that MPs intervened in making decisions which had previously been theirs, and increasingly controlled access to and distribution of resources held by the state. This process reached its apogee during the SLFP-dominated United Front government of the 1970s.

The development of MPs' patronal powers depended on a number of factors. First were the steadily deteriorating external resources of Sri Lanka which made control over imported goods more and more important. Second was the rapidly growing population and the appearance of large numbers of young people who had to be absorbed into the economy. Third was the growth of education and the widespread raising of aspirations for previously elite jobs which were now, in theory at least, open to all. Finally, there was the competitive escalation of electoral promises, promises which in practice could not be fulfilled.

It would, I think, be wrong to view the steady politicisation of the economy as a deliberate attempt to increase the patronal power of MPs. Under SLFP administrations there was an honest effort to introduce some form of socialism and to move power away from the elite and to the people. But in a situation where resources are too few to meet the demands made on government in general and MPs in particular, there is little option for MPs except to become patrons: to become if not founts of honour then founts of resources, and to use these resources both to reward past loyalty and to attract future support. Furthermore, these MPs were not working in a social or cultural vacuum, and as various writers on Sri Lanka have pointed out, the models of status and prestige which they were using owed something to pre-British and colonial times in which concepts such as *pirisa*, 'following', were important markers of position and political superiors were meant to be centres of distribution and redistribution (Obeyesekere 1967: 218). But there was a crucial difference between the system in the past and what emerged after Independence. In the past, political leaders were part of a patrimonial hierarchy centred on the king or the British state, and their status and power depended upon their position in the hierarchy. After Independence, there was always a certain ambiguity about the position of the MP. On the one hand, he too was dependent on the centre – on the prime minister or president. But on the other hand he was the autonomous leader of his electorate, validated through votes and not delegated authority. And for obvious reasons, ambitious MPs pushed the second factor rather than the first, and this, I would argue, is one of the reasons for the frequency of MPs switching party since Independence.

The result of all this was that, first, MPs became patrons surrounded by sets of personalistic dyadic ties which existed autonomously from all other ties. Indeed, a feature of all patron-client systems is this emphasis on isolated, unmediated dyadic relationships, at least in the way they are represented. And this is what places them apart from bureaucratic or patrimonial systems of delegation in which each relationship is represented as part of a larger system of relations. Secondly, the value which is stressed in this relationship is that of loyalty. Followers should be loyal to their patron; the patron should be loyal to his followers. The ideal is one of a reciprocity in which each party considers the exchange balanced, and this of course causes problems for the MP. Thirdly, the system is a zero-sum game, or at least is seen that way. Thus if X receives patronage it is at the expense of Y. And if X is loyal to A he cannot be loyal to B.

Returning to religion, there are two important ways in which these developments in the polity are related to changing religious forms. The first is that in Sinhala Buddhism there has always been a close relationship between religion and the polity. This is clearly seen in a number of ways, but for the present the most significant is the congruence in pre-modern Sri Lanka between the organisation of the state and the pantheon of the deities (Obeyesekere 1963, 1966). Thus the Kandyan kingdom was in some ways similar to what Weber called a 'patrimonial state'. Authority and honour in theory flowed from the centre down through a hierarchy of officials, and their position depended upon this downward flow. Similarly, the pantheon of the gods was organised in terms of a parallel hierarchy down which flowed authority and which encompassed a gradation of morality. Central to both was the concept of *varam*, delegated authority. With the growth of electoral politics the metaphor began to change: instead of kings and the patrimonial hierarchy, the world of the gods began to be talked of, at least by some, in terms of the prime minister and his ministers (Gombrich 1971: 172). Again there was a congruence between the polity and the world of the gods.

Yet such a vision of the gods fits uneasily with the realities of an increasingly strong patronage system in which dyadic ties, not hierarchical ties, are all important; in which loyalty to a particular patron and the balanced exchange of benefits are dominant. Furthermore, in this world of patrons and clients, the only morality is one of loyalty and calculated exchange. It is within this context, I would argue, that the rise of the god Kataragama amongst Sinhala Buddhists has to be understood. The god of thieves, rogues and vagabonds, has risen to prominence because he exemplifies all the qualities of the ideal patron. He has no interest in moral issues: in return for loyalty he will produce the goods. And *bhakti* religiosity, devotion to Kataragama, is the analogue of loyalty to the patron, for Kataragama is the patron *par excellence*. Today, the power of an individual god no longer depends upon his position in an over-arching hierarchical totality: today, gods such as Kataragama and Huniyam are increasingly autonomous beings. Thus the relationship of person to god is no longer the lowest rung in one all-encompassing systematic structure but rather an independent dyadic relationship.

In the case of Sinhala Catholics, the situation is rather different. In the first place, there was never the same congruence between the polity and the pantheon of the saints. In a sense, the administrative hierarchy of the Church played the role for Catholics that the hierarchy of the gods played for Sinhala Buddhists. Furthermore, none of the saints have quite the amoral qualities enjoyed by Kataragama, although St Anthony of Padua runs him quite close at times. But what can be seen is the tendency first, for exclusive devotions to grow, and secondly, for saints to lose their particular functions and become general patrons. Thus in Pallansena individuals chose particular saints as patrons and ignored the others, and turned to this saint for all purposes. At a less spectacular level, the same process is taking place amongst Catholics as amongst Buddhists.

There is, however, another aspect of this relationship between the polity and religious expression which is perhaps better worked out amongst Sinhala Catholics than amongst Buddhists, and that is the personalisation of power.

Earlier, I remarked that the 'holy men' of Sinhala Catholics were true charismatics in that they embodied divine power as a result of being chosen by the divine. They stand out as individuals who make and have made for them unique claims, and their charisma becomes part of their person. Thus their power depends upon no other people: they are unique

G

foci of divine energy and effectiveness. Returning to the MPs, if they represent themselves and are seen as simply rungs in the ladder of authority and power, then they cease to have any power in themselves. But given the nature of patronage, what these MPs are always trying to do is to turn their position in a structure into a personal fief in which they are the autonomous foci of power. Their power becomes part of their personhood which, like the power of the holy men, depends on no other people. In effect their aim is the sort of charisma that the Catholic holy men already possess, but the latter are only representations of the logic not yet realised in processes in the Sri Lankan polity: the rise of a charismatic super-patron.

**Conclusion**

Following Weber, writers such as Bryan Wilson have argued that with modernisation the role of religion in society is bound to decline. With the breakdown of the isolated rural community, with the spread of modern commerce and industry and the concomitant increase in 'rationality', they have argued that religion becomes increasingly compartmentalised and separated out from the mainstream of social life. Such an argument may have some relevance for the Western European situation, but to generalise from one specific historical trajectory to the world is surely extremely dangerous. Rather, in comparative perspective it could be argued that what has happened in Europe, in particular Britain, is exceedingly odd, and that rather than be treated as the model which other societies are bound to follow, it is perhaps the exception to the rule.

In Sri Lanka, the Buddhist tradition has always been an integral element in what has become labelled as politics. Such is the relationship that to separate the two is to run the danger of imposing a particular set of cultural categories on a context in which such categories are unsuitable. As writers such as Seneviratne (1978) and Nissan (1988) have shown, what are conventionally described as 'religion' and 'politics' are bound up to such an extent that any distinction between the two is little more than formalistic. This is not to say that relations of power and authority are defined in any simple way by what is conventionally described as Buddhism, nor that there is some timeless concept of the Buddhist state which continues through time irrespective of changes in power relations. As Nissan has shown, within contemporary Sri Lanka, there are at least three visions of the Buddhist state, of relations of power, authority and causality, each associated with a major pilgrimage shrine in Buddhist Sri Lanka, and each with different sets of forces in the island as a whole.

These visions are in part the result of changing sets of power and authority relations, yet at the same time, these relations are themselves partly defined and conceptualised in terms of differing, and at times conflicting strands in the Buddhist tradition.

Returning to the shrines of the Sinhala Catholics, here there are at least two contrasting political visions. On the one hand there is a vision of a return to the past; of a polity in which Catholics recovered their past. On the other is a vision of a new polity, a situation in which patronage rules supreme. Only in villages such as Ambakandawila has the compartmentalisation between religion and the rest of life which writers such as Wilson expect actually occurred, and this can be seen as the exception rather than the rule. But there is also another vision in which being Sinhala becomes increasingly important, and where the barriers between Sinhala Buddhists and Sinhala Catholics become increasingly blurred. This is the topic of the next chapter.

# 9

## On the borders

### Introduction

Looking back at the shrines discussed in previous chapters, a distinction has to be made between short-term cyclical processes and long-term trajectories. If we take Kudagama for instance, as the shrine grew in popularity so pressures were generated which increasingly undermined its existence. As the crowd of devotees grew, so did the amount of money given at the shrine. Suspicions grew that Father Jayamanne's assistants were misappropriating these funds thus tarnishing the shrine's sacred image. Similarly, as the number of pilgrims grew, it became increasingly difficult to control behaviour at the shrine, and the criticisms levelled against older places of pilgrimage such as Madhu and Talawila were increasingly directed against Kudagama. Such pressures were in part responsible for the growth of Suvagama and Katunayake, but as they grew in popularity so they too became the object of such criticisms. And in the case of Kudagama there was a further problem: the dangers of being co-opted into the mainstream of diocesan life.

Yet at the same time, another process was at work in the 1970s and increasingly in the 1980s which began to undermine not just particular shrines but also Catholic shrines in general. Clearly the sort of world hankered after by the faithful at Kudagama, Suvagama and Katunayake is a mirage. There can never be a return to the imagined golden age of the Catholic community in Sri Lanka. Today, Catholics form a small minority in a country dominated by tensions in which to be Catholic is increasingly irrelevant and ethnicity or political persuasion more and more important. In the long run shrines such as the ones discussed in this book are doomed to at best a marginal existence on the fringes of the Sri Lankan Catholic community. In themselves they do not present any long-term threat to the Church or the hierarchy. Rather they are elements in an entropic process which involves the slow fragmentation of the Church. In small but increasing numbers Catholics are turning to other forms of religious expression. These include various forms of Christian fundamentalism,[1] but what is perhaps most significant is the growing 'seepage' of Catholics towards the dominant religions of the country, most notably Buddhism.

What the missionaries called 'seepage' has always been a problem for the hierarchy. As was clear in earlier chapters, the Catholic community in Sri Lanka never formed a hermetically sealed, self-contained entity. Try as they might, the missionaries and their successors were never completely successful in controlling their congregations. From the beginning, the missionaries had to make compromises with the local situation, and many elements in 'popular Catholicism', most notably traditional forms of lay exorcism, display such a compromise. Only as long as the Church retained its power and the priests their authority over the laity could such compromises be kept under control. But with the political eclipse of the Church and the decline of priestly authority the ever-present problems associated with the minority status of Catholics have become more acute. Furthermore, the increasing involvement of Sinhala Catholics in the wider processes of Sri Lankan society, not just political but also cultural, has also had its effects. Resurgent Sinhala nationalism propagated by politicians, in the press and other media, and through the schools has led to an increasing sense of ethnic identity amongst Sinhala Catholics who are now more and more seeing themselves as Sinhala first and Catholic second. The assumptions of the wider Sinhala Buddhist community have increasingly become common currency amongst those who would describe themselves as Catholics.

Thus as well as the 'traditionalist', backward-looking shrines which I have concentrated on in this book, Sinhala Catholics are also investigating the possibilities inherent in contemporary popular Sinhala Buddhist practice. To some extent this has always been happening, and as previous chapters have made clear, even the most self-consciously 'traditionalist' devotees at Kudagama or Suvagama have more than a passing knowledge of what Sinhala Buddhists get up to. Growing numbers of Catholics are attending non-Catholic shrines, developing syncretic notions of religious practice, and questioning the basic tenets of the Church's teaching. Furthermore, in some ways such investigations and experiments have been encouraged by the form of Catholicism introduced by the nineteenth-century missionaries, particularly their stress on faith and their attempt to carve out a separate domain of the 'sacred'.

### Religion and scepticism

Throughout the history of the Catholic Church priests have worried about the degree to which the external rituals and teachings of the Church have been internalised by the laity. As was discussed in chapter 2, the nineteenth-century missionaries were no exception, and since then each generation of priests have accused their predecessors of concentrating on outward form rather than inner spirituality. Public performance was simply not enough: private faith was what was important. Doubt was an integral part of being a 'good Catholic' for without doubt there could be no faith. But to the extent that they were successful, the missionaries undercut their own position and encouraged their teachings to be questioned. And the more they were successful in encouraging inner reflection and thought, the greater the threat to the teachings of the Church and the greater the possibilities of what the priests saw as heterodox beliefs and practices.

On a number of occasions I have already mentioned Gabriel, my landlord in Pallansena. A man in his early sixties, he had never worked for a wage or salary but rather lived off his inherited money, some coconut small-holdings and minor activities such as growing orchids. With a lot of time on his hands Gabriel became something of a local intellectual. Besides dabbling in astrology and giving his services free to those who wanted them, he also spent a lot of time thinking about religion.

Like many people in Pallansena, Gabriel was outspoken in his criticisms of the modern Church. As far as he was concerned, today's priests were pale imitations of their missionary predecessors, and he found the modern liturgy abhorrent. On his infrequent visits to church he would return seething with anger at statements in the priest's sermon and change in the ritual of the mass. Yet whilst his most critical comments were reserved for these recent changes, at a more general level he criticised many teachings of the traditional Church. Thus he rejected the necessity of making even an annual confession to the priest and said he had not made confession for thirty years. Instead he claimed that he would confess to God and God alone. After all, he said, the priest is just a man no matter how good a priest he is. So how can a man forgive our sins? Similarly, he rejected the Church's teachings over the mass. As far as he was concerned the host and the wine did not become in any real sense the flesh and blood of Christ. Rather they were simply *lakunu*, 'symbols' or 'signs' which reminded us of Christ's passion and sacrifice.

Other people in Pallansena displayed varying degrees of scepticism towards the teachings of the Church. To take just one example, Bruno was an ex-village-headman who lived on the far side of Pallansena from Gabriel. He went much further than Gabriel, rejecting not only much of the role of the priest and the nature of the mass but also such ideas as heaven, hell, life after death, purgatory and so on. These, he claimed, were all 'lies' (*boru*). How could we know what happened after death, he asked. If heaven, hell and purgatory had any meaning then they referred to the here and now. Thus the rich lived in heaven, the poor in hell and the middle-classes in purgatory. Bruno still went to church occasionally, particularly at the feasts of obligation and during the annual patronal feast. But he did so, he said, not out of any great belief or faith but because it was customary and because he would feel 'shame' (*lajjava*) if he didn't go.

For people like Bruno and Gabriel, the crucial distinction was between *agama*, 'religion' and *viswasa*, 'faith'.[2] Religion denoted the teachings of the Church: what priests said was right or wrong, what they said would happen after death, what they prescribed as proper behaviour and proscribed as improper behaviour. Faith, on the other hand, was an individual matter which might or might not coincide with the teachings of the Church. It was not that Gabriel or Bruno viewed religion as wrong or as unnecessary. Indeed, they saw religion as essential to society. Thus Bruno argued that without religion, without the teachings of the Church, there could be no society. Religion for him existed as a set of rules without which society could not exist and without which 'we would all be animals'. Gabriel described religion as being 'like a ship to cross the sea' of life. But as individuals, they saw no direct fit between what the Church taught and demanded of them on the one hand, and what they personally believed and acted upon in their own lives. Personal faith and belief was something that each person had to work out for themselves. It was a private matter, a matter for one's own conscience not something to be talked about to the priest but rather discussed with one's friends. To them, religion was ultimately an arbitrary matter, a set of rules expounded by the Church. There was no proof that it was correct: 'How do we know if it is true? We are just told ...' In contrast, individual faith was something which was learnt through experience and reflection and which was developed as part of one's life. Both claimed that as children and young men they had believed what they had learnt in school or in church, but that as they grew older their own experiences had led them to reject much of what they had been told. And they accepted that because people had different experiences of life, so individuals came to different conclusions and individual faith would differ. What was right for one person would not be right for another.

Such attitudes as these are not unusual in contemporary Catholic villages, and individual faith and belief differ widely. As a general rule, men tend to be more sceptical than women: they are less frequent attenders at church and less willing to accept what they are told by the Church. Yet even so, whilst many women simply accept the teachings of the Church on the basis of priestly authority, some women are as sceptical as Bruno. For both men and women, the great attractions of shrines such as Kudagama are the miracles and exorcisms which provide visible proof of what is otherwise open to doubt.

Whether or not there was a similar degree of scepticism in the past is extremely difficult to ascertain: there are simply no reliable records. But talking to older people in Pallansena, Ambakandawila and elsewhere, it does seem that throughout the present century and probably earlier, at least a sizeable minority did not accept totally the teachings of the Church. Whilst willing to perform the outward rituals demanded of them, in private they held rather different views from those the missionaries wished of them. However, given the power of the priests in the traditional Church, given the tight parish organisation and given the control the Church exercised over education, it may well be that personal faith more closely approximated to public religion in the past than it does today.

### Religion and culture

If one age-old problem faced by the Church has been to create congruence between inner spirituality and outward practice, a second has been to demarcate the boundaries between 'religion' and 'non-religion': between the domain over which the Church has authority, and the domain over which the Church does not claim any special competence. Perhaps the most famous manifestation of this problem is St Augustine's letter to Pope Gregory requesting advice on how far to allow the people of sixth-century Kent to retain their traditional practices over such things as marriage. In the Counter-Reformation Church strenuous efforts were made to strengthen this distinction, and the missionaries who came to Sri Lanka were quite clear in their own minds not only that such a distinction be made, but also that it was universally valid.

In the Sri Lankan context, however, such a distinction was extremely problematic and there was no neat conceptual division between religion and culture, between the sacred and the secular. The closest approximation was the Sinhala-Buddhist distinction between *laukika* and *lokottara*, yet this was highly unsatisfactory for it put the cults of the gods on the same level as the profane world, an equation which the missionaries could not accept. It was only with the rise of so-called 'Protestant Buddhism', itself a reaction to and strongly influenced by Christian dualistic notions, that 'religion' became a distinct category in Sinhala-Buddhist cultural representations.

Partly in response to these difficulties, the missionaries generated a further distinction: between what was 'opposed' to religion (*agamata viruddha*), and what was simply 'outside' religion (*agamata piten*). The latter could be tolerated but the former could not. However, the question remained as to where precisely to draw the line, and individual priests differed as to what was 'outside religion' and what was 'opposed to religion'. Some saw astrology as dangerously opposed to religion: others saw it as something which had nothing to do with religion and even dabbled in it themselves. Similarly, ayurvedic medicine was a problem to many priests. In so far as it was closely tied up with the cults of the gods, some priests condemned it outright, but others thought that it could be freed from such influences and turned into a neutral science. Such distinctions varied not just between individuals but also over time. Thus attempts to control the behaviour of the laity were probably strongest in the early twentieth century when attendance at Buddhist funerals or other family rituals was widely condemned by the priests. Later such events became less problematic and began to be seen as 'cultural' and not 'religious' matters. And of course, the widespread changes in the sixties marked a major rethinking not just of the content of religion but also of where the boundary between religion and the secular lay.

If there were problems for the priesthood, then for the laity the situation was even more unclear. Put in its most general terms, the problem was how to marry the specific teachings of the Church with the particularities of the Sinhala cultural context. No matter how successful the missionaries were in creating a self-conscious, Catholic identity in Sri Lanka, people still had contact with non-Catholics. Individuals still attended Buddhist and Hindu festivals and still had recourse to the gods. Some still had non-Catholic relations or lived in close proximity to Buddhists. Whilst the missionaries may have celebrated the exorcism of demons the very exorcism itself only worked to reinforce concurrence in more general Sinhala ideas about demons. To a greater or lesser extent

Catholics were always aware of what was happening beyond the religious boundaries.

Given the stress on inner spirituality, on reflection, thought and belief rather than on a blind performance of externals, it was inevitable that whilst some Catholics, the forebears as it were of the faithful at Kudagama, vigorously rejected any compromise with the local cultural context, other individuals were always investigating the ways in which what might be called the assumptions of Sinhala life could be brought into relationship with the peculiarities of the Catholic Church.

### Gabriel's synthesis

Gabriel was much more than just a sceptic rejecting certain aspects of Church teaching. Rather he was attempting to make sense of what he had been taught by the Church within the wider Sinhala context. Whilst Bruno was content with simply rejecting those elements of Catholic teaching in which he had no faith, Gabriel went much further in trying to reconcile what he considered to be self-evident truths with his somewhat idiosyncratic views of Catholic teaching.

One of the problems which Gabriel spent a lot of time worrying about was suffering. He could reproduce the story of Job, talk of the unknowable nature of God's will and so on, but ultimately he found such approaches to suffering unsatisfactory. For him they did not answer basic questions of existence: why were some people born poor and others rich? Why did some people suffer from incurable ailments while others didn't? Why were some people's lives happy and others a series of disasters? Admittedly, there was sorcery and the demonic, and Gabriel fully accepted the powers of sorcerers and the existence of demons. But for him such explanations did not go far enough: they were only contingent causes of suffering, useful in certain contexts, but not ultimate explanations.

Gabriel found the solution to his problems in the idea of *karma*. According to Gabriel, it was *karma* which determined one's fate in life. One's existence in this life depended upon one's actions in previous lives, and whilst the rich were reaping the benefits of good actions in previous lives, so the poor were suffering for their past misdeeds. Gabriel himself had learnt from an astrologer something about his past lives. He claimed that in a previous life he had been a Hindu *sannyasin* in the Himalayas. Furthermore, *karma* involved not just human beings but also animals who also had souls. Thus a human being who had led a particularly evil life might be reborn as an animal, whilst an animal which had led a good life could be reborn as a human being. What distinguished man from the animals was not the presence or absence of the soul (*atmaya*), but the power of thought (*gnanasaktiya*) and the presence of a conscience (*hrudasaksiya*).

Yet in adopting the doctrine of *karma*, which he knew very well was rejected by the Church and was accepted by Hindus and Buddhists, Gabriel did not see himself as denying Catholic teachings. As far as Gabriel was concerned, the principle of *karma* was not a matter of religion but of science (*vidyava*). Furthermore, the teachings of the Church were quite correct as far as Catholics were concerned, for *karma* only worked until one was reborn as a Catholic. Then, depending on one's actions in this life, after death one would go to heaven, purgatory or hell. There was no second chance.[3] In other words, being born a Catholic was to escape from *karma*. Buddhists and Hindus had to wait until they were born as Catholics before they could escape rebirth and have a chance of salvation.[4]

Similar ideas concerning the superiority of being a Catholic and also the relationship between Catholic and non-Catholic also came out in one of Gabriel's favourite stories about St Francis Xavier, the famous 'apostle of the east' whose incorruptible body is now kept in Goa.

According to Gabriel, Francis Xavier was originally a Buddhist monk called Sri Rahula from Totagamuva in southern Sri Lanka. As a young monk, Sri Rahula was befriended by an older monk who had amazing powers of knowledge and rhetoric. Before he gave a sermon, the elder monk would always drink a little oil which he kept locked away, and which he wouldn't allow Sri Rahula to drink. One day, Sri Rahula got hold of the oil and drank it. He immediately collapsed as if dead, and the villagers sent for the older monk. He announced that the only cure was mothers' milk. This was forced down Sri Rahula's throat and he recovered. From then on he also shared these powers of rhetoric and knowledge because the oil was *Saraswathi tel*, 'Saraswathi oil'.[5] Sri Rahula then became a famous monk, but decided he wanted to travel. He went to Europe and there became a Catholic priest, taking the name of Francis Xavier. Returning to Sri Lanka, he died on board ship, but because he was such a holy and respected person he wasn't buried at sea but was packed in a box filled with salt. When the sailors opened the box a few weeks later, they found the body as fresh as when Francis Xavier had died, and in fright they threw the box into the sea. It was washed ashore in Goa, and that is why he is there and not in Sri Lanka.[6]

Gabriel claimed that he had been first told this story when a boy, and I have no reason to disbelieve him. It appears to be part of a larger corpus of stories which relate Catholicism to Buddhism and Hinduism but which firmly set up a hierarchical relationship between Catholicism and the other religions. Another common story is that St Sebastian (sometimes St Anthony) is Kali Amma's (sometimes Mari Amma's) elder brother. St Sebastian was a soldier in the employ of a king, sometimes said to be the king of Constantinople, who was a Buddhist. Sebastian became a Christian but his sister rejected him and the king executed him. Thus it is said that St Sebastian is particularly effective in dealing with afflictions caused by Kali. Other stories similarly relate saints to Hindu and Buddhist gods, the saints always occupying a superior role and enjoying superior powers to the gods.

Gabriel is, it must be admitted, somewhat exceptional in his attempts to produce a logically coherent synthesis of what he had been taught by the Church and the wider context of Sinhala cosmology. Yet in Ambakanda-wila too there were individuals who wondered about such matters and attempted in less rigorous ways to produce similar syntheses. It is probable that throughout the history of the Catholic Church in Sri Lanka individuals such as Gabriel have continually been making efforts to deal with the problem of being Sinhala and Catholic. Gabriel's solution was intellectual, but others have taken a more pragmatic approach, attending non-Catholic shrines, using non-Catholic exorcists and approaching non-Catholic deities.

The existence of such variation in popular Catholic belief and practice was not in itself a threat to the teachings of the Catholic Church. Gabriel's synthesis firmly placed Catholicism in a superior position. Thus one only escaped from *karma* when one was born a Catholic; St Sebastian was Kali's elder brother and could control the diseases Kali inflicted; the Buddhist monk became a Catholic priest, and so on. Similarly, attendance at the occasional Buddhist festival or using a Buddhist sorcerer were simply isolated acts, the individuals involved knowing that the Church disapproved but seeing their actions as not being 'opposed' to religion but simply 'outside' religion, no matter what the priest might say. However, the existence of such variation in popular Catholic belief and practice did set up certain potentials for change, and with the shifting power relations between Catholics and non-Catholics in Sri Lanka the potentials implicit in such variation and the stress that is laid on individual faith could lead to new forms of religious expression.

**Political power and cultural dominance**

Gabriel's attempt to bring together his Catholicism with the local cultural context was not a threat to the Church. It was very much his own private construction, and although he might argue with friends and neighbours over the nature of *karma* he in no way went out to convert others to his views. Indeed, his wife and son thought he was talking nonsense. As long as the Catholic community retained its privileges such a view of the world could be maintained, but as it declined so the sort of synthesis Gabriel was constructing became less and less tenable.

Much of the argument of previous chapters has been that the growth in popularity of shrines such as Kudagama and Suvagama has been largely concerned with recovering the past privileged position of the Catholic community in Sri Lanka. This history of post-Independence, particularly post-1956, Sri Lanka is frequently presented in terms of the growing hegemony of Sinhala Buddhists. Yet in the case of Catholics at least, the situation is more complex and for some purposes a distinction has to be made between *Sinhala* nationalism and *Buddhist* resurgence. For whilst much of the religious practice at these new shrines is anti-*Buddhist*, at the same time Catholics in Sinhala Sri Lanka were becoming increasingly aware of their identity as members of the *Sinhala* nation. Thus objections to changes in the Catholic liturgy or styles of church architecture were based on the laity interpreting them as a Buddhicisation of Catholic ritual for all that the clergy might present them as Sinhalisation. Yet at the same time, the growing sense of Sinhala nationalist identity amongst Sinhala Catholics exposed them to wider influences which in some cases undermined the distinction between Catholic and Buddhist practice and led to a growing congruence between the religious practices of Catholics and Buddhists.

The increasing integration of Sinhala Catholics into the wider context of the Sinhala nation took place through a number of channels. As has already been mentioned, the defeat of the Church over the schools issue and the attempts by the clergy to indigenise the Church led to a decrease in attempts to insulate Catholics from the wider society. Indeed, Catholics were now encouraged by the Church to see themselves as part of Sri Lankan society. At the same time, the changes in the political structure of Sri Lanka described in the last chapter further integrated Catholics into the wider polity. The increasing dominance of Sinhala nationalist rhetoric in political discourse, in newspapers, radio and more recently television, also had its effects, whilst after the state took over the schools it is not surprising that much more emphasis was put on the history of the Sinhala people and the deeds of the great mythical heroes of the Sinhala nation rather than on the saints and martyrs of the Catholic Church. Finally, the increasing polarisation in Sri Lanka between the Sinhala and the Tamil people meant that there was little room for alternative identities. 'Race' and 'ethnicity' became the dominant identities in the country as a whole, and there simply was no room for Catholics to assert their separate status within the country.[7]

Thus throughout Sinhala Catholic Sri Lanka, Catholics have increasingly asserted their identity as members of the Sinhala nation. In Vahacotte, for instance, until the late 1950s or early 1960s they still claimed that 'really' they were Portuguese, and on one celebrated occasion were even visited by the Portuguese ambassador to Sri Lanka.[8] But by the 1970s, such claims were generally rejected. All but the oldest inhabitants now claimed to be Sinhala and looked askance at the Estate Tamil pilgrims who came to the annual feast.

Elsewhere, language was an increasingly important matter. In Ambakandawila, as in many of the Catholic fishing villages along the west coast of Sri Lanka, even though people claimed to be Sinhala, Tamil was in widespread use until the 1960s.[9] From then on, fewer and fewer people continued to speak it. Although schooling in Ambakandawila had always been in Sinhala, in other villages demands were made to change the language of instruction from Tamil to Sinhala. Even two small groups in the Negombo region who did claim to be Tamil, the Bharatha and the Chettiar, also began to use Sinhala and have their children educated in Sinhala. In part such language shifting was a matter of pragmatics: Sinhala was now the official language and a knowledge of Sinhala was essential for jobs, particularly in the state sector. Yet at the same time it was also seen as a matter of identity – and of prudence. After all, as one man said to me in Ambakandawila, who wants to be mistaken for a Tamil? In churches too, the language issue could at times be important. In some parishes there were status distinctions between the Tamil-speaking and the Sinhala-speaking sections of the congregation, the former claiming precedence. With the growing predominance of Sinhala in the country as a whole, efforts were made to replace Tamil with Sinhala as the language of the services. In two or three cases this led to violence, Tamil-speakers seeing the linguistic change as an attack on their prerogatives.

By the late seventies, the Church in Sri Lanka was effectively split between a Tamil Church in the north and east and a Sinhala Church in the south (Stirrat 1984a). In Tamil areas, individual priests and large sections of the laity became increasingly involved in violence directed against the Sinhala-dominated state. Priests on both sides of the divide talked in terms of a 'Palmyrah curtain' dividing the north from the south, whilst amongst the laity any sense of a common identity linking Tamil Catholics and Sinhala Catholics was extremely weak. Admittedly, both Tamils and Sinhalese, attended the feasts at Madhu and Talawila, and a few Tamils, mainly Estate Tamils, would go to Kudagama. But by then, ethnic or racial identity far outweighed common religion affiliation. In the riots of 1983, some of the worst violence directed against Tamils took place on the west coast in predominantly Catholic areas such as north Colombo, Ja Ela, Negombo and Kochchikade, areas in which Catholics had once been predominantly Tamil-speakers. It was almost as if Sinhala Catholics had to outdo Sinhala Buddhists in asserting their Sinhaleseness.

The increasing importance of a Sinhala ethnic identity amongst Sinhala Catholics did not, of course, imply a necessarily increasing acceptance of Buddhism. After all, the majority of pilgrims to shrines such as Kudagama come from the sorts of towns mentioned above. Yet what it does imply is an increase in what is shared in common by Sinhala Catholics and Sinhala Buddhists. Exposed to the same mythical history with its tales of heroes and gods, and having increased contact with non-Catholics and their religious practices, Sinhala Catholics are increasingly exposed to the assumptions, the 'non-debatable' in Sinhala Buddhist society. Furthermore, it is now quite clear that Sinhala Buddhists are politically, economically and culturally dominant, at least in the south of Sri Lanka. If one reaction amongst Catholics is to retreat into an imagined past, another is to investigate more fully the gods of the Buddhists. But now the sort of synthesis constructed by Gabriel is anachronistic and fails to fit with present realities. The new syncretisms make the gods at least the equals, and sometimes the superiors, of the saints.

**Return to the gods**
Basil was born in 1946 in Pallansena. He was brought up in a poor Catholic family, his father earning a living as a labourer. After leaving school, Basil managed to learn how to drive and earned a living driving a hire car first in Colombo and then in Kochchikade, a town a couple of miles inland from Pallansena. He appears to have been involved in various sorts of petty crime including working as a bookie's runner. Through this he got involved in a gang fight and was arrested for murder. Whilst in prison he met various Buddhists who persuaded him of the power of Kataragama and so Basil made a vow to the god Kataragama promising that he would visit his shrine and perform penance if he was found not guilty. Basil was released because of lack of evidence and he started going to Kataragama. Since then he has been to the shrine of the

god each year at the annual festival in August. When he's there he says that he feels 'as if a great weight has been lifted from his chest' and when he comes home he has no worries. At first he simply took part in the *kavadi* dancing in honour of the god, but recently he has started walking the fire 'in thanks for all the help the god has given me'. When I knew him he was planning to hang on hooks to show his faith to Kataragama. Outside his house there is a small oil lamp which he lights each night in honour of the god. But besides Kataragama he also has a devotion to the goddess Kali and has visited her shrine at Munesseram on a number of occasions.

Despite what might appear to be rather heterodox behaviour, Basil still describes himself as a Catholic and denies he is a Buddhist. After all, he says, he does not worship the Buddha: all that he does is invoke the gods asking them for help. He admits that the priests would describe what he does as 'opposed to religion' (*agamata viruddha*), but he says that he still goes to church on occasional Sundays and each Tuesday attends the weekly mass in honour of St Anthony at Dalupota church. He sees the gods and the saints as two distinct entities, similar (*ekavage*) but not identical (*ekayi*), both of whom have power. Thus he tells a story of how he used to have his picture of the god Kataragama inside his house next to a small statue of St Sebastian. One night when he was lighting the lamp to Kataragama there was a sudden flash of fire and he collapsed. In a dream he discovered that pictures or statues of the saints and of the gods cannot be placed next to each other. So Kataragama got moved out into the garden. The point for Basil is that it is not enough to believe in the gods: one must have devotion (*bhakti*) to them, and this has to be expressed through such activities as hook-hanging or walking on fire.[10] But, he says, there is no point in doing this in honour of the saints: all that would happen is that your flesh would tear and your feet burn. More generally, however, Basil didn't really think that the saints were much use. They didn't give help all that often, and when they did it was only for small things like recovering mislaid money, regaining lost objects or curing children's minor illnesses.

For Basil, religion, the saints and the gods are basically a matter of pragmatic interest. He said that he had no idea which religion was correct – after all, Buddhism and Hinduism are very old religions and they must have some truth in them. He still calls himself a Catholic however, but this he claims is a matter of birth, 'like caste or race'. And because he doesn't know which religion is correct he has recourse to all of them. Yet at the same time, he has little faith in concepts such as the soul, heaven or hell.

Rather, he says that what happens after death is a mystery and no one knows until they die.

As far as Basil is concerned, the basic point about the gods is that they have power and the saints don't. As he says, 'Look at all the big people who go to Kataragama. Look at the help they have received. Not just Buddhists but also Catholics.' For him, there is no need for theological attempts to justify his actions: the power of the gods is self-evident. Thus rather than reject these sources of power as do the pilgrims who go to Kudagama or Suvagama, he actively seeks them out. Put on a wider stage, Basil is implicitly accepting the changing power relations in Sri Lanka: the political impotence of the Catholic community. But whilst perfectly willing to accept that what he is doing is 'outside religion', he is quick to tell the story of Mary Magdalene: after all she was a sinner, but Christ still loved her.

### Conci's shrine at Dalupota

One of the shrines Basil visits on a fairly regular basis is about five miles away from Pallansena in a village called Dalupota. This is a mixed Catholic–Buddhist area, most famous amongst Catholics for a shrine of St Anthony to which pilgrims go every Tuesday. For Basil, however, the attraction of Dalupota is a shrine run by a young woman called Conci.

Conci was born in 1955, the second child of a fairly prosperous tobacco trader. She was brought up as a Catholic, attending the local Catholic school and going with her parents to the annual feasts at Madhu, Talawila and so on. When she was seventeen, her mother's mother, of whom she was extremely fond, died. Around the same time her father's business began to fail. They were already involved in a land dispute with a neighbour, and so they began to suspect that sorcery might well be the cause of their problems. So they called in Father Zoysa, the licensed exorcist in Colombo diocese. He came, blessed the house and announced that they were now free of maleficent influences. For three months things were better, and her father's business began to recover. But then things started to go wrong again.

This time, rather than call in a priest, Conci's family decided to look elsewhere. Through a friend of Conci's elder brother they heard about a fortune teller, a 'light reader' (*anjamankaraya*), just outside Negombo.[11] Conci went with her parents to see the light reader, and much to her surprise she found that like the fortune teller she could also see into the light. They discovered that they were the victims of sorcery, and where their neighbour had buried the ensorcelling material. Conci was also told that she had to light a lamp to the god Huniyam each day, and that she had to stop eating meat and fish.

Each morning before she went to school, Conci lit the lamp to Huniyam. One day as she was lighting it, she collapsed into a trance. During the trance she had a vision (*darshana*) of her dead grandmother. Conci was told that her grandmother was now a servant (*sevaka*) of the god Kataragama. Then Kataragama appeared and told her that she had to go to the shrine of Kataragama in southern Sri Lanka. Conci persuaded her parents to take her, and they went the next weekend. There Conci had more visions both of her grandmother and of the god. She was told that she had the 'warrant' (*varam*) of the god who taught her a series of prayers (*gata*) through which she could become possessed by Kataragama. She learnt that she had to tell fortunes (*sadhara*) for forty-nine days without charging for them. At first she was apprehensive of obeying the god's orders, but then she became more frightened that if she did not obey his commands then her family would experience further problems. She started telling fortunes and also found that she could cure people, deal with those suffering from sorcery and demonic possession, find lost and stolen goods and so on.

At first, Conci carried out her 'work of the gods' (*deviyange vada*) in a hut in the garden of her parents' house. But as she became more and more popular, more room was needed. With the money she received from her shrine, the family built a new house about a quarter of a mile away, and their old house became Conci's shrine (see figure 4). Every day, except for Good Friday and Poya Days when her shrine is closed, she receives a steady string of clients, both Buddhist and Catholic, some coming from up to fifty miles away from Dalupota. As well as being possessed by Kataragama, she also gets possessed by Kali. Wednesdays and Saturdays are reserved for Kataragama; Tuesdays and Fridays for Kali.

By the time I met her, Conci was an extremely self-possessed, self-confident young woman. She was clearly in charge of her own household, her father and mother acting in effect as her servants. Furthermore, she was making a good living out of her shrine. Every day at least twenty clients, split equally between Catholics and Buddhists, would arrive seeking her services.

In many ways, Conci's story is remarkably similar to some of those discussed by Obeyesekere in *Medusa's Hair*. Yet Conci was, and still claims to be, a good Catholic. She still goes annually to Madhu and, if she has time, to Talawila and Teewatte as well as the annual feast at her local church in Dalupota, but the 'work of the gods' makes such demands on her that she can't go as often as she would like. She still prays to St Anthony and sends alms every Tuesday to be distributed to the poor at Dalupota church. At the same time, she goes to the shrine of Kataragama every three months, holds a festival in honour of Kataragama on 15 August each year, and visits the shrine of Kali at Munesseram every few months. Continually, she claims that because she was brought up as a Catholic, she knows very little about Buddhism, and that all her knowledge has been imparted to her by the gods when she is in trance. The result is a fascinating system in which there is both separation and integration of elements drawn from the two systems.

Figure 4    Conci's shrine at Dalupota

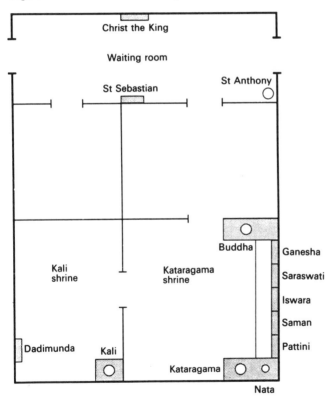

In the new house there are only Catholic pictures, but the old house, which she uses as a shrine, is divided into Catholic and Buddhist areas. In the waiting room are pictures and statues of Christ, St Anthony and St Sebastian. In the inner rooms where she meets clients and enters trances are images of the gods. Kali has one room to herself whilst Kataragama shares a separate room with other minor gods and a small Buddha shrine. Outside the main shrine is a small separate shrine to Huniyam, as well as an even smaller shed which she uses to 'cut sorcery' (*huniyam kapanava*). At these shrines, Conci performs a daily series of rituals. Each of the gods receives a daily *puja*, offerings of food and recitations of *gata* in their honour. The statue of Buddha receives the same food offerings as it would in any Buddhist shrine.

In this context, Conci presents the gods and the saints as belonging to two separate systems. As far as the saints are concerned, she claims that they have no power in themselves, and that all their power comes from God. Furthermore, she says that the saints are not very powerful. In part she says that this is because they have little interest in people, and in part because they are always moral and can't be used for things like revenge. As for the gods, they have power in themselves. They are much less moral and more involved in the world. Thus in relations with the gods people enter into direct exchange relations: they demand sacrifices or transfers of merit. With saints, all that one has to do is offer them lights or give alms to the poor 'in their name'. As Conci put it, 'The saints don't depend on people. They don't need people. But the gods do. They need merit.' And the merit comes from making offerings to Buddha. Yet even if the gods are more powerful than the saints, Conci's advice to her clients depends in part upon their religion. If they are Catholics, then Conci usually advises them to light candles to the saints or give alms in the saint's name as well as invoking the gods. If Buddhist, then as well as advising the invocation of the gods, Conci frequently recommends the performance of a *Bodhi-puja* (Seneviratne and Wickremeratne 1980).

However, in other contexts Conci and some of her followers go much further in attempting to integrate the gods and the saints. At other times, Conci claims that the gods and the saints are really identical. It is simply that different names are used by Catholics and Protestants. Thus she claims that the Virgin Mary, St Anne and Kali Amma are simply different ways of addressing different aspects of the *maniyo*, the 'mother'. St Anthony and Kataragama are similarly identified with one another, as are St Sebastian and the god Huniyam.[12]

Conci is, however, rather unwilling to be drawn into such questions of comparative theology. What for her is important is that the gods have power, that she has the *varam* of Kataragama, and that through this *varam* she can satisfy the needs of her clients. But some of her followers are willing to venture much further. One man, a regular attender at the shrine, claimed that all religions are really the same. Thus for him, Kataragama and the Virgin Mary are in some way siblings (*sahodarayo*). This, he said, was made clear in the Old Testament where one can find out the truth about the gods. But Catholic priests have withheld the Old Testament from the people for reasons which he did not know. If the priests were honest then they would tell the people and not keep it a secret. Another man, also a regular attender at the shrine, claimed that the first page of the Bible had been torn out and that it was there that the 'truth' was to be found.

**The future of popular Catholicism**
I found no other shrines similar to that run by Conci, but that does not mean that they do not exist or will not emerge in the future. In a sense Conci's shrine rather than Kudagama or Suvagama is a key to the future for at Dalupota the realities of political power are accepted in a way they are not at the other shrines I have discussed in this book.

One way of highlighting what is happening at her shrine is to compare it with the sort of synthesis produced by Gabriel. For him, there was no problem with the superiority and ultimate efficacy of what he saw as Catholicism. The problem for Gabriel was how to integrate his knowledge of Sinhala Buddhism with those teachings of the Church which he accepted, and the result was a vision in which the Virgin, the saints and Christ ruled supreme. He accepted that the gods existed but saw them as irrelevant and lacking the power of the saints. He accepted that *karma* determined one's life-chances, but only until one was born a Catholic. Such views were perfectly compatible with a world in which Catholics were a privileged minority, where their religion promised and supplied certain advantages over non-Catholics. But in the Sri Lanka of the 1970s Gabriel's synthesis was becoming anachronistic. Increasingly the realities of power were shifting in such a way that Catholics were becoming a beleaguered minority. Not surprisingly, a more pluralistic situation began to emerge in which people like Basil rejected the traditional claims of the Church to a monopoly on the truth and began to investigate other possibilities. The saints were losing their powers; the gods were reasserting theirs.

So far, attempts at producing new accommodations between the

Catholic and the Sinhala Buddhist traditions are in their early stages. Even Conci was unsure as to whether or not the saints were identical with the gods, and the answers she gave were contradictory. At times she would make half-hearted suggestions that Buddha and Christ are the same; at other times she would deny it.[13] If one treats religion as a matter of elite theology, then quite clearly such attempts are doomed to failure because entities such as 'Catholicism' and 'Buddhism' are based on different epistemological and ontological assumptions. But at the level of popular religion, religion as practised and reflected upon by ordinary people, the situation is much less clear. Given the sort of world in which they live, a world in the process of rapid change, of discontinuities and contradictions, it would be strange indeed if the result was a worked-out and internally consistent personal theology.

On the other hand, there is a certain internal consistency in the views of the faithful at a shrine such as Kudagama. Here the power of the Sinhala Buddhist gods is accepted and recognised, but this is only achieved by creating a fantasy of resurrecting the past. In the long run, to put it crudely, no matter how many miraculous cures of the demonically afflicted take place at Kudagama or Suvagama, these shrines cannot deliver the goods. They cannot lead to a recovery of a past which, after all, only exists in the imagination of the faithful. Consistency is achieved at the cost of failing to recognise reality.

Thus in the long run, it would appear that Kudagama and the other 'traditionalist' shrines are doomed to decline in popularity. Catholics are already declining as a proportion of the population in Sinhala Sri Lanka. In part this is due to a lower birth rate than other groups, but it is also a result of a slow drift towards Buddhism. At the same time, it must be expected that increasing numbers of people who claim to be Catholic become more and more involved in activities which are, in terms of the teachings of the Church, decidedly heterodox. Sinhala Catholics have always attended non-Catholic shrines, had recourse to the gods or approached sorcerers. But now, as the power of the Church declines and as Sinhala Buddhist hegemony in southern Sri Lanka becomes more and more dominant, increasing numbers of Catholics are turning to such alternatives and more and more shrines such as that run by Conci may well emerge. Alternatively, they simply start calling themselves Buddhists.

# 10

## Conclusion

In his 1984 article on apparitions and the Cold War in Europe, Christian raises the issue of the degree to which religious phenomena can be seen in national terms:

Perhaps in the seventeenth to nineteenth centuries nation-states with national churches somewhat compartmentalised European religion, but in many respects the nation-state is no longer the real arena of culture. In 1947 a circuit of mutual influence could probably have been detected that linked the visions of Mercedes Trejo in Aldeamoret to the *fanshen* of a Chinese commune. (1984: 259–60)

There is always a temptation to view the sorts of phenomena I have been discussing in this book in terms of narrowly defined Sri Lankan parameters. After all, as has been pointed out throughout, there are many parallels between the behaviour of Sinhala Catholics and their Buddhist co-nationals, whilst the rise of shrines such as Kudagama can easily be paralleled by similar developments amongst Buddhists in Sri Lanka. It could be argued that despite well over a century of European missionary effort, and over three centuries of a Catholic presence, all that has transpired is a thin and ultimately fragile veneer of Catholic teachings over an essentially Sinhala style of popular religion.

This sort of conclusion has been reached by Susan Bayly in her massive work on Islam and Christianity in South India. She argues that, 'the manifestations of Islam and Christianity which took root in south India' should not be 'dismissed as alien or marginal implants of European colonial rule' but rather as 'fully "Indian" religious systems' (Bayly 1989: 454). Bayly shows that despite formal allegiance to different religious traditions, 'The sharing of ... themes and principles of worship transcended divisions of community or confessional attachment' (1989: 455). Indeed, whilst recognising that it would be an 'oversimplification to represent every form of South Indian Hindu, Muslim and Christian worship as part of a single undifferentiated pattern of worship' (1989: 330), she could be interpreted as arguing that Christianity and Islam are little more than thin veils over an underlying autochthonous South Indian 'folk religion'. In Bayly's approach, the international 'circuits of mutual influence' have little relevance: foreign influence is submerged in an all-pervasive Indian sump.

Whatever the case in south India, in Sri Lanka these 'circuits of mutual influence' have had a long history. The Sinhala Buddhist tradition has for centuries been part of an international circuit which includes India, Burma and Thailand. More recently, modern Sinhala Buddhist practice has been strongly influenced not just by developments in other Theravada Buddhist countries in Southeast Asia but also by new movements in India and the West. Furthermore, throughout the history of Sinhala Buddhist society, the relationship between 'folk religion' and the religion of the Buddhist elite has been much more dynamic and mutually transformative than Bayly's interpretation of the South Indian material would allow.

In the case of the Sinhala Catholic tradition, such international circuits are even more clearly important. Introduced as part of the Portuguese colonial adventure, Catholicism in Sri Lanka has always existed at the point of intersection between indigenous Sri Lankan forces and the wider world of the Catholic Church. And whilst the missionaries and local priests have never been totally successful in instilling their various brands of Catholicism into the laity, it would be wrong to view the would-be converters as themselves being converted. Rather, between priest and layperson there was and is a continual dynamic, a continual process of teaching, accommodation and rejection in which forms of religious practice were and continue to be developed, reproduced and transformed.

Prior to the early nineteenth century, the dominant external influence on the Sinhala Catholic community came from the Goan Oratorian missionaries. Coming from a specific Indian context with its particular ideas of religiosity, the result was a form of Catholicism which later missionaries found repellent. In the nineteenth century, most missionaries working in Sri Lanka came from France and were strongly influenced by Counter-Reformation thinking. They in turn expounded a very different form of Catholicism, and although there was some resistance, for instance in the form of the 'Goan schism', through the authority and control they were able to exercise over their congregations the missionaries' vision of 'true' Catholicism became dominant. By the late twentieth century new versions of Catholicism were becoming increasingly important, and even if missionary priests were now of marginal importance, models of religion developed in Europe and the Americas had their effect on the Sri Lankan clergy. At the same time, the increasing dominance of Sinhala Buddhists led to new accommodations being worked out in the local domain. However, just as there had been resistance to the efforts of the nineteenth-century missionaries, so too there was resistance to reforms within the Sri Lankan Church, and once more recourse was made to the outside world: to Fatima, Garabandal and Lourdes, the points of reference for conservative Catholics.

What animates these 'circuits of mutual influence' is power, and a central theme running through this book has been the importance of power in understanding religious phenomena. Here it is not just a matter of asking, as does Talal Asad, 'How does power create religion? . . . [What are the] social disciplines and social forces which come together at particular historical moments to make particular religious discourses, practices and spaces possible[?]' (Asad 1983: 252). What also has to be asked is how what is called 'religion' constitutes power and authority: how particular religious discourses create and legitimate certain ways of envisaging power and power relationships. Thus from one angle, much of the discussion in this book has been concerned with the ways in which 'social disciplines and social forces' in contemporary Sri Lanka have worked to create specific forms of religiosity exemplified by the new Catholic shrines. But at the same time, a complementary theme has been the ways in which the forms of religiosity found at these shrines have helped constitute power relations in the world, in Sri Lanka and in the household, in particular ways.

Historically, the importance of power in the constitution of religious discourse and practice is quite clear. The sort of religiosity introduced by the Oratorians which emphasised saints and miracles was associated, as Bayly has argued, with the particularities of South Indian polities in the eighteenth and nineteenth centuries. Similarly, the variety of Catholicism introduced by the European missionaries of the nineteenth century was closely related to power struggles in Counter-Reformation and post-Revolutionary France (Hoffman 1984; Kselman 1983; Pope 1985). And finally, the teachings of the post-Vatican II Church owe much to the changes brought on by the end of colonialism. In such ways changing power relations reconstitute religion; the particular religious practices found in eighteenth-century south India or nineteenth-century France owe much to the specificities of the particular polity and the struggles for power within such polities.

Yet at the same time, the religiosity of devotees at Kudagama, Suvagama or wherever is not simply constituted by some externally defined set of power relations. Whilst the faithful come from particular social contexts and whilst the forms of religious expression found at these shrines can be linked to those contexts, their participation in particular rituals and practices contributes to their view of the world: to how they understand relations of power and domination. At Kudagama for instance, these relations are viewed in a very different way from what one would find in a post-Vatican II seminary. Central to this different view of the world is the way in which power itself is constituted by the discourses and practices of Kudagama. Here, power is not seen in terms of class or exploitation, but rather in terms of hidden spiritual forces which can only be made manifest in certain specific places at certain times by certain people.

The rise to fame of the shrines examined in this book depended upon their success as centres for exorcism. Peter Brown writing about exorcism in the late Roman period has described it as an 'operetta' and 'the late Roman operetta is ... brutally simple. It is on the theme of violence and authority ... The demon in the possessed abuses and even attacks the holy man; and the holy man shows his power by being able to bring into the open and ride out so much pent-up rebellion and anger' (Brown 1971: 88–9). But at shrines such as Kudagama or Katunayake, exorcism is more than an operetta: it is the process through which power and authority are created. This is most clearly seen in the way in which the exorcism process re-establishes relations of domination and subordination within the family. Through possession and exorcism the authority of parents over children and men over women is re-established and reproduced. At the same time, exorcism acts to establish the existence of demons and sorcerers as well as displaying the superior *potentia* of the divinely-chosen holy men. Those invisible threads of power which underlie the seemingly mundane world are thus made manifest. Where once the miraculous exorcisms performed by eighteenth-century missionaries were means by which Oratorian priests attempted to gain control over their converts, now miracles are one means of expressing resistance to the increasingly marginal role of Catholics as Catholics in contemporary Sri Lanka. Through exorcisms and other miracles which take place at these shrines, believers are pulled into Christian's 'circuits of mutual influence'. Overcoming the trials and tribulations of family life in contemporary Sri Lanka can be linked to the wider promises held out at the great shrines of the modern Catholic Church such as Fatima, Garabandal and Lourdes.

The believer is presented with a vision of the world in which relations of spiritual power are dominant and in which they become part of a universal community of believers. As Caplan has pointed out for Madras Protestants, 'Power [belongs] no less to the spiritual than to the material realm' (Caplan 1987: 256). With this the devotees at Kudagama would wholeheartedly agree – and indeed might go further. For them, 'real' power is spiritual power, and the shrines and holy men of modern Sri Lanka are means of tapping that power.

The recognition of the central importance of power in the realm of religious practice raises the question of the relationship between 'religion' and 'politics'. Such a distinction clearly does exist in the contemporary world, but it has arisen in particular historical contexts and is always open to challenge. Thus as far as Sri Lanka is concerned, the distinction only became important during colonial rule and was introduced as part of a particular European way of viewing the world, itself ideological and the result of struggles between Church and state over the boundaries of their respective jurisdictions. In the process of generating this distinction there has been a tendency for power to be subsumed under politics, or at least for distinctions to be made between the sorts of power associated with religion and politics.

The missionaries of the nineteenth century found themselves entering a world where there was already a continuing argument between Sinhala Buddhist activists and the colonial authorities over the boundary between religion and politics. Whilst the British rulers attempted to adopt a stance of neutrality in religious matters, which they wanted to be governed by 'customary' practice, they found themselves continually called upon to arbitrate in what they considered religious affairs. Although ostensibly about such matters as the control of ancient sites, temple succession rights, or processional routes, these arguments were also about the legitimacy of the colonial government's interventions and its ability to impose a certain set of categories through which to govern colonial Sri Lanka. As far as the Catholic missionaries were concerned, the neutrality of the colonial authorities towards religion allowed the Church space to re-establish and strengthen a specific Catholic community and was a feature of British rule which the Church firmly supported. Yet when it was in their interests, the missionaries were not averse to calling in the state to support what the Church saw as its religious rights.

In the twentieth century, however, the lines were redrawn and the nature of the colonial categories of religion and politics increasingly contested. The turning point was probably the introduction of the electoral system and the increasing use of the popular franchise by Buddhists to forward their interests. At first, both laity and priests refused to acknowledge this new situation and continued to fight for what they saw as a legitimate distinction between religion and politics. Despite claiming to be politically neutral, the Church sent questionnaires to candidates addressing what it saw as religious issues, and issued directives to Catholic voters as to which candidate they could and could not support. Yet under increasing pressure from the Buddhist majority, among which rather different concepts of the nature of politics and religion and the boundaries between the two developed, the Church was forced to withdraw. The schools takeover was only the most spectacular incident in this reluctant acceptance by the Church of definitions being generated and imposed by the Buddhist majority.

The complexities of this process have to be recognised. Not only have there been battles between Catholics and non-Catholics over the nature of the relationship between politics and religion, but also amongst Catholics. Today, many priests accept a strong distinction between religion and politics which allows them to be involved as individuals in what they recognise as secular politics. For others, the distinction is either irrelevant or is drawn in a different way. For them, their spiritual role necessarily involves them in activities which others would see as political. And for many of the laity, both positions are seen as unbecoming to a priest because they insist on a firm distinction between the world of religion and the world of politics, a distinction which isolates the priest on the spiritual side of the divide.

In sum, the opposition between politics and religion cannot be taken for granted and just as Asad has cogently argued against the possibility of a universal definition of religion, so too a universal definition of politics must be rejected. Rather than view the two as separate analytical domains which influence each other, they have to be viewed in terms of a wider, all-inclusive framework in which processes may at times involve the creation of separable categories of politics and religion, but when this distinction is made the questions that have to be asked are how this distinction is made, when it is made, who makes it and who contests it.

The contingent nature of definitions of politics and religion is related to wider issues of the nature of 'culture' in anthropology. There is still a tendency in the anthropology of Sri Lanka, as elsewhere, to talk in terms of particular, self-enclosed, clearly defined cultures, and to approach social phenomena in terms of such isolated cultures. Critiques of such an approach have, of course, a long history. Leach (1954) argued against the concept of 'unit societies', arguing that wnat could be represented as discrete entities had to be understood in terms of wider fields. More recently, Wolf has pointed out that 'The notion of separate and integral cultures' is itself a product of the rise of the concept of the nation, and that 'culture is ... better seen as a series of processes that construct, reconstruct and dismantle cultural materials' (Wolf 1982: 387). Building on these comments, Spencer has argued that what now passes as Sinhala Buddhist culture was constructed by resurgent Sinhala groups in the course of their struggle against the British and later in reaction to Tamil separatists (Spencer 1990). Running through all these critiques have been a recognition of Christian's 'circuits of mutual influence', an acknowledgement of the temporal dimension of the social and an acceptance of the importance of power in the ways in which cultural content and cultural difference are created.

The case of the Sinhala Catholics exemplifies in a particularly clear fashion those 'processes that construct, reconstruct and dismantle cultural materials'. Situated at the point of intersection of a series of powerful forces, Sinhala Catholics have developed a set of cultural trajectories through which they express claim and counterclaim, resistance and acceptance. Using elements derived from various different traditions, alternative forms of expression have been, and continue to be, created. The result is a series of competing forms of religious expression, a fragmentation which is to be expected given the declining role of the Catholic community in Sri Lanka as a whole. Such centripetal and entropic tendencies have always been present, but with the decline in the authority of the priesthood, the erosion of the position of the Catholic community in Sri Lanka, and the growing domination of Sinhala Buddhist cultural forms, the pace of such processes has accelerated whilst countervailing centripetal forces have declined in strength.

However, Sinhala Catholics are only a privileged instance of a more general tendency, for this process of cultural fragmentation is not restricted to marginal situations such as the Catholics of Sri Lanka but is rather a general feature of the modern world. In the past there possibly were isolated, autonomous societies, each of which possessing a shared culture, a shared set of meanings, to which all subscribed. Yet today, such societies if they exist are rare indeed. With the growing importance of transcultural and transnational processes, and with the involvement of most societies in wider economic and political processes, the prevailing picture is increasingly one of disintegration. Alternative cultural forms are in increasing competition with one another, and in the process transforming themselves, 'cultural materials' being reused and reformed in new and novel ways.

At any particular time one cultural form may become dominant, but such dominance tends to be shortlived and there are always alternatives at large. Thus to take Sinhala Buddhist Sri Lanka as an example, present-day cultural images of the nation stress two themes. The first of these is the identification of race, language, land and religion at the national level, various images being used to present a picture of homogeneous unity. The second is the image of village, tank (irrigation reservoir) and temple to constitute an ideal of the Sinhala village community, the essence of Sinhalaness. Such images have been accepted by some anthropologists as timeless cultural representations of Sinhala culture. Yet as has been shown by many writers, they evolved in a particular nationalist setting, itself a response to colonial rule and employing cultural materials from colonial ideology as well as from the Sri Lankan past. Furthermore, there are various alternative representations of Sinhala Buddhist society which stress other features, for instance class relations or relations of patronage. The dominance of particular cultural images is the result of particular historical processes. Genealogies of the elements which go to produce such images can be constructed which relate them to the activities of specific social groups engaged in struggles for domination at particular times. What has to be accepted is that what appears to be cultural homogeneity in contemporary Sinhala Sri Lanka is not unproblematic. Rather it is the result of a set of centrifugal forces, most notably the power of nationalism, which are for the moment dominant.

Such an approach has implications for the way in which I have approached religious phenomena in this book. Just as I have found it necessary to discard essentialist notions of culture, so too I have had to abandon essentialist notions of religion. The questions which I have found myself asking are concerned with how religious practice is constituted and constructed. Thus rather than see religious behaviour as a chorus of harmony, I have viewed such behaviour as a language of argument, a means through which claims to power are made, legitimated, accepted and rejected. The history of the so-called 'world religions' is a history of flux between centripetal and centrifugal forces. The history of the Catholic Church is a continual story of the rise and fall of 'heresies', and a measure of the strength of the institutional Church has been its success in keeping heresies under control. Yet at the same time what is represented as the core of orthodoxy, of unchanging dogma, is itself continually changing as new groups gain positions of power and authority within the Church and as the wider context in which the Church exists is changing. Thus approaches to religion which start off from the assumption that there is a 'true' Catholicism, Buddhism or whatever are doomed to failure. What is true or orthodox religion is itself a site of struggle. Similarly, approaches to religious phenomena which are couched in terms of syncretism have similarly to be abandoned, for ultimately they too are based on essentialist views of the nature of religious traditions.

In sum, rather than focus on culture or religion *per se*, I have found myself returning to two of the central themes in traditional British social anthropology. The first of these is a focus on social relations. Culture and religion are constituted in social processes, arise out of social relations and are transformed by social processes. Forms of religious and cultural expression do not exist in a vacuum but in the actual relations between people and social groups. The second of these themes is the stress on social order: on what makes society possible and the roots of social solidarity. Admittedly, traditional functionalist approaches tended to assume coherence as the norm and social change and conflict as aberrant phenomena. Yet only by addressing the problem of coherence as an issue can we begin to understand the processes by which cultural materials are constructed, reconstructed and dismantled; those situations in which order and coherence are maintained and reproduced and those in which fragmentation becomes the norm.

# Notes

**Introduction**

1 Except for some historical writings, very little work has been done on Tamil Catholics in Sri Lanka. The conflict between Tamil separatists and the Sinhala-dominated government has widened the gap between Tamil Catholics and Sinhala Catholics. On this see Stirrat 1984a.

2 This literature includes Ames 1964, 1966, Gombrich 1971, Gombrich and Obeyesekere 1988, Kapferer 1983, Malalgoda 1976, Obeyesekere 1966, 1970a, 1975a, 1977, 1978a, Seneviratne 1978, Southwold 1983.

3 The most explicit version of the 'great' and 'little' distinction is to be found in Obeyesekere 1963. See also Gombrich 1971.

4 On the nature of the 'Buddhist' state, see Tambiah 1976, 1977, and the early work by Heine-Geldern 1956.

5 See Obeyesekere 1963, 1966, Seneviratne 1978, and Gombrich and Obeyesekere 1988.

**2 The colonial Church**

1 There is some little evidence that there were Nestorian Christians in Sri Lanka in the medieval period, but they have had little if any influence on later Christian groups in Sri Lanka. The literature on missionary activity during the Portuguese period includes Abeyasinghe 1966, Boxer 1960–1, Don Peter 1978 and Queyroz 1930.

2 The situation is and was rather different on the east coast where even today there are communities speaking a Tamil-Portuguese creole (McGilvray 1982, Smith 1979). On the west coast Portuguese remained the language of domestic servants well into the nineteenth century.

3 As well as Boudens' historical work, the major source on the Catholic Church in Sri Lanka during the Dutch period is Perniola's collection and translation of documents (Perniola 1983–5). See also Arasaratnam 1958.

4 In 1826 there were only 12 priests to cater for perhaps 60,000 Catholics; in 1832 only 14 (Saverimuttu 1980: 14). By 1871 the number had risen to 61 for 173,000 Catholics, and by 1911 there were 233 priests, 122 brothers and 512 sisters to serve a Catholic population of almost 340,000 (Kuruppu 1924: 51).

5 This led to the infamous 'Goan schism', a schism concerned with authority rather than dogma. In Sri Lanka one church, 'Our Lady of a Good Death' in Colombo remained loyal to Goa until the 1940s. But in general after the 1870s the schism was unimportant in Sri Lanka. For details, see Boudens 1979, Saverimuttu 1980.

6 The Oblates were particularly important on the west coast. In the south and east, Jesuits had a significant presence whilst in the central highlands Sylvestrine Benedictines were important.

7 These terms are originally Tamil, as are many of the terms used by Catholic Sinhala speakers. In part this is because the Oratorian missionaries first worked in Tamil areas of Sri Lanka, but also because in the heartland of Sinhala Catholics, around Negombo, Sinhala Catholics frequently used Tamil as their first language until very recently. Boudens (1957: 174) describes *muppus* as 'native wardens of the local church in charge of temporal affairs' and *annavis* as 'catechists'.

8 Novenas are ideally the nine evening services leading up to the annual feast of the patron saint. Besides the ones described here there were also *bara* or 'vow' novenas given by individuals or groups in fulfilment of vows to the saint.

9 Thus in fishing disputes, the crucial factor was often church membership rather than physical residence.

10 The Durava are traditionally associated with toddy tapping, the Karava with fishing and the Goyigama with farming. The standard work on caste in Sinhala Sri Lanka remains Ryan 1953 whilst Roberts 1982 is important for the coastal areas. On the peculiarities of caste in Ambakandawila, see Stirrat 1981a.

11 One of the more blatant examples of caste affiliation was just north of Pallansena where two churches belonging to different castes faced each other across a main road.

12 There is some uncertainty over numbers. Kuruppu claims that there were 81 Catholic-run schools in 1861, a figure rising to 725 by 1911 (Kuruppu 1924: 51).

13 There are very few records of conversions to Catholicism in the nineteenth century. Where missionaries tried to convert Buddhists they generally failed. See Boudens 1979.

14 This is to over-simplify grossly a very complex process. The best treatment of the 'Buddhist revival' of the nineteenth century is Malalgoda 1976. See also Gombrich and Obeyesekere 1988 and Wickremeratne 1969.

15 Although the groups involved in these clashes were defined in terms of religious affiliation, this of course does not mean that they were simply the result of religious differences. A full analysis of these clashes has yet to be written.

16 For details of the riot, see Dep 1969: 203–7, Malalgoda 1973, Rogers 1987: 176–9, Somaratna 1991, Sumathipala 1969–70 and the government report of the Committee of Enquiry. By one of those ironies of history, the troops used to restore order were from a predominantly Catholic Irish regiment.

17 Significantly, the only groups which did not clash with one another during this period were the Buddhists and the Hindus. Violence between these groups,

redefined in racial terms, is a post-Independence phenomenon. See Nissan and Stirrat 1987, 1990 and Rogers 1987.

18  The importance of space is also apparent in more serious clashes such as that in Anuradhapura in 1903. See Nissan 1985, Rogers 1987: 183–7.

19  On the impact of the Donoughmore constitution, see Russell 1982, Nissan and Stirrat 1987, 1990.

20  In a sense, there is some historical backing for Malalasekera's view. Many of the Catholics along the western seaboard claimed to be Sinhalese yet spoke Tamil as their first language. It appears that a large proportion, particularly of the Karava caste, were relatively recent immigrants from South India (Roberts 1980).

21  Similar criticisms were probably also levelled by Hindu Tamil activists against Tamil Catholics, but work on the Hindu revival is still in its early days. See Hellmann-Rajanayagam 1989, Kailasapathy 1985.

22  Thus in Pallansena and many other Catholic Sinhala villages, primary education was in Tamil rather than Sinhala. At the great Catholic festivals such as at Madhu and Talawila, Sinhalese and Tamils mixed freely. Marriages between Tamil and Sinhala Catholics were much more frequent than marriages between Catholics and non-Catholics who shared the same ethnic identity.

23  'Catholic Action' was and is a blanket term for the lay apostolate and includes such organisations as the Catholic Union, formed in Sri Lanka in 1896 'to protect religious and social interests'.

24  Thus in France in the seventeenth century, writers such as Cardinal du Perron argued that, 'the king held his crown from God alone and ... no power in the world, be it spiritual or temporal, had any rights over his kingdom' (Heyer 1969: 19).

25  This perhaps goes some way to explaining why in areas such as Latin America where Catholicism owes most to the first wave of missionary activity, marriage and family relations are relatively unstressed, whilst in Sri Lanka the Church did and does put an inordinate amount of stress on 'correct' matrimonial and family relations.

26  The missionaries were scandalised by the practice of close kin marriage common in Sri Lanka. Throughout Catholic areas such marriage was banned, and in the main the ban was successful.

27  This is symptomatic of the superior status given to anything European by Sinhala Catholics during this time. The use of puppets was seen as 'backward' and 'primitive'.

28  Priests varied in their attitudes towards these plays. Some saw them as dangerously idolatrous: after all, the water used to wash the statue of Christ was often treated as supernaturally charged, whilst other people would measure the statue with thread and wear the thread as a prophylactic throughout the succeeding year. In the main, however, such dramas were seen as being in line with the general theological preoccupations of the age.

29  Pallansena church is dedicated to Our Lady of Sorrows, (sometimes known as Our Lady of Seven Doulours) *Viksopa Maniyo*, whilst one of the other churches in the mission is dedicated to Our Lady of Good Expectation

(*garbavasa maniyo*). As in South India, Our Lady of the Snows is particularly associated with the Parava people (Bayly 1989). Over 20 per cent of churches in Sri Lanka are dedicated to one form or another of Our Lady.

30 Thus at Fatima, the Virgin asked for 'the consecration of Russia to my immaculate heart and the communion of reparation on the first Saturdays'. She went on to promise that, 'if people attend to my requests Russia will be converted and the world will have peace'. But if not, then 'Russia will spread its errors throughout the world, fomenting wars and persecutions of the Church' (Johnston 1980: 33–4).

31 In 1820 a Methodist wrote, 'the great majority of the Catholics in this country know nothing but how to cross themselves and repeat Pater Noster and Ave Maria'. A year later another Protestant claimed that Sri Lankan Catholics, 'hardly knew the Bible, their religious services often turning into worldly festivals with drums beating, flags flying, bells ringing, guns firing, feasting ...' (Boudens 1979: 34–5).

32 The only exception to this division of labour appears to be the *pirit* ceremonies of protection which are concerned with Buddha rather than the gods (Gombrich 1971).

33 For fuller details of these and other shrines, see Stirrat 1982 and the references therein. Both shrines appear to have been constructed on earlier, non-Catholic, shrines.

34 By the middle of the nineteenth century it was such an important source of income that the two vicariates fought bitterly over its control. See Boudens 1979: 66.

35 In the 1840s Madhu came under the control of the Goan schismatics, the Church only retrieving it after a series of civil court cases.

36 As late as 1914 there were no non-European bishops in the Catholic Church – excluding the four Thomist Catholic bishops of Kerala, in India, who were something of a special case (Neill 1964: 259).

37 An example of this attitude is shown in a series of fishing disputes in the early twentieth century. The government asked the Church to intervene and the Archbishop decided in favour of Pitipana parish. The *muppu* of the other parish, 'whilst obedient as ever to the authority of the ... [Church]', complained bitterly that his parish had the disadvantage of a local priest (SLNA 59/2464).

38 Thus parishioners often objected to lower caste priests. It is said that the first priest from the Washerman caste found a bundle of dirty washing left on his verandah by irate high-caste Goyigama parishioners. Reportedly, when a Durava (toddy tapper) priest was promoted, a statue of a priest climbing a coconut tree was delivered to his house.

### 3 The Church in crisis

1 Further details of Teewatte can be found in Stirrat 1982. It started off as a small Lourdes shrine, but during the Second World War, Bishop Joulain promised to build a basilica there if Sri Lanka was spared attack from the Japanese. The attempt to link the shrine with a national version of the Virgin Mary has not been a success: it remains a large but relatively unpopular Lourdian shrine.

2 The best discussion of the 1956 election remains Wriggins 1960. See also the discussions in Jupp 1978, Manor 1989, Moore 1985 and Wilson 1974.

3 Some further discussion of the political changes after 1956 will be found in chapter 8.

4 As we shall see in the next chapter, this pamphlet is still remembered today.

5 *Poya* days are the four quarter-days of the Buddhist lunar calendar. In the 1970s there was a return to Sundays as the weekly holiday.

6 The details of the schools take-over are discussed at length in Abeysingha 1976. See also Houtart 1974, especially pages 286–94.

7 Thus opposition to the take-over was often strongest amongst Catholic groups such as fishermen who had benefited least from the Church-run schools.

8 Various Protestant translations of the Bible had been available since the nineteenth century, but none were deemed suitable for Catholics. Attempts were made to work with Protestants on new translations, but these were not completely successful.

9 *Hevisi* bands are basically marching bands using traditional Sinhalese instruments. They appear to be an invention of the twentieth century.

10 The development of patronage in post-Independence Sri Lanka will be examined in some detail in chapter 8.

11 Thus appointments to vacant sees are always surrounded by rumours as to the political linkages of the candidates involved.

12 By far the best discussion of radical Catholicism in Sri Lanka is Ulrich Dornberg's recent thesis (Dornberg 1985).

13 This led to a minor scandal once the names of the so-called 'Sixty-one Group' had been leaked to the press and aroused widespread anger amongst the laity.

14 Bishop Leo had earlier been Bishop of Kandy but he resigned as he wanted to regain the status of an ordinary parish priest. Rome refused his request and offered him the newly created diocese of Badulla in which he could experiment with radical Catholic alternatives in the liturgy and priestly formation.

15 The radical movement in Sri Lanka culminated in the Asian Theology Conference organised by Tissa Balasuriya and held in Sri Lanka in 1979. However, this attempt to produce a specifically Asian 'Liberation Theology' had little impact in Sri Lanka.

16 It was also rumoured that Father Paolicci was responsible for leaking to the press the names of the sixty-one priests who had come out against clerical celibacy in 1971. Father Paolicci died in 1976.

17 The term 'pariah' relates to the poor Indian Tamil estate labourers who formed the majority of Catholics in the Badulla diocese. For Father Paolicci and his like, poverty was unfortunate but inevitable.

18 Usually this involved a conversion to Buddhism. There are a number of large nineteenth and early twentieth-century Buddhist temples along the west coast in close proximity to churches built by these converts as challenges to the Church.

19 Priests were only too well aware of such criticisms, and many went to extreme lengths to avoid being alone with women. Others claimed that simply because they were priests they became the objects of amorous pursuit by women.

20 Secular priests are diocesan priests as distinct from religious priests who are

members of religious orders. Whilst the latter take a vow of poverty, secular priests can continue to own private property of their own. Given that many Sri Lankan priests come from middle class backgrounds, a number are quite wealthy in their own right.

21 In one case, a priest was chased out of his parish after a series of fiery sermons attacking the evils of capitalism and espousing socialism.

22 For a similar tension between the laity and the clergy amongst South Indian Protestants, see Caplan 1987: 185.

23 It also appears that the proliferation of statues of Buddha in public places, what Obeyesekere (1970a) refers to as 'Buddha in the market place', was sparked off in imitation of Catholic practice.

24 Another *suruvama*, by a main road about thirty miles north of Pallansena, consists of a statue of St Antony of Padua. Around the base of the plinth is a frieze of pigs! The local Catholic village is surrounded by Muslims, and the pigs are a reference to a miracle performed by St Antony which led to a group of Moors being turned into swine.

**4 The rise of Kudagama**

1 It should be noted that these details come from priests who were opposed to Father Jayamanne's style of religion. Alternative versions of his past are mentioned in later pages. Unfortunately, Father Jayamanne was unwilling to talk to me about his past.

2 The earliest mention I have found of Kudagama is in D'Oyley's account of the Kandyan kingdom where he lists the dues owed the Crown by the inhabitants. See D'Oyley 1929: 16.

3 The Kegalle district was a particularly troubled area during the 1971 Insurrection. It is claimed that this was partly due to Batgama antipathy to the pretensions of the Goyigama caste. Be that as it may, when I first knew Kudagama people were very reluctant to talk of the Insurrection and young men were few.

4 It appears to have been quite common for missionaries from Europe to bring relics to Sri Lanka and for them to be left in the island when the missionaries returned home.

5 More will be said about the social composition of the pilgrims in chapter 8. But it should be noted at this point that we have no reliable data on the class composition of Catholics in Sri Lanka.

6 First Fridays have been particularly associated with the cult of the Virgin since the Marian revival of the nineteenth century.

7 There was also a certain amount of fear that the demons exorcised by Father Jayamanne at the shrine remained in the village and attacked the locals.

8 This appears to be an almost universal feature of shrines – at least Catholic shrines. Dahlberg reports the same sorts of comments about traders at Lourdes (Dahlberg 1987) and similar comments are made at Sri Lankan shrines such as Madhu and Talawila (Stirrat 1982).

9 See Turner 1969, 1974, Turner and Turner 1978. For criticisms of Turner, see Pfaffenberger 1979, Sallnow 1981 and 1987.

10 These verses of the Way of the Cross are from one of the English-language prayer books sold at the shrine.

H

11 When it rained, the congregation would crowd into the church for the Way of the Cross. In the late seventies when numbers began to decline, it was only held in the open air on the first Friday of each month.

12 Father Jayamanne claimed that at first he allowed people to kiss the Thorn but stopped this practice for hygienic reasons.

13 This is a not uncommon way of dealing with priests and other religious who have in one way or another incurred the wrath of the clerical authorities. During the seventies, however, government restrictions on foreign travel meant that this threat had lost its power, and many priests would have dearly loved to be exiled for a year or so.

14 How he obtained this relic is a mystery to me. I am told that it was presented to him by a conservative missionary, but Father Jayamanne refused to confirm or deny this story.

15 It should also be remarked that the diocese of Galle was the only diocese in Sri Lanka that did not possess a major pilgrimage centre. How far this influenced the bishop in his attitude towards Kudagama is not clear.

**5 Demonic possession and the battle against evil**

1 Thus Huniyam is said by some Sinhala Buddhists to be unambiguously a god, by others to be a demon, and for others to be a god when the moon is waxing and a demon when waning. See Gombrich and Obeyesekere 1988: 112–32.

2 Even today, *agama*, the word used to denote religion in Sinhala-speaking Sri Lanka, is used by Catholics to refer to Catholicism alone.

3 The opposite appears to be the case amongst Protestants of Madras where the category of evil is undifferentiated. See Caplan 1985 and 1987: 225–6.

4 Again, for the same sort of debate, see Caplan 1987: 226–7.

5 For fuller details on Sinhala Buddhist ideas concerning *peretayo* see in particular Gombrich 1971: 163–7, as well as Kapferer 1983. Clearly, the *peretayo* of Sri Lanka are related to the *pret* of North India and the *pey* of South India. See Caplan 1987: 201.

6 For details of these demons – and others – see the work of Obeyesekere and Kapferer.

7 Not surprisingly Father Jayamanne and his helpers attempted to stop such practices, but not with much effect.

8 I came across no evidence of Muslim demons. Why this is so is not clear – after all, there is no love lost between Catholics and Muslims in Sri Lanka. But there is a certain ambiguity over attitudes towards Islam amongst Sinhala Catholics. Some Catholics do claim that Muslims worship the moon, but given the absence of Jews in Sri Lanka, most Catholics see Muslims as adhering to the religion of the Old Testament and are thus afforded some recognition.

9 See Kapferer 1983 and Obeyesekere 1970b, 1975b, 1981, for discussions of this in Sinhala Buddhist contexts.

10 Clearly all these times and states-of-being are open to all sorts of structuralist interpretations. See Kapferer 1983 amongst others.

11 Jonathan Spencer reports that in the Sinhala Buddhist village he worked in during the early 1980s *bhikkhus* were frequently thought to be sorcerers, whilst

Chris Fuller tells me that Malayalis have this same reputation in India. See also Caplan 1987: 198.

12 This story appears to refer to the sorcerer discussed by Gombrich and Obeyesekere (1988: 61). Clearly, in 1978 when Gombrich and Obeyesekere appear to have met him, he was very much alive. Furthermore, they report that he was an *ex*-monk and that many of his clients were Roman Catholic.

## 6  Suffering and sacrifice

1 Clearly, this case of demonic possession can be seen in terms of Lewis' argument that malevolent possession, is 'a means by which women, and sometimes other subject categories, are enabled to protect their interests and prefer their claims and ambitions' (Lewis 1966: 322).

2 This may be a harsh judgement, but it is one which was widely shared in Pallansena even by those who were most willing to accept the reality of demonic possession. I should add that Neil was one of my neighbours in Pallansena, and it struck me, too, that his possession was an important factor supporting his life of studied inactivity.

3 In contrast, Jonny Parry tells me that the aim of much exorcism in Hindu India is not to turn bad possession into good possession but rather to turn bad supernatural beings into relatively good ones.

4 See below, chapter 7, for a discussion of these prayer men.

5 Gold (1988) refers to much of the recent literature. For better or worse, Lewis (1971) remains the most widely cited work on possession in a comparative perspective.

6 Summarising Kapferer's argument is extremely difficult because of the way in which caveats and modifiers are scattered through the text, often denying what appears to be the main thrust of his argument.

7 Thus his use of the nature/culture distinction is extremely problematic, particularly when he can produce no evidence that this distinction is made by Sinhala Buddhists in the manner which his analysis demands. Secondly, his treatment of pollution is also questionable as he lumps together a number of distinct phenomena under the heading of 'pollution', even claiming that cooking is 'polluting'.

8 What follows is of course only one variation on the representation of women in the Catholic tradition. See Caroline Bynum's work on medieval women which suggests that the 'humanity of Christ' could be viewed as denying men a share in Christ's holiness which women enjoyed (Bynum 1982).

9 Thus most people at Kudagama consider that the Virgin Mary never menstruated. She was immaculately conceived and a few even claim that she gave birth without pain or afterbirth. Finally, being bodily assumed into heaven her body failed to go through the period of decay with which death *killa* is associated.

10 See once more the arguments of Caroline Bynum concerning female religiosity in medieval Europe (Bynum 1982; 1987).

## 7  Holy men and power

1 This and other quotations are from a transcript of his life story. Lambert likes

talking: the transcript covers twenty-three pages of single-spaced typescript, so what follows is heavily edited. I would like to thank Ben Sooriyabandara for recording and translating this data.

2  This appears to be modelled on a similar sand pit inside the church at Madhu which is also thought to contain supernatural sand.

3  I have no idea what Father Jayamanne's views on Suvagama are. However, some critics of Suvagama claim that Lambert is possessed by a *mala peretaya*, the spirit of his dead father. Similar comments are made of Lalith Aponsu at Katunayake.

4  The quotations that follow come from interviews with Bishop Aponsu's brother, a homeopathic doctor in Colombo. Bishop Aponsu was extremely loath to be interviewed, at least by me.

5  This is not an uncommon miracle amongst Sinhala Catholics. In 1979 the eyes of a statue in Wattala just to the north of Colombo were seen to move and attracted large crowds for a week or so.

6  This is one of the most popular churches in Colombo amongst 'traditional' Catholics, famous for its perpetual novena.

7  On some of the problems in dealing with hagiographic literature, see Bell 1985, Bynum 1987: 24–5, Geary 1978: 9–16, Keyes 1982, Tambiah 1984 and Weinstein and Bell 1982: 8–15.

8  Almost certainly the histories of Lalith and Lambert are modelled on such popular versions of Father Jayamanne's life. After all, both of their shrines grew up after Kudagama, and Lambert at least was a devotee of Kudagama before he started his activities at Suvagama.

9  I should add that there have been cases of the Virgin appearing to women and children in Sri Lanka, either as dreams or apparitions, but these have not, as far as I know, become the centres of cults or shrines.

10  Also, it would appear that the categories of those who experience apparitions in Europe tend to get possessed by demons in Sri Lanka. A more ambitious contrast between holiness in European and Sinhalese Catholicism would have to take into account differing constructions of gender and the demonic in the two areas.

11  The *pasan pot* were either recited in private during Holy Week or, when political circumstances allowed, formed the basis for public Easter dramas. Such translations are particularly associated with Father Jacob Goncalvez. They are discussed in Peiris 1943.

12  Occasionally these people were also known as *thiyannichchikarayo* or *orsam kiyana minissu*. I have been unable to obtain a direct translation of the first term, but the second literally translates as 'prayer-saying men'.

13  In general, it appears that European missionaries were more tolerant of such activities than were their Sri Lankan counterparts.

14  Fuller details of this shrine are given in Stirrat 1981b.

15  In imitation of parish organisation, Norbert's helpers are organised into a *dayaka mandalaya*. Furthermore, his chief helper is known as an *annavi*.

16  It should also be noted at this point that the fasting Norbert went through prior to being possessed is reminiscent of the ban on eating after midday for Buddhist monks.

**8 Patronage and religion**

1 On one celebrated occasion a *bhikkhu* turned up at Kudagama. His sister had been ill but had recovered after visiting the shrine. The *bhikkhu* sat by the altar looking somewhat bemused and embarrassed whilst Father Jayamanne led the congregation in prayer and devotion to the Virgin Mary.

2 I have written at length about Ambakandawila elsewhere. See in particular Stirrat 1988.

3 This is not an unusual form of sorcery in Sri Lanka and elsewhere in South Asia.

4 These lists were more or less the same as those found in the *araksha pot* mentioned in the last chapter.

5 Thus whilst at Kudagama, the term *lakuna* was used to denote the signs demons used to indicate their presence within their victims, in Ambakandawila the term was used to denote objects used to change the inner state of the observer.

6 Pallansena is one of the few parishes in Sri Lanka to still perform an annual Passion Play. This is attended by thousands of visitors even though it does not rival the more famous Passion Play put on in Duva a few miles to the south.

7 Today, such cycles of devotions are discouraged by the priests. One is reminded here of Christian's comment that what is now seen as part of the 'little tradition' was often first introduced as elements of the 'great tradition' (Christian 1972).

**9 On the borders**

1 I know too little about these groups to make any sensible comments on them. On Protestant fundamentalist groups in Madras, see Caplan 1987.

2 *Viswasa* is a particularly interesting concept and 'faith' is an imperfect translation. The term also denotes 'trust' and 'belief'.

3 Gabriel was a bit unsure about purgatory. On the one hand he would dismiss it as the 'treasury of the Church' or the 'Church's elephant goad' and deny that it existed, but at other times he would quite happily talk as if it existed.

4 *Karma* is used in a number of ways by Catholics to talk about one's situation in life. Thus as well as Gabriel's version, some people claimed that it was simply 'luck', whilst others said that one's *karma* depended on the actions of seven generations of ancestors.

5 Saraswathi is, of course, the goddess of learning.

6 A Sinhala Buddhist version of this story is given by Gombrich and Obeyesekere: 'According to popular tradition the fifteenth-century monk Totagamuve Sri Rahula, a poet and scholar, practiced black magic and composed versified spells' (1988: 49). A far cry from the holy St Francis Xavier!

7 On the ways in which Sinhala and Tamil identities became all-embracing categories in Sri Lanka, see Manor 1984 and Nissan and Stirrat 1987, 1990. An alternative approach is to be found in Kapferer 1988. Muslims clearly form an exception to the picture I have presented of the Catholic situation, but they could and did claim a separate ethnic as well as religious identity: they claimed to be 'Moors'.

8 Luckily for them, the myths of origin of the village talk of Portuguese refugees marrying high-caste Sinhala women, so it was a simple matter to change their ethnic claims.

9 The use of Tamil amongst these coastal groups probably indicates their

relatively recent origin as South Indian immigrants (Roberts 1980). However, there are various other stories as to why they used Tamil. One common one is that they are the descendants of prisoners brought back from India by the Sinhala hero Gajabahu (Obeyesekere 1978b). Another is that they became Tamil speakers because they were converted to Catholicism by missionaries who spoke Tamil. A third is that they adopted Tamil to escape paying the fines imposed on the Sinhala people by the British after the anti-Muslim riots of 1915.

10 Interestingly, he compares hook-hanging with Christ's crucifixion. More generally, at times Basil claims that it is through such *tapasa* that people can gain supernatural powers.

11 Light reading is also a frequent component in traditional Sinhala Catholic healing rituals.

12 In the case of Huniyam and St Sebastian, iconographic representations of both feature horses, and this may be the basis of this identification. More generally, St Sebastian is seen as a particularly dangerous saint capable of revenge if promises to him are not fulfilled. As for St Anthony and Kataragama, it is more difficult to find iconographic elements in common, although St Anthony's reputation as a 'miracle worker' may be at the basis of this identification.

13 Gombrich and Obeyesekere mention similar attempts at syncretism amongst Sinhala Buddhists. See Gombrich and Obeyesekere 1988: 305–6, 341.

# References

Abeyasinghe, T. 1966. *Portuguese Rule in Ceylon, 1594–1612*. Colombo, Lake House

Abeysingha, N. 1976. 'The 1960–1961 schools' crisis in Ceylon'. *Journal for Missiology and Religious Studies* 60: 217–26

Ames, M. 1964. 'Magical animism and Buddhism: a structural analysis of the Sinhalese religion system'. In E. B. Harper (ed.), *Religion in South Asia.* Seattle, University of Washington Press

    1966. 'Ritual prestations and the structure of the Sinhalese pantheon'. In M. Nash (ed.), *Anthropological Studies in Theravada Buddhism.* Yale, University Press

Anderson, B. 1983. *Imagined Communities: Reflections on the Origin and Spread of Nationalism.* London, Verso

Arasaratnam, S. 1958. 'Oratorians and predikants: the Catholic Church under Dutch rule'. *Ceylon Journal of Historical and Social Studies* 1: 216–22

Asad, T. 1983. 'Anthropological conceptions of religion: reflections on Geertz'. *Man* 18: 237–59

Aubert, R. 1978. *The Church in a Secularised Society.* London, Darton, Longman and Todd

Balasuriya, T. 1972. 'Some consequences of the nationalization of schools in Ceylon'. *Outlook* 5: 19–22

    1975. *Reflections on the Nationalization of the Catholic Schools in Sri Lanka.* Colombo, Centre for Society and Religion, Dossier 17

Bax, M. 1990. 'The madonna of Medjugorje: religious rivalry and the formation of a devotional movement in Yugoslavia'. *Anthropological Quarterly* 63: 63–75

Bayly, S. 1989. *Saints, Goddesses and Kings: Muslims and Christians in South Indian Society, 1700–1900.* Cambridge, Cambridge University Press

Bell, R. M. 1985. *Holy Anorexia.* Chicago, Chicago University Press

Bendix, R. 1966 [1959]. *Max Weber: An Intellectual Portrait.* New York, Doubleday

Boudens, R. 1955. 'Negombo, un centre de resistance catholique à Ceylan sous l'occupation hollandaise'. *Neue Zeitschrift fur Missionwissenschaft* 11: 81–91

1957. *The Catholic Church under Dutch Rule.* Rome, Catholic Book Agency

1979. *Catholic Missionaries in a British Colony: Successes and Failures in Ceylon 1796–1893.* Immensee, Nouvelle Revue de Science Missionaire

Boxer, C. R. 1960–1. 'A note on Portuguese missionary methods in the East, 16th–18th centuries'. *Ceylon Historical Journal* 10: 77–90

Brown, P. 1971. 'The rise and function of the holy man in late antiquity'. *Journal of Roman Studies* 41: 80–101

1981. *The Cult of the Saints.* Chicago, Chicago University Press

1989. *The Body and Society: Men, Women and Sexual Renunciation in Early Christianity.* London, Faber and Faber

Bynum, C. 1982. *Jesus as Mother: Studies in the Spirituality of the High Middle Ages.* Berkeley, University of California Press

1987. *Holy Feast and Holy Fast: The Religious Significance of Food to Medieval Women.* Berkeley, University of California Press

Caplan, L. 1985. 'The popular culture of evil in urban South India'. In D. Parkin (ed.), *The Anthropology of Evil.* Oxford, Blackwell

1987. *Class and Culture in Urban India: Fundamentalism in a Christian Community.* Oxford, Clarendon Press

Casperz, P. 1974. 'The role of Sri Lanka Christians in a Buddhist majority system'. *The Ceylon Journal of Historical and Social Studies* NS 4: 104–10

Christian, W. A. 1972. *Person and God in a Spanish Valley.* London, Seminar Press

1984. 'Religious apparitions and the Cold War in southern Europe'. In E. Wolf (ed.), *Religion, Power and Protest in Local Communities.* Berlin, Mouton

1987. 'Tapping and defining new power: the first month of visions at Ezquioga, July 1931'. *American Ethnologist* 14: 140–66

Cupitt, D. 1980. *Taking Leave of God.* London, SCM Press

Dahlberg, A. 1987. *Transcendence of Bodily Suffering: An Anthropological Study of English Catholics at Lourdes.* Unpublished PhD thesis, University of London

1991. 'The body as a principle of holism: three pilgrimages to Lourdes'. In J. Eade and M. Sallnow (eds.), *Contesting the Sacred.* London, Routledge

Dep, A. C. 1969. *A History of the Ceylon Police,* vol. 2. Colombo, Times of Ceylon

Don Peter, W. L. A. 1978. *Education in Sri Lanka under the Portuguese.* Colombo, Colombo Catholic Press

Dornberg, U. 1985. *Contextual Theology in Sri Lanka. Presentation and Analysis of Recent Theological Developments.* Unpublished Diploma thesis, Wilhelm's University of Westfalia, Munster

D'Oyley, J. 1929 (reprinted 1975). *A Sketch of the Constitution of the Kandyan Kingdom.* Colombo, Tisara Prakasakayo

Flannery, A. P. 1975. *Documents of Vatican II.* Grand Rapids, William B. Eardmans Publishing Company

Geary, P. J. 1978. *Furta Sacra: Thefts of Relics in the Central Middle Ages.* Princeton, Princeton University Press

Gold, A. G. 1988. 'Spirit possession perceived and performed in rural Rajasthan'. *Contributions to Indian Sociology* 22: 35–63

Gombrich, R. 1971. *Precept and Practice*. Oxford, Clarendon Press
Gombrich, R. and G. Obeyesekere 1988. *Buddhism Transformed. Religious Change in Sri Lanka*. Princeton, Princeton University Press
Hebblethwaite, P. 1975. *The Runaway Church*. London, Collins
Heine-Goldern, R. 1956. *Conceptions of State and Kingship in Southeast Asia*. Ithaca, Cornell University Press
Hellman Rajanayagam, D. 1989. 'Arumuka Navalar: religious reformer or national leader of Eelam'. *Indian Economic and Social History Review* 26: 235–57
Heyer, F. 1969. *The Catholic Church from 1648 to 1870*. London, A & C Black
Hoffman, P. T. 1984. *Church and Community in the Diocese of Lyon, 1500–1789*. Yale, Yale University Press
Horowitz, D. L. 1980. *Coup Theories and Officers' Motives*. Princeton, Princeton University Press
Houtart, F. 1974. *Religion and Ideology in Sri Lanka*. Colombo, Hansa
Johnston, F. 1980. *Fatima: The Great Sign*. Chulmleigh, Augustine Publishing Company
Jupp, J. 1978. *Sri Lanka: Third World Democracy*. London, Frank Cass
Kailasapathy, K. 1985. 'Cultural and linguistic consciousness of the Tamil community'. In Social Scientists' Association (ed.), *Ethnicity and Social Change in Sri Lanka*. Colombo, SSA
Kapferer, B. 1983. *A Celebration of Demons: Exorcism and the Aesthetics of Healing in Sri Lanka*. Bloomington, Indiana University Press
1988. *Legends of People, Myths of State*. Washington, Smithsonian
Keyes, C. F. 1982. 'Introduction. Charisma: from social life to sacred biography. In M. R. Williams (ed.), *Charisma and Sacred Biography. Journal of the American Academy of Religious Studies* Thematic Studies 48, Nos. 3 & 4: 1–22
Kreisler, B. R. 1978. *Miracles, Convulsions and Ecclesiastical Politics in Early Eighteenth-Century Paris*. Princeton, Princeton University Press
Kselman, T. A. 1983. *Miracles and Prophecies in Nineteenth-Century France*. New Brunswick, Rutgers University Press
Kuruppu, D. J. B. 1924. *The Pearl of the Indian Ocean: A Handbook of Ceylon*. Colombo, Catholic Messenger Press
Leach, E. R. 1954. *Political Systems of Highland Burma*. London, G. Bell & Sons
Lewis, I. M. 1966. 'Spirit possession and deprivation cults'. *Man* 1: 307–29
1971. *Ecstatic Religion*. Harmondsworth, Penguin
Lewis, J. P. 1917. 'Some folklore from the Northern Province'. *Ceylon Antiquary and Literary Register* 2: 179–81
McGilvray, D. 1982. 'Dutch Burghers and Portuguese mechanics: Eurasian ethnicity in Sri Lanka'. *Comparative Studies in Society and History* 24: 235–63
1988. 'Sex, repression and Sanskritization in Sri Lanka?' *Ethnos* 16: 99–127
Malalgoda, K. 1973. 'The Buddhist-Christian confrontation in Ceylon, 1800–1880'. *Social Compass* 20: 171–200
1976. *Buddhism in Sinhalese Society 1750–1900: A Study of Religious Revival and Change*. Berkeley, University of California Press
Manor, J. (ed.) 1984. *Sri Lanka in Change and Crisis*. London, Croom Helm

1989. *The Expedient Utopian: Bandaranaike and Ceylon*. Cambridge, Cambridge University Press

Modder, F. 1908. *Gazetteer of the Puttalam District of the North-Western Province of Ceylon*. Colombo, Frank Cottle

Moore, M. 1985. *The State and Peasant Politics in Sri Lanka*. Cambridge, Cambridge University Press

Neill, S. 1964. *A History of Christian Missions*. Harmondsworth, Penguin

Nissan, E. 1985. *The Sacred City of Anuradhapura: Aspects of Sinhalese Buddhism and Nationalism*. Unpublished PhD thesis, University of London

1988. 'Polity and pilgrimage centres in Sri Lanka'. *Man* 23: 253–74

Nissan, E. and R. L. Stirrat 1987. *State, Nation and the Representation of Evil: the Case of Sri Lanka*. Sussex Occasional Papers in Social Anthropology No. 1

1990. 'The generation of identities: Sinhala and Tamil'. In J. Spencer (ed.), *The Power of the Past*. London, Routledge

Obeyesekere, G. 1963. 'The great tradition and the little in the perspective of Sinhalese Buddhism'. *Journal of Asian Studies* 21: 139–53

1966. 'The Buddhist pantheon in Ceylon and its extensions'. In M. Nash (ed.), *Anthropological Studies in Theravada Buddhism*. Yale, Yale University Press

1967. *Land Tenure in Village Ceylon: A Sociological and Historical Study*. Cambridge, Cambridge University Press

1970a. 'Religious symbolism and political change in Ceylon'. *Modern Ceylon Studies* 1: 43–63

1970b. 'The idiom of demonic possession: a case study'. *Social Science and Medicine* 4: 97–111

1975a. 'Sinhalese-Buddhist identity in Ceylon'. In G. de Vos and L. Romanucci-Ross (eds.), *Ethnic Identity: Cultural Continuities and Change*. Mayfield Publishing Company

1975b. 'Psychocultural exegesis of a case of spirit possession in Sri Lanka'. *Contributions to Asian Studies* 8: 41–89

1977. 'Social change and the deities: the rise of the Kataragama cult in modern Sri Lanka'. *Man* 12: 377–96

1978a. 'The firewalkers of Kataragama: the rise of bhakti religiosity in Buddhist Sri Lanka'. *Journal of Asian Studies* 37: 457–76

1978b. 'Gajabahu and the Gajabahu synchronism: an inquiry into the relationship between myth and history'. In B. L. Smith (ed.), *Religion and the Legitimation of Power in Sri Lanka*. Chambersburg, Anima Books

1981. *Medusa's Hair*. Chicago, Chicago University Press

Peiris, E. 1943. 'Sinhalese Christian literature of the XVIIth and XVIIIth centuries'. *Journal of the Royal Asiatic Society (Ceylon Branch)* 35: 163–81

1948. *Marian Devotion in Ceylon*. Colombo

Perniola, V. 1983–5. *The Catholic Church in Sri Lanka: The Dutch Period* (3 volumes). Colombo, Tisara Prakasakayo

Pfaffenberger, B. 1979. 'The Kataragama pilgrimage: Hindu-Buddhist interaction and its significance in Sri Lanka's polyethnic social system'. *Journal of Asian Studies* 38: 253–70

1982. *Caste in Tamil Culture: The Religious Foundations of Sudra Domination in*

*Tamil Sri Lanka.* Syracuse, Maxwell School of Citizenship and Public Affairs, Foreign and Comparative Studies/ South Asian Series No. 7

Pope, B. C. 1985. 'Immaculate and powerful: the Marian revival in the nineteenth century'. In C. N. Atkinson, C. H. Buchanan and M. R. Miles (eds.), *Immaculate and Powerful: the Female in Sacred Image and Social Reality.* Boston, Beacon Press

de Queyroz, F. 1930. *The Temporal and Spiritual Conquest of Ceylon* (translated by S. G. Perera). Colombo, Government Press

Roberts, M. 1980. 'From southern India to Lanka: the traffic in commodities, bodies and myths from the thirteenth century onwards'. *South Asia* 4: 36–47

1982. *Caste Conflict and Elite Formation. The Rise of the Karava Elite in Sri Lanka, 1500–1931.* Cambridge, Cambridge University Press

Rogers, J. 1987. *Crime, Justice and Society in Colonial Sri Lanka.* London, Curzon Press

Russell, J. 1982. *Communal Politics under the Donoughmore Constitution, 1931– 1947.* Dehiwala, Tisara Prakasakayo

Ryan, B. 1953. *Caste in Modern Ceylon: The Sinhalese System in Transition.* New Brunswick, Rutgers University Press

Sallnow, M. 1981. 'Communitas reconsidered: the sociology of Andean pilgrimage'. *Man* 16: 163–82

1987. *Pilgrims of the Andes: Regional Cults in Cusco.* Washington, Smithsonian

Saverimuttu, P. N. M. 1980. *The Life and Times of Orazio Bettacchini, the First Vicar Apostolic of Jaffna, Ceylon (1810–1857).* Rome, Urbaniana University Press

Seneviratne, H. L. 1978. *Rituals of the Kandyan State.* Cambridge, Cambridge University Press

Seneviratne, H. L. and S. Wickremeratne 1980. 'Bodipuja: collective representations of Sri Lankan youth'. *American Ethnologist* 7: 734–43

Smith, I. R. 1979. 'Convergence in South Asia: a Creole example'. *Lingua* 48: 193–222

Somaratna, G. P. V. 1991. *Kotahena Riot 1883: A Religious Riot in Sri Lanka.* Colombo

Southwold, M. 1983. *Buddhism in Life. The Anthropological Study of Religion and the Sinhalese Practice of Buddhism.* Manchester, Manchester University Press

1985. 'Buddhism and evil'. In D. Parkin (ed.), *The Anthropology of Evil.* Oxford, Blackwell

Spencer, J. 1990. 'Writing within. Anthropology, nationalism and culture in Sri Lanka'. *Current Anthropology* 31: 283–300

Stirrat, R. L. 1977. 'Demonic possession in Roman Catholic Sri Lanka'. *Journal of Anthropological Research* 33: 133–57

1981a. 'Caste conundrums: views of caste in a Sinhalese fishing village'. In D. McGilvray (ed.), *Caste Ideology and Interaction.* Cambridge, Cambridge University Press

1981b. 'The shrine of St Sebastian at Mirisgama'. *Man* 16: 183–200

1982. 'Shrines, pilgrimages and miraculous powers in Roman Catholic Sri Lanka'. In W. J. Shiels (ed.), *The Church and Healing.* Oxford, Blackwell

1984a. 'The riots and the Roman Catholic Church in historical perspective'. In J. Manor (ed.), *Sri Lanka in Change and Crisis*. London, Croom Helm

1984b. 'Sacred models'. *Man* 19: 199–215

1988. *On the Beach. Fishermen, Fishwives and Fishtraders in Post-colonial Lanka*. Delhi, Hindustan Publishing Corporation

1989. 'Money, men and women'. In J. Parry and M. Bloch (eds.), *Money and the Morality of Exchange*. Cambridge, Cambridge University Press

Sumathipala, K. H. M. 1969–70. 'The Kotahena riots and their repercussions'. *Ceylon Historical Journal* 19: 65–81

Tambiah, S. J. 1976. *World Conqueror, World Renouncer*. Cambridge, Cambridge University Press

1977. 'The Galactic Polity: the structure of traditional kingdoms in Southeast Asia'. In S. Freed (ed.), *Anthropology and the Climate of Opinion*. New York, New York Academy of Sciences

1984. *The Buddhist Saints of the Forest and the Cult of the Amulets*. Cambridge, Cambridge University Press

Tennent, J. E. 1850. *Christianity in Ceylon, its Introduction and Progress under the Portuguese, the Dutch, the British and the American Missions; with a Historical Sketch of the Brahmanical and Buddhist Superstitions*. London, John Murray

Turner, V. 1969. *The Ritual Process*. London, Routledge

1974. *Dramas, Fields and Metaphors*. Ithaca, Cornell University Press

Turner, V. and E. 1978. *Image and Pilgrimage in Christian Culture*. Oxford, Blackwell

Vidler, A. 1961. *The Church in an Age of Revolution*. Harmondsworth, Penguin

Weerawardena, I. D. S. 1960. *Ceylon General Election 1956*. Colombo, Gunasena

Weinstein, D. and R. M. Bell 1982. *Saints and Society*. Chicago, Chicago University Press

Wickremeratne, L. A. 1969. 'Religion, nationalism and social change in Ceylon, 1865–1885'. *Journal of the Royal Asiatic Society (Ceylon Branch)* 56: 123–50

Wilson, A. J. 1974. *Politics in Sri Lanka, 1947–1973*. London, Macmillan.

Wilson, P. J. 1967. 'Status ambiguity and spirit possession'. *Man* 2: 366–78

Wolf, E. 1982. *Europe and the People without History*. Berkeley, University of California Press

Wriggins, W. H. 1960. *Ceylon: Dilemmas of a New Nation*. Princeton, Princeton University Press

# Index

# Cambridge Studies in Social and Cultural Anthropology

Editors: ERNEST GELLNER, JACK GOODY, STEPHEN GUDEMAN, MICHAEL HERZFELD, JONATHAN PARRY

* Available in paperback